NEW YORK CENTRAL

3-2712

NEW YORK CENTRAL

STITUTION"
tury Limited
NTRAL LINES

Walter L. Greene

Library of Congress Catalog Card Number
73-92249

ISBN: 0-89024-024-8

FRONTISPIECE PAINTING
Missouri Pacific's Sunshine Special is shown along the bluffs
of the Mississippi River in a 1926 painting by William Harnden
Foster, an artist renowned for his railroad calendar paintings.

FRONT ENDSHEET PAINTING
"A National Institution," a portrait of the Twentieth Century
Limited by Walter L. Greene, was used by New York Central for
its 1926 calendar, one of a series of Twentieth Century paintings
shown on NYC calendars. An H-10 crosses the bridge overhead.

First printing, 1974. Second printing, 1975.

THE SUNSHINE SPECIAL

MORE CLASSIC TRAINS

BY ARTHUR D. DUBIN

KALMBACH BOOKS

For Lois, Peter, and Polly.

Foreword

1   A RECENT visit to Boston to attend the Annual Meeting of The Railway & Locomotive Historical Society provided an opportunity for a reunion with Arthur Dubin and brought me the good news that MORE CLASSIC TRAINS would soon go to press after years of intensive work assembling the illustrations and writing the text.

During the many years of our friendship I have recognized Arthur Dubin as the foremost historian of the great railroad passenger trains of North America and their equipment. Great passenger trains have such distinctive and vibrant personalities that they are transformed into living beings in the eyes and minds of the true lovers of them. Each great train has a history and an individuality that sets it apart from every other train, just as great men and women have their own individual characteristics and personalities. However, it takes a Boswell or a Herodotus to view these differences in the human personality and find the appropriate words and phrases to illuminate and distinguish their subjects so that all who read carefully may understand them. Arthur Dubin is the Boswell and Herodotus of the railroad passenger train.

His book, SOME CLASSIC TRAINS, which was published by Kalmbach in 1964, immortalized in its text, photographs, and other descriptive material, the personalities of its historic subjects. The sequel, MORE CLASSIC TRAINS, not only continues this significant work, but advances it to a new plateau of achievement.

It is highly important that this record of great trains has been produced because even though Amtrak is striving valiantly to emulate the great passenger-train standards of the past, and is deserving of credit for its ambitions, efforts, and achievements, let no one assume that the passenger services of today are more than a facsimile of those from the glory days of the standard bearers of times past. As one who has clear recollections of train travel dating to 1906, I can speak with the authority of personal experience.

The great named trains of this nation began to emerge in the "elegant eighties" and "gay nineties." They grew continuously in number and prestige, even throughout the depression years of the 1930's and during the highly competitive years following World War II, until the national super highways and jet planes sounded their death knell — one by one — beginning in the late 1950's. Travel on these named trains was a delightful experience in the comforts, amenities, and conveniences of the good life. The pleasures were reinforced by the kaleidoscopic panorama of scenery to be enjoyed through the car windows, a delight that highway and air travel do not provide. However, to most travelers, the reduced time for air transportation and the freedom from schedules that are the highway mode's advantage appear to take precedence over other considerations. The Cunard Line's philosophy that "getting there is half the fun" is still valid although most travelers disregard it. A similar observation appeared 60 years ago on an item of Pennsylvania Railroad travel literature that quoted a personage of the time, "The purpose of travel is not merely to reach the goal, but to find enjoyment en route."

Regrettably, it is not economically possible to restore the "Golden Age" of travel by train, but its passing means that something precious has gone out of our lives. Those persons who loved to travel on the great trains as well as those who were born too late to know the standard bearers of the premier railroads have been denied one of life's joys. It is, therefore, of great consequence that the aura and glamour of railroad travel aboard the "classic trains," as Arthur Dubin refers to them, should be preserved in a graphic and understandable manner so that future generations of Americans can learn of their heritage and can discover the graces and amenities of life en route which once were far superior to those that are experienced aboard the public conveyances of today.

Just as it takes biographies of great men and histories of great events to impart to them life and interest and to relate their significance, so it is necessary for biographies and histories of great trains and the services they provided at their pinnacle to relate the important role occupied by the passenger trains in the cultural, social, and technological development of North America.

Fortunately the need for adequate literature on this subject is filled by a growing output of books. As a collector of volumes on or about railroads that date back nearly 60 years, my library has never been growing more rapidly than it is now. However, there are always works that are pre-eminent in their field and Arthur Dubin's SOME CLASSIC TRAINS, and now the sequel, MORE CLASSIC TRAINS, are among them. SOME CLASSIC TRAINS, for example, has taken me on a series of delightful trips down memory lane. I have ridden every one of the trains described in that book except the Santa Fe's *De-Luxe*, *Saint*, and *Angel*, the special *Cardinals Train*, and the *Cuban Special*. Moreover, I am able to recall many of the scenes shown along the routes over which these trains ran.

Ever since I read the advance pages of the manuscript for MORE CLASSIC TRAINS, I have become increasingly impatient to read the finished work. Now, at last, I shall be able to make it a cherished and treasured addition to my collection.

John W. Barriger III

1973
St. Louis, Mo.

Contents

Introduction

1 THE PERIOD of North American history dating from mid-19th to mid-20th century has been termed the "Railway Age." For more than 100 years — from the zenith of the stagecoach to the advent of the jet airliner — the railway passenger train offered the most luxurious form of overland transportation in the United States, Canada, and Mexico.

The decades of railroad expansion that followed the Civil War in America and Confederation in Canada were marked by the prosperity of the industrial revolution. Concurrently, during what has been called the Victorian Era, royalty exercised great influence in North America as well as in Europe. The term "palace" gained wide commercial appeal. Cities boasted of Palace Hotels and Palace Theaters; steamships carrying passengers from the Old World to the New were described as palatial; and railroads exulted over their trains of palace cars. Indeed, many North Americans first experienced architectural beauty and elegance in hotels, theaters, ships, and trains.

MORE CLASSIC TRAINS is the author's second book that seeks to document the history of the great passenger trains during the era of the palace car — the "Railway Age" in North America.

THE five locomotives and 11 cars of Denver & Rio Grande train 6, the eastbound San Francisco and Chicago Limited, pose for a portrait (note the conductor standing by the steps of the second coach and the white-jacketed figure on the steps of the dining car) on Soldier Summit, Utah, on April 6, 1911. Photo by Bill Shipler Photo.

Railroading's golden age—when travel time meant train time

THE DeWitt Clinton, built in the summer of 1831 by John Jervis at the West Point Foundry in New York City, puffed out of Albany, N. Y., in August 1831 on its first regular run over the Mohawk & Hudson Railroad (later New York Central). The first passenger coaches in the train were ordinary stagecoaches, 15 feet long and mounted on flanged wheels. Shown here is a replica of the train, built in 1893 for the Chicago World's Fair. It was faithfully reproduced from a silhouette —a popular fad of the day—made on August 9, 1831, by William H. Brown, an artist and writer who was present at the first 12-mile run to Schenectady.

THE Limited Mail, an early Pennsylvania Railroad passenger train, paused above a barge canal after crossing the Rockville Bridge over the Susquehanna River near Harrisburg, Pa., in the 1870's. Trailing the 4-4-0 were two white mail cars, two baggage cars, two day coaches, and three Pullman Palace cars.

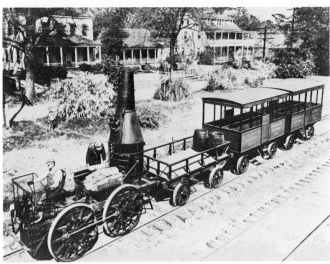

THE Baltimore & Ohio was the first common-carrier railroad in the U.S. to serve as a public conveyor of passengers, transporting the first revenue riders on January 7, 1830, with horses furnishing the motive power. The South Carolina Railroad (later Southern Railway) was the first common-carrier railroad operated by steam power. Above is a replica of the first train, operated at Charleston, S. C., on Christmas Day 1830. The locomotive was the vertical-boiler Best Friend of Charleston.

AFTER completion of the Union Pacific and the Central Pacific in 1869, transcontinental passengers riding CP's Express at Corinne, Utah (left) could choose accommodations among the "Lincoln car" (the former Presidential car), a CP coach, Pullman Palace cars that included the Wahsatch and Denver, and Silver Palace car D.

NYC.

THE New York Central & Hudson River's white Fast Mail was photographed at Albany, N. Y., in the 1890's, with the railroad YMCA in view.

Author's collection.

TWENTIETH CENTURY LIMITED mailing labels were furnished by New York Central. As late as the 1950's, 7500 pieces of mail were delivered daily to the Century in New York; 3800 pieces in Chicago. In addition, 175,000 letters were collected daily in special mail drops in Post Offices. The service was used mostly by business houses seeking safe, swift mail delivery.

George R. Lawrence.

AC&F.

SOUTHERN Railway Post Office car No. 28 (AC&F 1924) displays the pigeonhole cases and steel racks used for sorting mail en route. The U. S. Mail first was transported by rail on the South Carolina Railroad in 1831. The first special car equipped for handling mail was operated on the Hannibal & St. Joseph Railroad in 1862. Chicago & North Western introduced the first permanent RPO car in 1864. At the peak of RPO service about 1915, 20,000 clerks in nearly 4000 cars annually distributed 14 billion pieces of mail on the move.

NIGHTTIME on the Milwaukee Road. A locomotive headlight beam points the way down the track in a 1902 photograph by Chicago photographer George R. Lawrence.

THE Kansas City Southern's Flying Crow was inaugurated on June 15, 1928, for Kansas City-Shreveport-Port Arthur service. Here Pacific No. 807 heads seven steel-sheathed cars.

Author's collection.

PRR from Paul T. Warner.

A 4-4-0 speeds the Pennsylvania Limited (above), predecessor of the Broadway Limited, through Merion, Pa., in 1899. The train was known as "The Yellow Kid" because of its colors — cream above the window sill, green below, with the letterboard in red.

MICHIGAN CENTRAL No. 8, the eastbound Wolverine, rolls over Illinois Central trackage along Chicago's lakefront in 1923.

Alfred W. Johnson.

Author's collection.

STEEL CARS with sheathing grooved to resemble wood were in vogue in 1916 when gentlemen repaired to the observation car of the Royal Palm, a Chicago-Cincinnati-Jacksonville train introduced by Big Four, Queen & Crescent Route, and Southern in 1913.

ADVERTISED AS "The Rolls-Royce of American Railroading," Milwaukee Road's Pioneer Limited (below) operated between Chicago, Milwaukee, and the Twin Cities. Pacific 6109 led the re-equipped orange-and-maroon train on its exhibition run in 1927.

Kaufman & Fabry, courtesy CMStP&P.

SOMEWHERE along the coast of Connecticut a white-frocked young lady waves a nosegay at the engineer and fireman of a New Haven train.

DIXIE FLYER made first leg of Chicago-Florida run over C&EI.

GREAT TRAINS were closely associated with great hotels. In the 1890's passengers alighting from Santa Fe's California Limited at Pasadena, Calif., were adjacent to the lawn of the Hotel Green, one of many California hotels catering to tourists.

16

ALONGSIDE its namesake river, a Hudson-type locomotive of the New York Central has the famed Twentieth Century Limited in tow.

BALTIMORE & OHIO No. 6, the Capitol Limited, leaves Chicago in January 1930.

SPECIAL open-observation cars provided passengers on daylight rides aboard Milwaukee Road's Olympian with a perfect view of the Bitter Roots and a chance to breathe the bracing mountain air.

The Pony Express

GREAT NORTHERN'S Empire Builder departs St. Paul (Minn.) Union Depot under a plume of white in the glory days of steam.

BROADWAY LIMITED is drawn across the Delaware River on four-track stone arch bridge near Trenton, N. J., by one of Pennsylvania's K4s 4-6-2's. The structure was completed in 1903.

IT'S Broadway vs. Century and K4 vs. J-1 as rods and valve gear flash and the Pennsylvania's Broadway Limited and the

New York Central's Twentieth Century race from Englewood Union Station, Chicago, on 16½-hour schedules to New York.

Author's collection.

The great train races

Rice's Railroadograph.

EDITOR David P. Morgan described a great moment in railroading in TRAINS Magazine of May 1961: "It happened, doubtless, wherever competitive rails paralleled, even between steam roads and interurbans, but it took place most memorably between the titans. The Race, that is. All quite unofficial, to be sure. Management would have denied any knowledge of it — the ICC you know. Yet happily incriminating evidence is presented in this photograph (above right). Both Baltimore & Ohio and Pennsylvania scheduled

3 p.m. expresses out of Washington for New York, and this is the result as the rivals hit their stride on a June afternoon in 1930. On the outside iron is Pennsy No. 144, powered by K4 Pacific No. 5041; and slightly in the lead is B&O No. 22, under the cinders of 4-6-2 No. 5301, President Adams." More numerous, but also exciting, were the occasions when one train overtook another on the same railroad. (Above left) The Exposition Flyer passes Second No. 11 on the CB&Q between Clyde and Aurora, Ill.

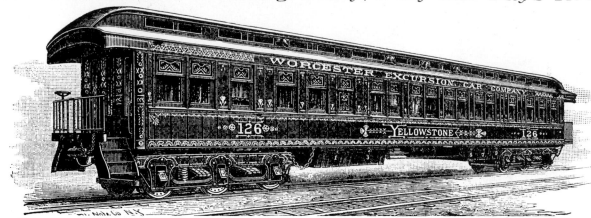

WORCESTER EXCURSION CAR COMPANY.

The 12th Annual Shooting Party, Fifty=Six Days Route.

From Worcester, Mass., to Beacon Cavern, Idaho, via Erie Railroad to Chicago, via C. & N. W. and U. P. Railroads to destination through Illinois, Iowa, Nebraska, Wyoming, to Idaho.

Leave Worcester, Sept. 6, 1890.   **PALACE HOTEL CAR "YELLOWSTONE."**

WHEN the West was still young, sportsmen (and women) from the East traveled by special cars equipped for hunting parties. Brochure cover from 1890 (above) advertised a 56-day excursion from Worcester, Mass., aboard car Yellowstone, built by Jackson & Sharp. Hunters alighted from Worcester Excursion Car Edwin Forrest (right) to pose beside an abundant supply of game for well-known photographer Haynes of Fargo in the Dakota territory.

Special trains for a special way of life

DURING the years when Americans traveled to work and to play aboard interurbans, a group of dandies prepared to leave Highwood, Ill., on a stag outing to Milwaukee, Wis. The railroad is the Chicago & Milwaukee Electric, predecessor of the North Shore, and the car is No. 29, built in 1907 by Jewett Car Company at Newark, O.

SPECIAL TRAINS featured special menus.

THE Cuban Special, an all-Pullman train, made weekly tours between Havana and Santiago from January to April 1925. The crew (below) posed in front of two observation cars. Palm trees (above) graced the dining car. Afternoon tea (left) was a social nicety.

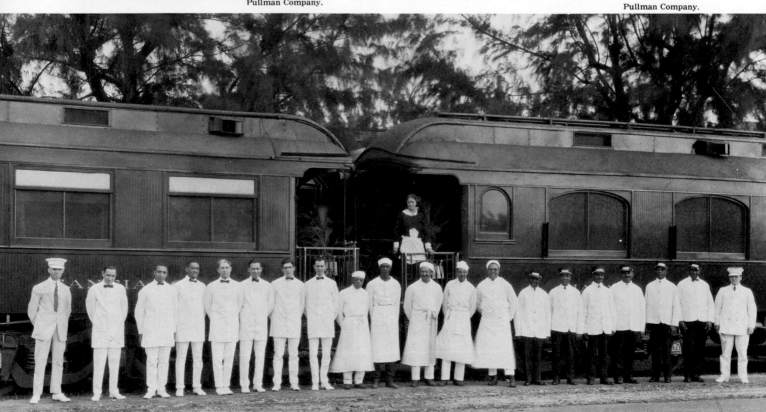

CANADIAN PACIFIC 3-foot-gauge tram, connecting the railroad-owned Chateau Lake Louise with CP's main line, operated from 1912 until 1930.

IN 1936 the United Drug Company, manufacturers of Rexall Products, decided to operate a coast-to-coast goodwill train in lieu of its state and national conventions of druggists. The Pullman Company outfitted the 12-car blue-and-white Rexall train, which covered 29,000 miles in 47 states. The drugstore on wheels (above) stands in Chicago. Car Bisma-Rex (below left) used a Rexall brand name, as did the Ad-Vantage (below right). At the far end of the car is the last word in soda fountains.

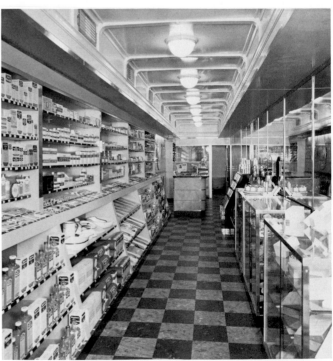

Pullman Company.

DEFENSE EXHIBIT TRAINS of World War II took off on 40-day trips which carried them into every manufacturing center where there might be available facilities for defense production. Three red, white, and blue eight-car trains left Washington, D. C., on November 10, 1941, crammed with special exhibits designed to help manufacturers, large and small, determine whether they could do defense work. Six of the eight cars on each train were filled with samples of needed defense equipment and parts, arranged for exhibit, and the other two cars contained living quarters for the staff of 36 Government representatives traveling on each train. The trains rode the rails at night, and were open for inspection during the day.

SILK SPECIAL is pulled by a bipolar gearless-type electric locomotive of the Milwaukee Road. Before the advent of synthetic textiles, silk specials raced across the continent from Pacific Coast ports in the United States and Canada with their precious cargoes destined for eastern manufacturing plants. During a peak year, 1929, more than 500,000 bales of raw silk worth 3¼ million dollars were transported by rail to the East. During August 1924 one of the fastest silk trains on record operated Seattle-New York City in 73 hours 25 minutes.

CMStP&P.

PRR.

ON March 4, 1924, the Pennsylvania Railroad ran a special train for the International News Reel Corp. that carried motion pictures of the Calvin Coolidge inauguration. The train prepares to leave Union Station in Washington, D. C.

Pullman Company.

THE inauguration of President Dwight D. Eisenhower in 1953 was a major operational exercise for Eastern railroads — especially those directly serving Washington. More than 600 coaches, sleeping and parlor cars, and diners converged on the city at the same time, and over 10,000 persons made their home in parked sleepers — 2100 alone at B&O's Eckington Yard (above). The railroads provided their guests with telephone service, steam heat and electricity, and 24-hour police protection.

RAYMOND-WHITCOMB
LAND CRUISES
IN AMERICA

SUMMER 1928

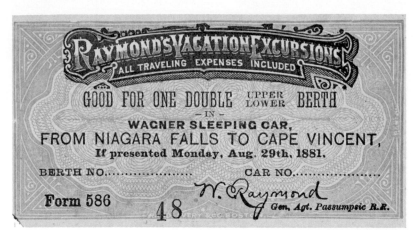

RAYMOND'S VACATION EXCURSIONS
ALL TRAVELING EXPENSES INCLUDED

GOOD FOR ONE DOUBLE UPPER LOWER BERTH
— IN —
WAGNER SLEEPING CAR,
FROM NIAGARA FALLS TO CAPE VINCENT,
If presented Monday, Aug. 29th, 1881.

BERTH NO.................... CAR NO....................

Form 586   48   W. Raymond
Gen. Agt. Passumpsic R.R.

BOSTON travel merchants W. Raymond and I. A. Whitcomb began their Raymond & Whitcomb excursions, "All Traveling Expenses Included," in the 1880's to show Easterners the wonders of the American West and Mexico by train. George M. Pullman provided luxurious equipment, including special dining car Raymond in 1886, one of the few Pullmans named for a living person. In 1926 Raymond & Whitcomb introduced Land Cruise Liners. Again, the Pullman Company co-operated by turning out six special cars: three entertainment-recreation cars, two all-room sleepers, and one open-section car. The Land Cruise Liners operated throughout North America, but were discontinued in 1931, victims of the stock market crash and hard times.

YOSEMITE PARK (left and below) was a special all-room sleeper for Raymond & Whitcomb that featured showers in two bedrooms, fixed lower beds in all rooms, and private toilet facilities. Point Willoughby (right) was a 10-section, 2-drawing-room Pullman built in 1926.

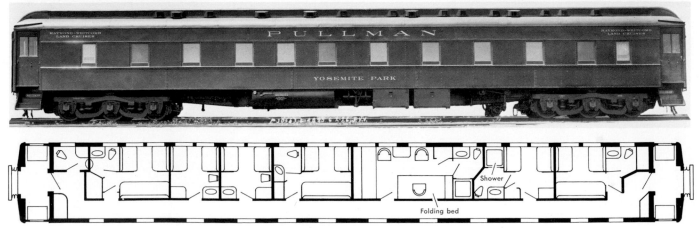

ENTERTAINMENT-RECREATION CAR Coliseum, built in 1926 for Raymond & Whitcomb Land Cruise trains, had a gymnasium complete with weights, mechanical horse, punching bag, lockers, and shower room; barbershop; library-lounge; and a recreation hall for lectures, motion pictures, and lantern slides. The 38-foot-long room also could accommodate 15 couples for dancing.

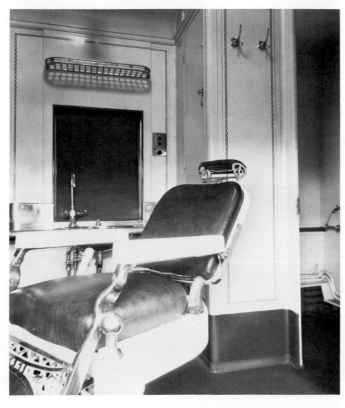

Interurban classics

DE LUXE Chicago North Shore & Milwaukee golf special for the Banker's Association pauses at Highland Park, Ill., circa 1925.

Author's collection.

THE Comet, luxury electric train of the Oakland, Antioch & Eastern (later Sacramento Northern) between San Francisco and Sacramento, crosses the Lake Temescal bridge in the Berkeley hills about 1915. Double-platform observation-parlor-buffet car Moraga was built in 1913 by Wason Car Company of Worcester, Mass.

Herbert Georg Studio, collection of George Krambles.

PRIDE of the Illinois Terminal System were the Peorian and the Capitol Limited, which operated between Peoria-Springfield-St. Louis. This view taken in 1935 shows one of the tangerine-colored beauties on the wye at Springfield. Reserved-seat observation-parlor-dining car Lincoln brings up the rear. IT and its predecessor, Illinois Traction System, operated over some 450 route miles.

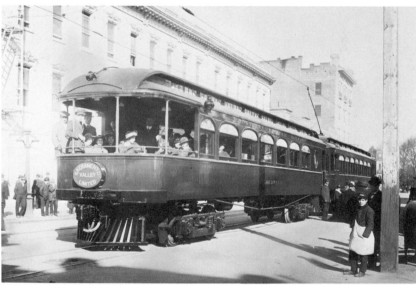

McCurry Foto Co., from author's collection.

THE maiden run of classic, de luxe observation-parlor car Bidwell was on Northern Electric's Sacramento Valley Limited from Sacramento, Calif., in 1915.

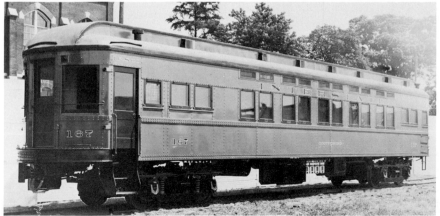

Both photos, collection of George Krambles.

ORANGE-AND-RED 10-section sleeping car Scottsburg, a trailer built in 1926 by American Car & Foundry, was operated by the Interstate Public Service Company between Indianapolis and Louisville until 1931, when it was sold to the Pacific Great Eastern along with sisters Indianapolis and Louisville for operation north of Vancouver, B. C.

The Streamliner
CITY OF LOS ANGELES

THREE great trains of the streamliner era: From left to right, Santa Fe's extra-fare Super Chief made the daily run between Chicago and Los Angeles in 39¾ hours; Union Pacific-Chicago & North Western City of Denver covered 1048 miles in 16 hours at an average speed of 65 mph; the red, green, and silver Green Diamond of Illinois Central ran the 294 miles from Chicago to St. Louis in 5 hours.

ROCK ISLAND'S Rockets meet near Englewood, Ill.

D. W. Yungmeyer.

Sleek and swift—the streamliner era

PRR.

THE Pennsylvania Railroad's Trail Blazer, photographed at Englewood in 1945, is pulled by S-1 6-4-4-6 No. 6100, one of the largest and fastest steam locomotives ever built. This four-cylinder giant was capable of sustained speeds of 100 mph.

FAMED NYC Hudson 5344, Commodore Vanderbilt, rebuilt in 1934 with a slipstream cowl for Century service, overtakes a Rock Island 4-8-2.

CRI&P AND SP operated the short-lived Arizona Limited. The streamlined, all-Pullman, extra-fare train ran every second day Chicago-Phoenix during the winter season of 1940-1941. On the rear is Pullman American Milemaster, which was exhibited at the New York World's Fair in 1939.

BURLINGTON'S Mark Twain Zephyr arrives at Hannibal, Mo., in 1952 during its daily round trip along the Mississippi River between St. Louis and Burlington, Ia. The train's tail sign is a bas-relief of Samuel L. Clemens (Mark Twain) and his signature.

A STREAMLINED version of a time-honored pose. Eastbound and westbound Twentieth Centuries meet in the night at Buffalo, N. Y.

IN 1947 General Motors' Electro-Motive Division, working with Pullman-Standard, produced an experimental train, the Train of Tomorrow, which was shown during a 6-month exhibition tour of the United States. The four-car train contained a day coach, diner, sleeper, and observation lounge, and was powered by a single EMD 2000-h.p. E7 diesel locomotive. Each of the four cars was equipped with the new Astra-Dome. The train, seen on the Monon near French Lick, Ind., was sold to the Union Pacific in 1950.

TRAIN-NUMBER board, green flags mark first section of SP's Cascade.

CENTURY lounge patrons (above) were served in a raised observation section. Broadway's Tower View (below) and Mountain View had buffet-lounges.

MISSOURI PACIFIC'S new Texas Eagle leaves St. Louis in 1948.

PIONEER LIMITED of early 1900's was sans observation platform.

PRETTY girls ride the Sioux to the Corn Palace, Mitchell, S. Dak., in 1930.

Posing on the platform

IT'S March 1, 1929, and passengers aboard the Miamian await 10 a.m. departure time while the conductor checks his Hamilton. In a few minutes, all-Pullman First 72 will depart Miami for New York.

A GROUP poses on the open platform of Northern Pacific's Yellowstone Comet in 1927. Barney & Smith originally built the observation car for the North Coast Limited.

WITH brass rail gleaming and scarlet-and-white drumhead sign aglow, the Florida-bound Dixie Limited of 1925 readies for its southward run from Chicago's Dearborn Station via the C&EI's Dixie Route.

The Miamian
NEW YORK—PALM BEACH—MIAMI

PASSENGERS happily bid adieu from the platform of the North Western Limited in 1923. It was about this time that new improved E-2 4-6-2 locomotives and the latest Pullman-Standard sleeping cars were placed in operation on "the shortest route to St. Paul and Minneapolis."

A LOUNGE-OBSERVATION CAR of the Denver & Rio Grande Western poses for 1926 Panoramic Special photo at Burnham Shops, Denver.

33

A COLLECTION of early Pullman sleeping-car tickets includes No. 1, an original ticket issued in 1859.

Origin and development of the sleeping car

THE first sleeping-car service in the United States is generally acknowledged to have been established in the winter of 1837-1838 on the Cumberland Valley Railroad (later part of the Pennsylvania Railroad) between Harrisburg and Chambersburg, Pa., where connection was made with the western stage-coach. The car was a remodeled day coach with crudely built berths or bunks. On each side of a center aisle near the middle of the car were two sections of bunks, three bunks to a section. The top bunk turned up toward the roof, the middle one folded down against the side of the car and formed the back of the seat, and the lowest bunk was used as a seat. By day the passengers occupied this seat facing the aisle. At one end of the car was a wash basin. A wood or coal stove furnished the heat and can-

dles provided illumination. The car was named *Chambersburg*.

Later, different types of bunk cars appeared on newly completed railroads, sometimes with slight improvements, but none offered a great deal of comfort. At first no bed coverings were furnished and passengers reclined on rough mattresses with overcoats or shawls drawn over them. Eventually, railroads began supplying travelers with bedding.

The sleeping-car business had its true inception in 1859 when George Mortimer Pullman completed his first car. Recognition must be given to Pullman for development of the comfortable and convenient passenger train. He conceived the luxury car and the network of through routes which enabled passengers to travel over long distances in comfort.

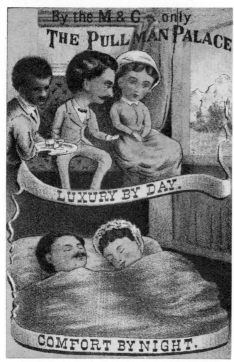

TRADE CARD advertised Pullman luxury.

AN EARLY Union Pacific tourist car reveals bare wooden seats and spittoons, indicating it was a man's world in the 1880's.

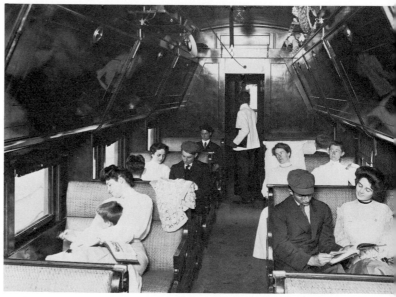

AFTER a reupholstering in rattan, this standard sleeper served as a tourist car on the Chicago, Milwaukee & St. Paul in 1900.

REFINED sleeping-car travel was apparent in the varnished woodwork, brass hardware, beautiful upholstered seats, and imported carpet that marked a first-class Pullman of the 1880's.

PHOTO depicts a model of a Cumberland Valley sleeping car.

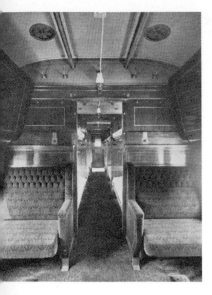
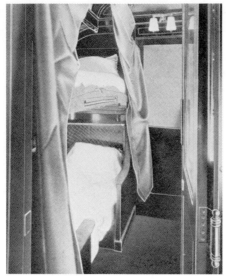

BARNEY & SMITH built Springfield (right) and Decatur for Illinois Traction in 1911. The interior (left) contained 10 sections.

CN.

THIS sleeping car owned by Canadian National had semi-enclosed sections with shaded lamps, carpet, and air conditioning.

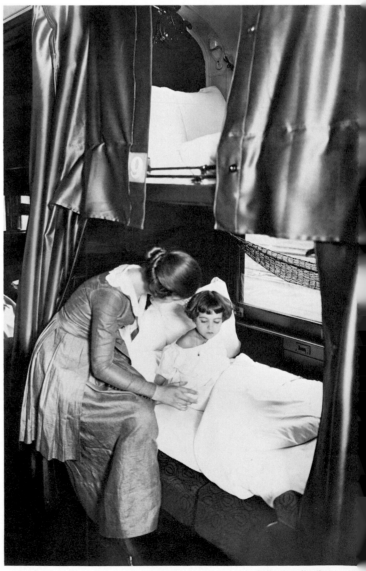

Author's collection.

UPPER and lower berths in section No. 9 are ready for occupancy as a young mother tucks in her child in this 1910 photo.

PULLMAN tourist-car passengers riding the Santa Fe early in the 20th century witnessed many happy scenes, such as this sing-along. Note the Gibson Girl look.

HORSE-DRAWN sleeping car (right and below) was built by Brill in 1887 for a 70-mile run on the **Tramway Rural** in Argentina.

AN IMPORTANT duty of the Pullman porter was the preparation of beds for passengers. Bed making was an art, and porters prided themselves on making beds that were as comfortable to sleep in as they were attractive to look at.

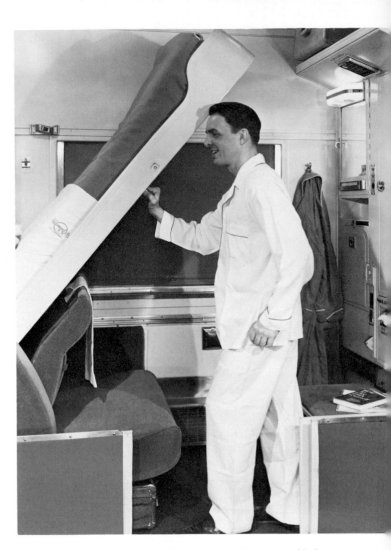

ALL the comforts of home. The roomette of 1937 provided an enclosed room with folding bed, crisp linen, and private toilet.

ONE of Pullman's most elegant cars was built in 1897 for the Mexican government. This suite was resplendent with gilt ornamentation and satin draperies with fringed tassels.

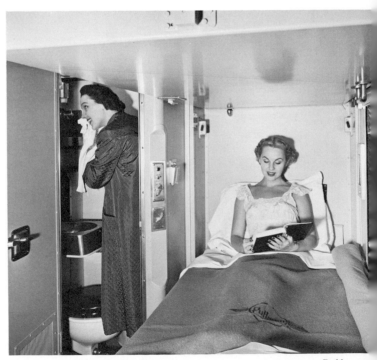

PRIVACY was a keynote of lightweight sleepers as enclosed quarters replaced open sections. Two women enjoy a double bedroom, with private toilet annex, on the CB&Q's American Royal Zephyr.

CMStP&P.

PASSENGERS who rode Milwaukee Road's Pioneer Limited coach to Chicago's "A Century of Progress" in 1934 slept in soft beds.

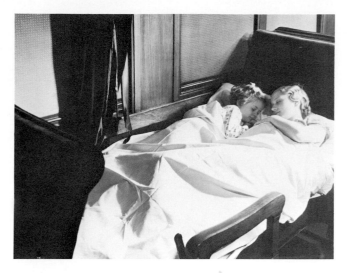

MOTHER and child doze in lie-down coach on Northern Pacific. Price was an important consideration during the depression.

How the travel-prone traveled prone

GN.

A POST-WORLD WAR II double bedroom (above) on Great Northern's Empire Builder was plain but modern, with many mechanical comforts. Harness was a protection in case of emergency stops.

(ABOVE RIGHT) Coach seats on a Baltimore & Ohio special for a Boy Scout outing in the mid-1930's were arranged for sleeping.

BUDGET-MINDED passengers were able to travel overnight in coaches. Reclining seats and adjustable leg and footrests, along with pillows, on a Burlington coach (right) made sleeping easier.

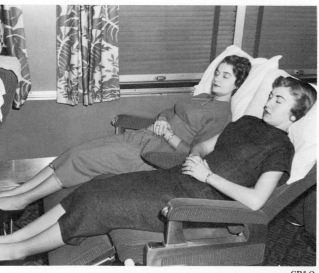

CB&Q.

All photos, author's collection.

Dinner in the dining car

EARLY travelers by rail were forced to take their meals at eating houses en route. Such meals generally were rushed and unpleasant experiences, although dining in houses operated by Fred Harvey along the Santa Fe was an exception.

To provide food service aboard the cars, George Pullman constructed the hotel car *President* in 1867. This car, which combined sleeping and eating, made its appearance on the Great Western Railway of Canada. One year later Pullman produced the first car exclusively made for dining and named it *Delmonico*, after the famous New York restaurateur. It entered service on the Chicago & Alton and proved such a success that it fostered a fleet of dining cars operated by Pullman Company.

Gradually the railroads established their own dining-car services, which were operated solely to attract passengers. Although dining cars rarely made a profit, they served as showpieces for the railroad, and on competitive runs passengers often selected trains because of their reputation for special dishes and good meals.

PULLMAN hotel cars Windsor, President, Buckingham, Marlborough, Rossmore, and Viceroy operated on the Pennsylvania during the 1870's and 1880's and offered such delicacies as quail and blue-winged teal in elegant surroundings (above left). Santa Fe dining car Gilsey (above right) was built by Pullman in 1888.

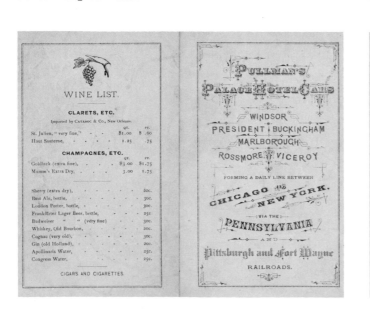

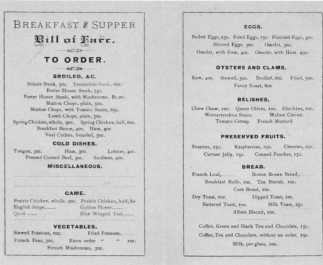

CB&Q. C&NW, author's collection. NP.

FLOWERS were featured both on dining cars (left) and on menus (center). Chef prepares NP's famous Big Baked Potatoes (right).

Collection of Andrew Merrilees.

DELMONICO (1868) was the first car built exclusively for dining.

TWENTIETH CENTURY LIMITED
ON THE NEW YORK CENTRAL.

DINNER

BLUE POINTS ON HALF SHELL

CONSOMME JULIENNE CREAM OF TOMATO

OLIVES SALTED ALMONDS CELERY

BOILED CHICKEN HALIBUT, VIN BLANC
POTATOES NATUREL

SMALL PATTIES OF CAPON, FINANCIERE
APPLE FRITTERS GLACE AU KIRSCH

PRIME RIBS OF BEEF AU JUS

BOILED POTATOES MASHED POTATOES BAKED SWEET POTATOES
BOILED ONIONS GREEN PEAS STRING BEANS

PUNCH CREME DE MENTHE

ROAST YOUNG GOOSE WITH DRESSING, APPLE SAUCE

LETTUCE SALAD, MAYONNAISE OR FRENCH DRESSING

BANANA CUSTARD, ORANGE CREAM SAUCE
ASSORTED CAKE FRUIT IN SEASON ICE CREAM

CANADIAN CLUB CHEESE ROQUEFORT CHEESE
BROWNSVILLE OR BENT'S WATER CRACKERS, TOASTED

COFFEE

No charge for coffee demi-tasse served in Buffet Smoking or Observation Car.
Please procure check from dining car conductor.

MEALS, ONE DOLLAR

"LITHIA POLARIS"—PURE SPRING WATER FREE."
The drinking water served on this car is from the celebrated "Polaris
Springs" of the Boonville Mineral Spring Co., on the Rome, Watertown &
Ogdensburg Division, in the foot-hills of the Adirondack Mountains. It has
been analyzed by eminent chemists and is absolutely pure.
A SOUVENIR MENU.
A copy of this Menu card in an envelope ready for mailing will be
furnished free on application, by the conductor in charge of this car.

Author's collection.

DINNER on the Twentieth Century Limited cost a dollar in 1904.

Pullman-Standard.

WAITERS such as the one on the Pennsylvania (left) would happily furnish customers with recipes for "specialties of the house." The 1897 oyster car (above) was designed by Arthur Stilwell to transport seafood delicacies north from the Gulf.

PRR.

THE NORTH SHORE SPECIAL

CHICAGO AND MILWAUKEE

VIA

THE NORTH WESTERN LINE

DINNER

LOBSTER COCKTAIL

CHESTNUT PUREE   CONSOMME, NEAPOLITAINE
SALTED ALMONDS   OLIVES

FILET OF SOLE, TARTAR
SLICED CUCUMBERS

SWEETBREAD AND FRESH MUSHROOM PATTIES

CELERY CROQUETTES

ROAST TURKEY, CRANBERRIES
SWEET POTATOES, KENTUCKY STYLE   ARTICHOKES, HOLLANDAISE

ROAST NATIVE BEEF, NATURAL
BROWNED MASHED POTATOES   SPINACH, A LA CREME

THANKSGIVING SHERBET

POINSETTIA SALAD

NEW ENGLAND PUMPKIN PIE

SWEET APPLE CIDER

PISTACHIO ICE CREAM   HICKORY NUT CAKE

ROQUEFORT   CAMEMBERT

COFFEE

DUBONNET, A TONIC AND APPETIZER, INDIVIDUAL, $ .20

WINES. ETC.

		SMALL
Champagnes	MOET & CHANDON (WHITE SEAL)	$2.00
	POMMERY SEC	2.00
	G. H. MUMM'S (EXTRA DRY)	2.00
	KRUG PRIVATE CUVEE	2.00
	RUINART, VIN BRUT	2.00
	IMPERIAL (COOK'S)	1.25
California Red Wines	ST. JULIEN (CRESTA BLANCA) — SPLITS, .25	.50
	CHATEAU MARGAUX (ALTA VISTA)	.75
	MEDOC (ALTA VISTA)	.50
	CHIANTI (ALTA VISTA)	.50
	ST. JULIEN (GOLD MEDAL CORDOVA)	.50
Imported Red Wines	ST. JULIEN (NATHANIEL JOHNSON & SON)	.75
	PONTET CANET " "	1.00
	CHATEAU LAROSE (HORRAMER, LEON & CO.)	1.75
	ST. JULIEN (HORRAMER, LEON & CO.)	.75
	PONTET CANET " "	1.00
California White Wines	SAUTERNE (GOLD MEDAL CORDOVA)	.50
	SAUTERNE (ALTA VISTA)	.50
Imported White Wines	SAUTERNE (NATHANIEL JOHNSON & SON)	.75
	CHATEAU LATOUR BLANCHE "	1.50
	RUEDESHEIMER (DEINHARD CO.)	1.00
California Sparkling Wines	BURGUNDY	1.00
	MOSELLE	1.00
Imported Sparkling Wines	CHAMBERTIN, RED (B. L. & CO.)	1.50
	CHABLIS, WHITE (B. L. & CO.)	1.50
Waters	HIAWATHA LITHIA — SPLITS, .15	.25
	IMPORTED CLUB SODA	.25
	DELATOUR CLUB SODA	.25
	CONGRESS OR HATHORN	.25
	WHITE ROCK LITHIA — SPLITS, .15	.25
	APOLLINARIS " .15	.25
	CLYSSMIC " .15	.25
	POLAND — UNCHARGED	.25
	SPARKLING APENTA — SPLITS, .15	
	RED RAVEN " .15	
	HUNYADI — PER GLASS, .15	.35
Beer	PABST "BLUE RIBBON"	.20
	SCHLITZ "PALE"	.20
	BLATZ "WIENER"	.20
	MILLER'S "HIGH LIFE"	.20
	SCHOENHOFEN EDELWEISS	.20
	LEISY "EXPORT"	.20
Whiskies	OLD FITZGERALD RYE OR BOURBON — INDIVIDUALS, .20	
	NATIONAL CLUB BOURBON " .20	
	SCOTCH OR CANADIAN CLUB " .20	
	WESTMORELAND RYE " .20	
	KING WILLIAM SCOTCH " .25	
	RYE OR BOURBON, FLASKS, 50c AND 75c	
Miscellaneous	COCKTAILS—WHISKY, MARTINI OR MANHATTAN " .20	
	HENNESSY BRANDY " .35	
	AMONTILLADO SHERRY " .20	
	BASS' ALE, WHITE LABEL OR DOG'S HEAD — NIPS, .15	.30
	BESLEY'S PALE ALE — NIPS, .10	
	GUINNESS' DUBLIN PORTER	.30
	BELFAST GINGER ALE " .25	
	WHITE ROCK GINGER ALE " .15	
	OLD TOM GIN — INDIVIDUALS, .20	
	CREME DE MENTHE " .20	
	BENEDICTINE " .20	
	EFFERVESCENT BROMO SELTZER " .10	
	MALT NUTRINE — SPLITS, .15	

IMPORTED AND DOMESTIC CIGARS, 10c, TWO FOR 25c, 15c AND 25c

All items, author's collection.

A THANKSGIVING DAY dinner with chestnut puree, roast turkey, and pumpkin pie was part of the menu on the North Shore Special of the North Western Line between Chicago and Milwaukee in 1909. Printed recipes for special dishes were available, compliments of the steward.

NORTH SHORE LINE
"The Road of Service"

Parlor Dining Car Service

Luncheon
65 Cents

Choice
Beef Stew with Vegetables
Red Currant Jelly Omelet
Broiled Lamb Chop, Currant Jelly

Cottage Fried Potatoes   Hot Pickled Beets

Bread and Butter

Home-made Pie

Coffee   Tea   Milk

Luncheon
75 Cents

Broiled North Shore Tenderloin Steak

Cottage Fried Potatoes   Cole Slaw

Bread and Butter

Home-made Pie

Coffee   Tea   Milk

MINIMUM SERVICE CHARGE 65c. PER PERSON

To Patrons:

When patrons occupy a parlor car chair longer than the time of serving a meal, the regular charge for such accommodations will be made.

A parlor car chair may be occupied, without the ordering of food, at the regular fixed charge.

Beverages

All Beverages are opened in the presence of our guests and
Served from the original individual sealed container.

COCKTAILS
Martini 30
Dry Martini 30
Old Fashioned 30
Manhattan 30

WHISKIES
Bourbon Bonded 40
Bourbon Bonded Highball 45
Bourbon 25
Bourbon Highball 30
Rye, Bonded 40
Rye, Bonded Highball 45
Scotch (Imported) 40
Scotch (Imported) Highball 45

(Highballs served with split of ginger ale or sparkling water as desired)

BRANDY
Cognac (Imported) 40

GIN
Distilled Dry (Domestic) 25

IMPORTED WINES
Port 30
Sherry 30

BEER
Bottle or Can 25

GINGER ALE
Splits 15

MINERAL WATER
White Rock Splits 15
Sparkling Water, Splits 10

CIGARS AND CIGARETTES
Cigars . . . . 2/25—15
Cigarettes 20

PLAYING CARDS
Club Special 50

IN 1939 the North Shore Line interurban featured broiled tenderloin steak for 75 cents. In 1909 a shot of aged rye whiskey cost 20 cents; 30 years later the price had doubled.

TOUR OF
THE PRESIDENT
TO THE NAVAL REVIEW
APRIL 26. 1893.

DINNER   WASHINGTON TO NEW YORK

BLUE POINTS — CELERY   AMONTILLADO SHERRY

GREEN TURTLE   CHATEAU YQUEM

FILLETS OF SOLE, TARTARE SAUCE — POTATOES A LA DUCHESSE

PHILADELPHIA CAPON, EGG SAUCE   CHATEAU MARGAUX

ROAST BEEF — NEW POTATOES

SPRING LAMB, MINT SAUCE

GREEN PEAS — ASPARAGUS

SQUAB ON TOAST — PINE APPLE FRITTERS

LOBSTER SALAD — DRESSED LETTUCE   POMMERY AND GRENO SEC

ENGLISH PLUM PUDDING, BRANDY SAUCE

STRAWBERRIES AND CREAM — FRENCH ICE CREAM

ASSORTED CAKE — PRESERVED FRUITS

CHILLED ORANGES — MALAGA GRAPES

ROQUEFORT AND EDAM CHEESE

BENT'S CRACKERS

CAFÉ NOIR

PULLMAN DINING CAR SERVICE

BILL OF FARE from a special train transporting President Grover Cleveland to a naval review on April 26, 1893, listed green turtle soup, squab on toast with pineapple fritters, and English plum pudding with a brandy sauce. The menu was autographed by the President, his wife Frances, and other dignitaries.

Dining Service
The George Washington
CHESAPEAKE AND OHIO LINES
☆
Mount Vernon Dinner $1.25

Celery Hearts   Green Olives
Tomato Juice or Oyster Cocktail
——— CHOICE ———
Philadelphia Clam Chowder   Consomme
——— CHOICE ———
Broiled or Fried Fish, Lemon Butter
Dinner Steak   Grilled Lamb Chops
Fried Oysters with Cole Slaw
Roast Young Turkey with Dressing, Cranberry Jelly
——— CHOICE OF TWO ———
Potatoes (as desired)   Creamed Cauliflower
Fresh Green Beans   Buttered Beets   Broccoli (Hollandaise)
Green Pepper and Cream Cheese Salad
French Endive Salad with French Dressing
Assorted Bread
——— CHOICE ———
Pumpkin Pie   Mince Pie   Baked Apple
Ice Cream with Cake   Grapefruit
Roquefort or Martha Washington Cream Cheese with Wafers
Tea   Coffee   Milk   Cocoa
☆
Tavern Dinner 75c
Broiled or Fried Fish or
Pot Roast of Beef, Browned Potatoes, Brussels Sprouts
Lettuce Salad, Assorted Bread, Pumpkin Pie
Tea, Coffee, Milk
☆
ꙮ *Suggestions* ꙮ

Oysters—On Half Shell 35, Stewed in Cream 50, in Milk 35
Oysters—Fried (6) 50, with Cole Slaw 60
Broiled or Fried Bass, with one Vegetable 85
Grilled Lamb Chops (2) with one Vegetable 85
Dinner Steak with one Vegetable 85
Roast Young Turkey, Dressing, Cranberry Jelly 75
Pot Roast of Beef, Browned Potatoes 65
Omelet with Mushrooms or Oysters 65
Imported Frankfurters, Potato Salad 60
Broiled French Sardines on Toast 60
Oven Baked Beans with Brown Bread 35

You are welcome to take this Menu Card with you.
The Steward will provide an envelope upon request.

ONE of the last great heavyweight trains, the George Washington, was placed in service by Chesapeake & Ohio on April 24, 1932. Colonial dining car featured a $1.25 Mount Vernon dinner.

AT&SF
De Luxe

· MENU ·
DEC 1 2 1911

OYSTERS—BLUE POINTS 25   FRIED 40   BROILED 40   MILK STEW 35
SARDINES 40   CAVIAR 40   CHOW CHOW 15   OLIVES 20
BROILED OR FRIED BACON 50   BROILED OR FRIED HAM 50
BACON AND EGGS 60   HAM AND EGGS 60
BOILED, FRIED OR SCRAMBLED EGGS 25   POACHED EGGS ON TOAST 45
SHIRRED EGGS 30   PLAIN OMELETTE 35; WITH HAM, PARSLEY, OR TOMATO 50
MUSHROOM OR RUM OMELETTE 50
TENDERLOIN OR SIRLOIN STEAK 90
WITH FRENCH PEAS 1.00   WITH MUSHROOMS 1.10   WITH BACON 1.00
WITH BORDELAISE OR BEARNAISE SAUCE 1.10
EXTRA SIRLOIN STEAK, FOR TWO 1.75
WITH FRENCH PEAS 2.00   WITH MUSHROOMS 2.00   WITH BACON 2.00
WITH BEARNAISE OR BORDELAISE SAUCE 2.00
BROILED YOUNG CHICKEN 65   FRIED YOUNG CHICKEN 65
MUTTON CHOPS 60
WITH BACON 70   WITH TOMATO SAUCE 70
POTATOES—FRENCH FRIED 15   AU GRATIN 25
HASHED, BROWNED, LYONNAISE OR JULIENNE 15
COLD OX TONGUE 40   COLD HAM 50   BOSTON BAKED BEANS, HOT OR COLD 30
LETTUCE SALAD 30   POTATO SALAD 25   CHICKEN SALAD 60
VIENNA BREAD 10   TEA BISCUIT 10   BOSTON BROWN BREAD 10
DRY TOAST 10   BUTTERED TOAST 10   MILK TOAST 25
SHREDDED WHEAT BISCUIT WITH CREAM 25
ASSORTED FRUIT 20   PRESERVED STRAWBERRIES 25   PRESERVED FIGS 25
ORANGE MARMALADE 20
ROQUEFORT CHEESE WITH WATER CRACKERS 25
COFFEE, PER POT, FOR ONE 15; PER POT, FOR TWO 25   DEMI-TASSE 10
COCOA OR CHOCOLATE WITH WHIPPED CREAM, PER CUP 15
TEA—CEYLON, YOUNG HYSON, ENGLISH BREAKFAST, OR SPECIAL BLEND
PER POT, FOR ONE 15; FOR TWO 25
MILK, PER BOTTLE 15   MALTED MILK, PER CUP 15
ONLY PURE SPRING WATER SERVED

GUESTS WILL PLEASE CALL FOR CHECK BEFORE PAYING AND COMPARE AMOUNTS CHARGED
A CHARGE OF 25 CENTS IS MADE FOR EACH EXTRA PERSON SERVED FROM A SINGLE
MEAT OR FISH ORDER

SANTA FE DINING CAR SERVICE
BY FRED HARVEY

THE "Extra Fast-Extra Fine-Extra Fare" Santa Fe de-Luxe operated once a week each way between Chicago and Los Angeles during the winter season. Occupancy was limited to just 60 persons. The menu, offering Fred Harvey dining service, is from the inaugural run of the train on December 12, 1911.

IN 1950 Santa Fe's new Super Chief offered the Turquoise Room, which was decorated with a sterling-silver medallion inlaid with turquoise and hand-fashioned by the Zuni Indians of New Mexico. Medallion replica was embossed on cover of elaborate 11 x 14-inch menu, which featured Double Sirloin for $7.75.

George L. Beam.

BROILED Rocky Mountain trout was a Denver & Rio Grande specialty in 1910.

Author's collection.

INTERURBAN railways prided themselves on their dining service. Chicago & Milwaukee Electric parlor-buffet car No. 400 had immaculate linen, fresh flowers, and a smiling, congenial staff.

CMStP&P.

KITCHEN on Milwaukee Road dining car was scrupulously clean.

SP.

CONSTRUCTED by Pullman-Standard in 1949 for Southern Pacific's overnight San Francisco-Portland Cascade, the triple-unit Cascade Club (above) was an articulated diner and lounge, 203 feet 10 inches long. Dining car (below) was outshopped by Budd for Chicago, Burlington & Quincy's 1936 stainless-steel Denver Zephyr, one of the country's great overnight streamliners.

Hedrich-Blessing.

44

DINING CAR Giacobini (named for a comet) ran on Central Railroad of New Jersey's famed blue-and-white special, the Blue Comet, inaugurated in February 1929 on the New York-Atlantic City run. Blue Comet paved the way for all-coach trains such as the Trail Blazer and El Capitan.

WAITERS carry dinners on Rock Island's crack Golden State Limited.

SPECIAL Pullman Company dining-room car D-100 operated in tandem with dorm-kitchen car K-100. In 1937 the nine-year-old cars respectively were named Angel's Camp and Donner Lake for service on UP's Forty-Niner.

FRESH ROSES welcomed early risers to breakfast on the Golden State.

BOISTEROUS politicians aboard New York Central's Albany-New York City "Legislative Train" made ladies tremble with fear.

Club car cavalcade

THE social center of the de luxe train was either the club car or the lounge car. On truly posh trains there was one of each: a club car, usually for men; and a lounge car for ladies. In the early days of the limited, drinking hard liquor and smoking was confined to the club car. This pattern prevailed until passage of the Volstead Act in 1919 (commonly known as pro-

hibition), which precluded the sale of liquor. Notable exceptions were the limiteds which operated in or through parts of Canada.

"Repeal" of the Volstead Act in 1933 and the popularity of smoking by women changed life on the cars. In time the men's club car disappeared; only the lounge car remained.

PASSENGERS rode in style on Pennsylvania Railroad parlor cars between New York and Philadelphia during 1876.

PARLOR CAR Maud, replete with oil lamps and tassels, was built by Pullman for service on Boston & Maine in June 1893.

WAGNER drawing-room car Pinzon was finished in satinwood in Louis XVI style; library at far end of car was English oak.

PARLOR CARS such as CMStP&P's Ripon were affected by the private automobile as businessmen took to the highway.

AT the turn of the century, Burlington club-car patrons enjoyed liquid refreshment or a cigar while reading publications such as Leslie's or Harper's Weekly. Women were not to be found in the masculine atmosphere of whiskey and nicotine.

CANADIAN NATIONAL lounge car James Bay was built in 1929 for the Toronto-Vancouver Confederation. It boasted English silver harewood paneling and blue-and-silver upholstery. Adding to the pleasures of travel were a shower, barbershop, and gym.

NO prohibition here! The smoking room of Canadian Pacific's Trans-Canada Limited was one of the places where a man could freely order scotch and soda in the prohibition year of 1929.

BARNEY & SMITH club car of the Milwaukee Road was built in 1909 and served nearly 40 years on the Pioneer Limited. Interior contained Spanish leather chairs, leaded-glass windows.

Pullman-Standard.

ALTON LIMITED observation car featured a Tea Room, where Japanese girls dressed in kimonos served tea.

NEATLY ARRANGED spittoons were part of the decor in the club car of Reading Company's speedster, the Rocket. In 1932 a reserved seat on this train cost 35 cents.

BROCHURE listed services, prices.

CARD was used to make up a passenger list on Panama Limited.

CMStP&P.

TAPESTRY and polished wood grace this cozy nook in the lounge car of CMStP&P's Chicago-Omaha New Arrow in July 1929.

48

TRAVELERS on their way to fun and games in Colorado in 1929 are absorbed in their various hobbies aboard the Burlington's Aristocrat.

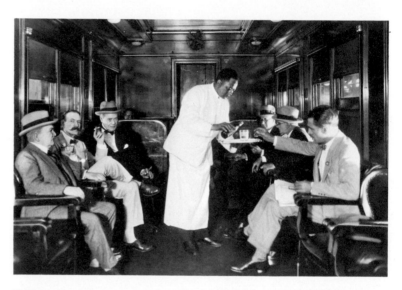

THE liquor cabinets on the Twentieth Century Limited usually were well-stocked, but during prohibition the club car served "near beer" and ginger ale. The only hard liquor available on New York Central lines was served aboard Michigan Central trains en route through Ontario, Canada.

THOUSANDS of postcards probably were written at this desk in the salon-lounge of sleeping car Happy Hollow Club on CB&Q's Ak-Sar-Ben (Nebraska spelled backwards), a train named after an Omaha civic group.

CHICAGO & NORTH WESTERN lounge car was built by AC&F in 1949 for Overland Route service. In 1961, long after Overland Route trains had moved to CMStP&P, it was rebuilt to a commuter tavern car.

PASSENGERS faced each other instead of the scenery on this remodeled Illinois Terminal interurban parlor-buffet-observation car, which operated in Peoria-Springfield-St. Louis service.

UP-C&NW'S Columbine, named after Colorado's state flower, carried the solarium-lounge Colorado Club, which displayed the state shield (below) against a blue-and-cream exterior.

THE Spanish decor of Camaguey of the Havana Special set the mood for travelers bound for Cuba via Key West in 1926.

THE Pompeiian Room of CB&Q's Denver Limited was decorated in red, black, bronze, green, and ivory. Filipino attendant served mineral water and tea, but no hard liquor. The christening by Mayor William E. Dever of Chicago on June 16, 1926, marked the first time such a ceremony was broadcast on radio from coast to coast. The summer-only Denver Limited operated for several seasons.

INTERIOR DESIGNER S. B. McDonald gave the lounge of the 1937 Super Chief the full Navajo treatment by including colorful blanket upholstery, and authentic Navajo sand paintings on the pier panels.

En Route

B&O.

BALTIMORE & OHIO maintained a high standard in car equipment, as attested to by this observation-lounge on the Capitol Limited. It provided a relaxing atmosphere in which to spend part of the time en route to one's destination. The car was one of the Capitol-series observations built in 1929 and remodeled in 1938.

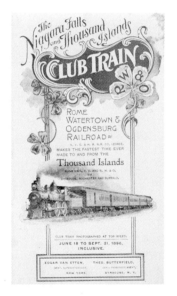

CLUB train was RW&O's bid for 1896 vacation trade.

CRI&P.

CLEANING women tidied the observation car on Rock Island's Golden State Limited.

PRR.

THE decor in the lounge car of the Pennsylvania Railroad's Chicago-Washington Liberty Limited extended to the traveler an invitation to relax, refresh himself, chat, read, or play cards.

Budd.

HIGH-SPEED Metroliner trains were placed in service on January 16, 1969 in the Penn Central's New York-Philadelphia-Washington "corridor." The 34-seat parlor car is called the Metroclub.

51

METROPOLITAN railroad passenger terminals were among the most imposing and expensive of architectural works. Chicago's second Union Station (above left) was built in 1880 to replace the building destroyed in the Great Chicago Fire of 1871. Known as the "General Passenger Depot," it was an outstanding Chicago landmark. The third Chicago Union Station and railroad office complex (above) was completed in 1925 to serve as terminus for four railroads: Pennsylvania, Burlington, Chicago & Alton, and Milwaukee Road. Designed by the firm founded by Daniel Burnham, architect for Washington Union Station, the 1925 CUS cost 90 million dollars. The tracks lead from the concourse building along the river; the main waiting room and offices are in the rear building. The mammoth main waiting room (facing page, top left) is graced with Corinthian columns. World War II crowds gather in the main concourse building (facing page, top right) which covered an area of 320 x 200 feet and rose to a height of 118 feet above street level. This portion of Chicago Union Station was demolished in 1969 and replaced by a high-rise office/concourse structure.

THE concourse at Pennsylvania Station, New York, could almost contain a regulation football field under its glass-and-steel roof. The station was replaced by a new building in the mid-1960's.

Of tickets and wickets

DENVER UNION STATION is located at the foot of Seventeenth Street in the Mile High City. C&S dual-gauge tracks at far right were still in use when this 1914 photo was taken.

CORDIAL CONDUCTORS check in a sleeping-car passenger for the Overland Limited in Chicago at North Western Terminal.

MILWAUKEE ROAD ticket offices at Cincinnati, O. (upper) and Omaha, Nebr. (lower) displayed travel folders and timetables that advised patrons of schedules, fares, and consists of trains.

DURING World War I the railroads of the United States were placed under Federal control of the United States Railroad Administration under direction of W. G. McAdoo. This wartime measure proved unpopular, however, and the railroads were returned to private ownership after the War. The USRA consolidated ticket office shown above was located on Jackson Boulevard in Chicago.

SP.

PRR.

THE train board at Oakland Pier (Calif.) station in the good old days of 1926 listed 40 departures (left). Gate 24 at Chicago Union Station in 1958 (right) shows departure time for Pennsylvania's all-Pullman Broadway Limited.

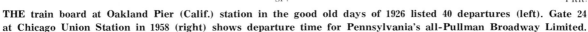

A SMOGLESS skyline greets Santa Fe's San Francisco Chief as it arrives Chicago's Dearborn Station in 1957 (above right).

CN.

CENTRAL STATION, Montreal, covers 27 acres; includes station, hotel, and office building, all built on air rights over tracks.

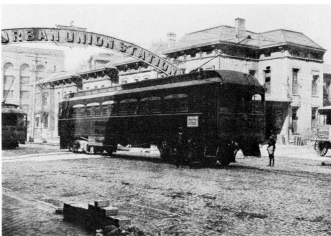

Author's collection.

A CONVERTIBLE parlor-sleeping car built by the Holland Palace Car Company prepares to leave Interurban Union Station in Columbus, O., on a demonstration run. Two such cars, Francis and Theodore, were built in 1903 for Columbus-Zanesville service before being sold to the Illinois Traction System in 1907.

CB&Q.

TICKET OFFICE of Chicago, Burlington & Quincy in Denver carried out the stainless-steel theme of its passenger trains.

THE station in El Paso, Tex., was designed in the Spanish Mission style popular throughout the southwestern United States. Rock Island-Southern Pacific westbound No. 3, the Golden State, is in the foreground; eastbound No. 2, the Sunset Limited, is in the background in this view taken in 1952.

A SOO LINE sleeping-car porter holds a lonely vigil as train No. 17, the Laker, prepares to depart Grand Central Station, Chicago, on June 8, 1959. The station was site of "the great trainshed party" held by the American Institute of Architects in June 1969 prior to demolition of the station.

55

All items, author's collection.

PHOEBE SNOW in immaculate white dress symbolized the cleanliness of travel on the Lackawanna Railroad — the Road of Anthracite.

Publicity, postcards, and a prospectus

BAGGAGE stickers for Los Angeles Limited, Olympian, Zephyr, and Santa Fe de-Luxe brought rails publicity. Coupon entitled passengers to refund of extra fare if the Broadway Limited ran over 55 minutes late.

SERVICE on Chicago North Shore & Milwaukee's new high-speed Skokie Valley Route officially was opened on March 28, 1925.

Last spikes and first runs

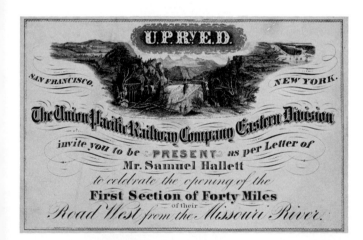

THE Chicago-New York Electric Air Line Railroad was incorporated in 1906 to build a high-speed line employing "lectromotive" motive power. The scheme failed in 1917.

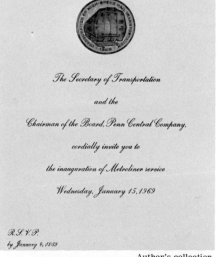

MORE than 100 years apart: invitations to opening of UP (top), first Metroliner run.

WORKERS and railroad officials stand by on May 19, 1909, as the last joint is bolted into place near Garrison, Mont., to complete the Milwaukee Road's Pacific extension.

57

Christening the classic trains

MP.

THE first run of the fabled City of Mexico was from St. Louis Union Station in June 1937. The de luxe, all-Pullman tourist special, advertised as "The Finest International Train In The World," operated once a week to Mexico City.

Author's collection.

EDWARD GOWEN BUDD (center), Budd Company founder and pioneer builder of stainless-steel equipment, attends the inauguration of NYC's new Empire State Express on December 7, 1941.

CB&Q.

ON October 23, 1936, the preservice, nonstop Chicago-to-Denver run of the new Denver Zephyr was made with the Gentlemen Adventurers of the Chicago Association of Commerce aboard. Crowds lined the station platform and right of way at Galesburg, Ill., as the speedster passed.

THE inauguration of the Chicago & North Western/Union Pacific Chicago-Denver Columbine was warmly greeted at Chicago with picture taking (far left), waving of the State of Illinois flag (left), and public viewing (right). Gov. William H. Adams of Colorado (above) christened the train at Denver on May 15, 1927.

A GALA Old Western reception, featuring cowboys, cowgirls, and Indians, was held at Phoenix, Ariz., on December 17, 1940, for the first run of the Chicago-Phoenix Arizona Limited.

ON September 6, 1929, Rock Island officials and Western guests introduced a new Rocky Mountain Limited. Ten years later, a streamlined Rocky Mountain Rocket replaced the heavyweight cars.

WITH Gen. Dwight D. Eisenhower, actress Beatrice Lillie, and New York City Mayor William O'Dwyer participating, the 1948 Twentieth Century Limited was dedicated in Grand Central.

59

PRR.

(LEFT) On the 25th anniversary of Milwaukee Road's Southwest Limited in 1928, the cake was cut by famed New York and Chicago restaurateur George Rector, who also was the railroad's Director of Cuisine. The Pennsylvania Railroad's Broadway Limited (above) celebrated its 50th birthday in 1952 by breaking through paper bunting as it rolled eastward from Chicago.

CMStP&P.

Rolling old in style . . . birthdays and anniversaries

CB&Q.

THE 50th anniversary of the Burlington & Missouri River Railroad's entry into Denver was commemorated on May 25, 1932.

Alfred E. Perlman and the Officers of

The New York Central System

request the pleasure of your company

at a ceremony and luncheon

in honor of

the Sixtieth birthday of the

Twentieth Century Limited

Friday, the fifteenth of June

at twelve o'clock

R. S. V. P.   Track 34, Grand Central Terminal
230 Park Avenue   Luncheon immediately following
New York 17   Biltmore Hotel

NYC.

ON June 15, 1962, the 60th birthday of the Twentieth Century Limited, the author received a slice of cake from noted steward Tommy Walsh at Chicago's La Salle Street Station.

MAINSTAY passenger locomotives on the Pennsylvania were 425 K4s Pacifics, built from 1914 to 1928. They had 80-inch drivers.

Portraits of power

THE tender (below) of Big Four K-3a Pacific No. 6500 sported a plate bearing the name of the St. Louis-New York Southwestern Limited. New York Central & Hudson River 4-4-0 No. 999 (right), the highly publicized locomotive of the Empire State Express and onetime holder of the world's speed record of 112.5 mph, is displayed at Chicago's Museum of Science and Industry.

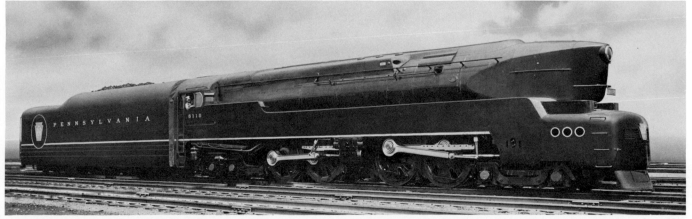

PENNSYLVANIA 4-4-4-4 No. 6110, ordered from Baldwin in 1940 and delivered in 1942, was designed to handle 880-ton passenger trains over the 713 miles between Harrisburg and Chicago at 100 mph with only one fuel stop. Length: 122 feet 9¾ inches.

61

UNION PACIFIC'S Pullman-built streamliner M-10000 attracted crowds at Chicago's "A Century of Progress" in 1934. Denver streetcar (below) ran to trainside during a popular 1933 exhibition tour.

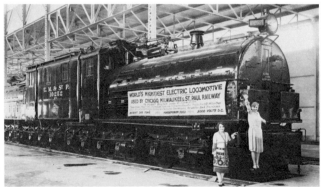

Hedrich-Blessing.

THE Chicago Railroad Fair of 1948 and 1949 commemorated 100 years of railroading in Chicago. On display was Pennsylvania 4-4-2 No. 7002 (actually No. 8063 in disguise) which made an unofficial world's speed record of 127 mph in 1905.

The fairest at the fairs

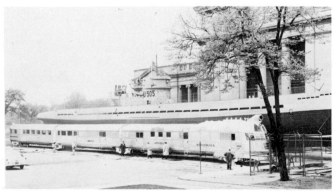

CM&StP.

ALL SET for the latest in buggy rides! Two Philadelphia visitors at the 1926 Sesquicentennial Exposition approve of the Chicago, Milwaukee & St. Paul Railway's exhibit of the world's newest and most powerful electric locomotive.

CB&Q.

AMERICA'S first stainless-steel diesel-powered streamliner, the Pioneer Zephyr of 1934, is on permanent exhibit at the Museum of Science and Industry in Chicago. The U-505, a captured World War II German submarine, is in the background.

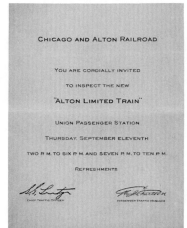

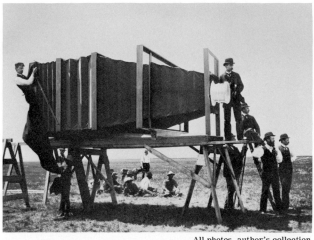

All photos, author's collection.

Donald Duke.

IN 1901 photography specialist George R. Lawrence photographed the Chicago & Alton's Alton Limited with what was termed "the world's largest camera" (top right). The result was an 8-foot 4½-inch photograph made from one plate (above). A cordial invitation was extended to view the train (top left). Free reclining chairs were part of the service (right).

Print promoters and pass masters

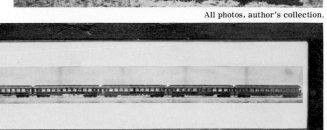

Author's collection.

FIRST totally air-conditioned train was B&O's Columbian.

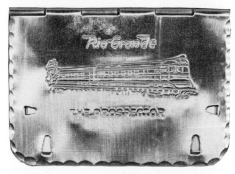

Hedrich-Blessing photo, author's collection.

THE lavishing of passes offering free transportation to dignitaries was one of the most notable publicity schemes developed by railroads. Probably the most unique passes were issued by Otto Mears, president of the Silverton Railroad and the Rio Grande Southern. Above is one of the rare silver-filigree Mears passes, presented in 1893. Nearly 50 years later the Denver & Rio Grande Western had a stainless-steel memento created for the 1941 inaugural run of the Prospector.

Reprinted with permission from Midwest, Chicago Sun-Times.

CHICAGO delegation members to the 1930 national Women's Christian Temperance Union convention depart Chicago on a special train (above). Chief Justice and Mrs. Charles Evans Hughes (above right) occupy North Coast Limited's rear platform at Spokane.

Name riders for name trains

CRI&P.

TWO motion picture actresses pose with humorist Will Rogers upon arrival in Chicago on the Golden State Limited.

CRI&P.

MISS AMERICA of 1927, Dorothy Britton (left), waves to admirers from the observation car of the Golden State Limited in Chicago.

64

NP.

PRR.

CM&StP.

(ABOVE LEFT) Field Marshall Foch of France (with hand extended) and General John Pershing of World War I fame share an observation platform on the Pennsylvania Railroad at Altoona, Pa., on October 30, 1921. (Above right) Inventor Thomas A. Edison visits an exhibition in 1926 of a Milwaukee Road bipolar electric locomotive built by General Electric.

CMStP&P.

CM&StP.

Herbert Georg, collection of George Krambles.

DRUMHEAD of Illinois Terminal's Illmo Limited sports a Cardinal insignia in honor of St. Louis baseball team riders in 1931.

(ABOVE LEFT) Notre Dame's 1930 football team rides the Pacific Limited. Coach Knute Rockne is fourth from left on the railing.

(LEFT) The first woman to swim the English Channel, Gertrude Ederle, is presented with flowers aboard the Columbian in 1926.

STRONGMAN Charles "I was a 97-pound weakling" Atlas was able to move the roller-bearing Broadway Limited of 1938. Such promotions thrust name trains into the public eye. The four-track (broad-way) tailsign motif appeared with the streamlined trains.

ONLY the Lone Ranger's sidekick, Tonto, and his nephew, Dan Reed, knew his true identity. Here the masked man, still incognito but probably Earl W. Graser, who played the part from 1933 to 1941, shakes hands with a Chicago & North Western train crew.

BARITONE John Charles Thomas takes a few moments to smile and wave in the traditional pose from the observation platform.

WORLD CHAMPION prizefighter Jack Dempsey waves from the solarium of Great Northern's Chicago-Seattle Empire Builder.

DIZZY DEAN, pitcher for the St. Louis Cardinals, occupies the engineer's seat of Illinois Central's Panama Limited.

C&NW.

CHIC SALE of outdoor plumbing fame and two actresses, Lillian Taez and Alice Derrell, attend ribbon-cutting ceremonies at the Chicago dedication of the Columbine in 1930. The locomotive is one of the Chicago & North Western's giant new Class H 4-8-4's.

AT&SF.

VENTRILOQUIST Edgar Bergen with Mrs. Bergen and dummy Charlie McCarthy ham it up for the camera aboard the Santa Fe. Celebrities often could be found on trains such as the Chief, and were frequently the targets of photographers and the press.

CB&Q.

FAMED composer and pianist Sergi Rachmaninoff relaxes on the Denver Zephyr. He wore gloves to protect his hands.

CB&Q.

MASTER of the violin, Fritz Kreisler, displays his priceless Stradivarius while traveling aboard a Burlington Zephyr.

NYC.

DON MC NEIL, host of the popular radio program Breakfast Club, is about to depart Chicago on the Twentieth Century Limited.

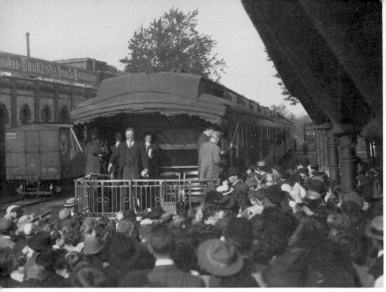

Author's collection.

THEODORE ROOSEVELT campaigns by train in Wisconsin.

The President of the United States of America
and Party
Enroute to St. Paul-Minneapolis, Minn.
via Chicago & North Western Line
Sunday, June 7, 1925

Ride with presidents and royalty

CM&StP.

PHOTO of Woodrow Wilson aboard the Pioneer Limited of 1912 was doctored with artist's drawing of old Chicago Union Station.

CM&StP.

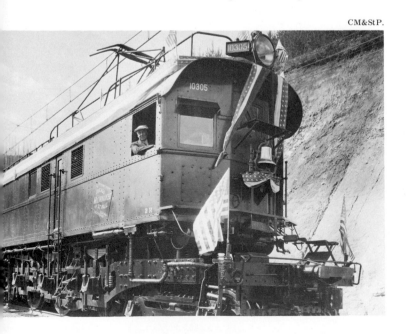

CB&Q.

FRANKLIN D. ROOSEVELT stood for this photograph while en route from Denver to Omaha aboard the Burlington on October 10, 1936. FDR was an enthusiastic railroad traveler.

ON JULY 2, 1923, President Warren G. Harding visited the cab of a CM&StP electric on his way to the Northwest and the opening of the Alaska Railroad. He died in San Francisco on his return trip.

B&O.

HARRY S. TRUMAN and Winston Churchill leave Washington in 1946 for latter's famous "Iron Curtain" speech in Fulton, Mo.

UPI.

PRESIDENT Richard M. Nixon (whose father was a trolley motorman) and Mrs. Nixon wave as they board a Penn Central Metroliner on January 24, 1970, for a trip to Philadelphia to attend a concert on the 113th anniversary of the Philadelphia Academy of Music. This was the first train ride by a Chief Executive, excluding campaign trains, since John F. Kennedy traveled from Washington to Philadelphia for an Army-Navy football game in 1962.

CHICAGO & NORTH-WESTERN Ry.

Special Train conveying the PRESIDENT and Mrs. CLEVELAND

CHICAGO TO MADISON Oct. 1887

J. M. WHITMAN, GENERAL MANAGER   S. SANBORN, GENERAL SUPERINTENDENT.

MOVEMENT OF TRAIN

BETWEEN

Chicago and Milwaukee.

THURSDAY, OCTOBER 6TH, 1887.

Lv. CHICAGO,	10.00 AM
Lv. CLYBOURN JUNCTION,	10.12 AM
Lv. DEERING,	10.14 AM
Lv. RAVENSWOOD,	10.20 AM
Lv. ROSEHILL,	10.23 AM
Lv. ROGERS PARK,	10.26 AM
Lv. CALVARY,	10.28 AM
Lv. SOUTH EVANSTON,	10.30 AM
Lv. EVANSTON,	10.34 AM
Lv. NORTH EVANSTON,	10.36 AM
Lv. WILMETTE,	10.37 AM
Lv. WINNETKA,	10.43 AM
Lv. GLENCOE,	10.47 AM
Lv. HIGHLAND PARK,	10.55 AM
Lv. HIGHWOOD,	10.57 AM
Lv. LAKE FOREST,	11.05 AM
Lv. LAKE BLUFF,	11.08 AM
Lv. WAUKEGAN,	11.21 AM
Lv. KENOSHA,	11.51 AM
Lv. RACINE JUNCTION,	12.10 PM
Lv. RACINE,	12.15 PM
Lv. COUNTY LINE,	12.29 PM
Lv. OAK CREEK,	12.38 PM
Lv. ST. FRANCIS,	12.47 PM
Lv. BAY VIEW,	12.50 PM
Lv. ELIZABETH STREET,	12.55 PM
Ar. MILWAUKEE,	1.00 PM

EDWARD J. CUYLER, Sup't.

Author's collection.

AN ornate time card was issued for the movement of special train of President Grover Cleveland and Mrs. Cleveland in October 1887.

CB&Q.

FORMER PRESIDENT Herbert Hoover boarded Chicago, Burlington & Quincy's Twin Zephyr bound for Minneapolis in the 1940's.

THE trai
the showe

IN 1939
toured

A PRIV
the obse

69

EXHIBIT CAR of Northern Pacific displayed agricultural and mineral products and wildlife to attract colonists to the West.

Chapel bells, funeral knells, and prison cells

Both photos, Pullman Company.

REED (above) was one of three sleepers Pullman rebuilt as traveling labs for the American Red Cross in 1917. Used to control epidemics, they were named for leaders in the field of communicable disease: Walter Reed, Louis Pasteur, and Elie Metchnikoff. (Below) In the 1930's, aliens and Federal prisoners were transported in Pullman tourist car No. 3195, equipped with barred windows.

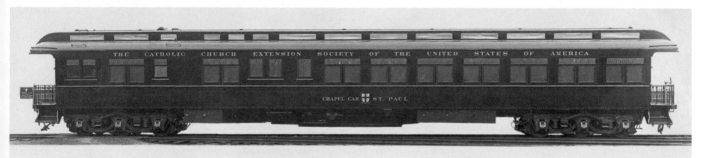

Barney & Smith, courtesy the Catholic Church Extension Society.

RAILROADS brought religion to many remote sections of the country. The chapel car St. Paul was operated by the Catholic Church Extension Society of the United States of America. Interior (below) had wood pews, leaded glass windows, and altar.

Author's collection.

THE black-draped funeral train of President William McKinley arrived at Washington, D. C. (far left) in September 1901 from Buffalo, N. Y., where the President had been assassinated. Special Pullman car Pacific (left) was arranged with catafalque for placement of the coffin.

Both photos, Pullman Company.

PULLMAN CAR Princeton (above) housed a field-trip deluxe during the summer of 1926 when 20 Princeton University students and their professor toured the West. By day, the rolling residence hall became a classroom (below) equipped for slide lectures.

SANDY RIVER AND RANGELEY LAKES RAILROAD

AN EXTRA dollar entitled vacationing Down Easters to one of 26 plush seats (right) in the parlor car Rangeley. Built by Jackson & Sharp for the 71-mile 2-foot-gauge Sandy River and Rangeley Lakes Railroad, the car served a popular lakes region of Maine.

Jackson & Sharp photos, courtesy AC&F.

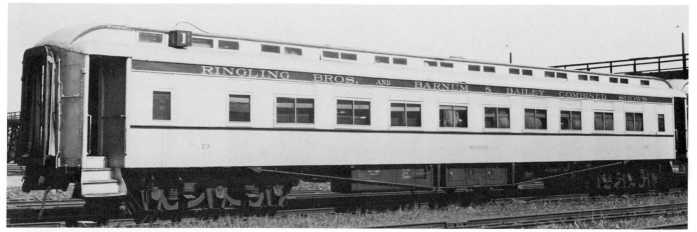

MICHIGAN (above), a former World War I Pullman hospital car, was delegated to happier duties when it joined the circus. Ringling Bros. and Barnum & Bailey Combined Shows boasted a roster of 90 railroad cars during the 1920's. Route card (left) of one of their circus trains for the 1927 season included a visit to Canada.

RINGLING BROS AND BARNUM & BAILEY COMBINED SHOWS

SEASON 1927

No. 6

OFFICIAL ROUTE

ALLOW MAIL ENOUGH TIME TO REACH POINTS NAMED BEFORE DATE GIVEN.
GENERAL OFFICES No. 221 INSTITUTE PLACE, CHICAGO, ILL.

DATE		TOWN	STATE	R.R.	MILES
			Nineteenth Week		
Aug.	15	Edmonton	Canada	C N R	350
"	16	Calgary	"	C P R	194
"	17	Lethbridge (Afternoon Only)	"	"	126
"	18	Cranbrook (Afternoon Only)	"	"	200
"	19	Spokane	Washington	C P R - S I	102
"	20	Wenatchee	"	Great Northern	174
		SUNDAY	Twentieth Week		
Aug.	22	Vancouver	Canada	Great Northern	253
"	23	Seattle	Washington	"	155
"	24				
"	25	Tacoma		Northern Pacific	40
"	26	Portland	Oregon	Union Pacific	144
"	27	Salem	"	Southern Pacific	53
		SUNDAY	Twenty-first Week		
Aug.	29	Chico	California	Southern Pacific	504
"	30	Sacramento	"	" "	86
"	31	Oakland	"	" "	132
Sept.	1		"		
"	2	San Francisco	"	" "	6
"	3	" "	"		
"	4	" "	"		
			Twenty-second Week		
Sept.	5	San Jose	California	Southern Pacific	51
"	6	Salinas (Afternoon Only)	"	" "	67
"	7	Santa Barbara	"	" "	253
"	8 to 12	Los Angeles	"	" "	104
			Total Mileage to date -		8964

THE *Jeffersonian*

COMPLETELY NEW ALL-COACH STREAMLINER

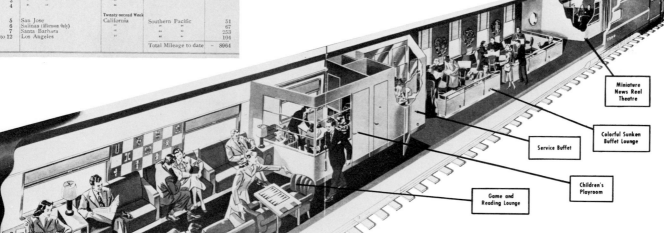

Miniature News Reel Theatre

Colorful Sunken Buffet Lounge

Service Buffet

Children's Playroom

Game and Reading Lounge

IMAGINE a game room, children's playroom, newsreel theater, and a sunken lounge (artist's rendering, top) all being found in

PRR 7302 (above). Such recreation cars appeared on the New York-St. Louis Jeffersonian when Pennsy re-equipped the train in 1948.

79

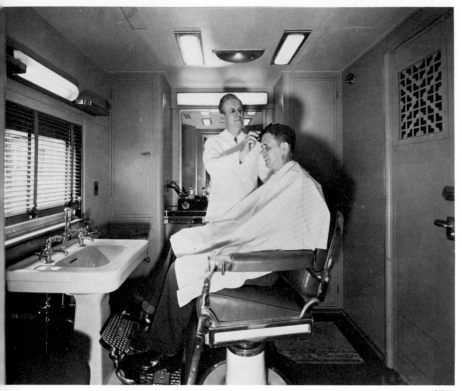

NYC.

"A LITTLE off the sides, please": a trim on the Twentieth Century in 1948.

Short on top, medium on the sides, and easy on the curves

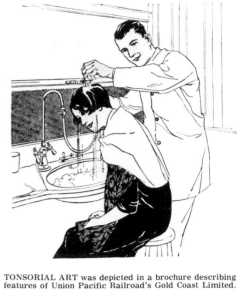

TONSORIAL ART was depicted in a brochure describing features of Union Pacific Railroad's Gold Coast Limited.

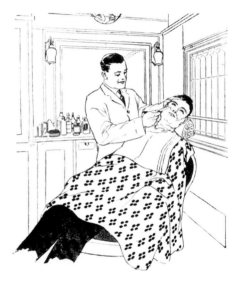

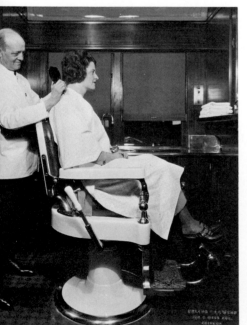

CRI&P.

CMStP&P.

CB&Q.

HAIRDRESSING on the Golden State in the 1920's was done for milady in the barbershop (left) instead of the Pink Poodle beauty shop. The morning ritual that never changes: after a good night's sleep on a gently swaying car, and before a hot breakfast in the diner, a shave is a must (center). The electric shaver has replaced the lather and razor, a dangerous instrument when traveling at over 80 mph. In the 1930's one could get a shave, a haircut, or a shampoo as this gentleman is doing on the CB&Q (right).

80

THE first transcontinental Movietorium was on the Olympian in March 1923 (left). An early experiment with train films was on the B&O entertainment car, which had a Victrola and a projector (above).

Reels on wheels

TRANS-CINEMA brochure on B&O.

IN-TRAIN movies were offered in a B&O coach (below) and in dining car (above).

BURLINGTON recreation car showed films.

THIS Chicago, Burlington & Quincy recreation car was arranged for card playing. Here passengers engage in a game of bridge.

The games that passengers play

CHILDREN had their own playroom on PRR's Jeffersonian of 1948.

THROUGHOUT the years, the Florida Special offered diversion from the scenery. In the 1930's the music of a three-piece orchestra (above right) made travel time seem short. In the 1960's, bingo, fashion shows, and television were offered (right).

Both photos, CMStP&P.

MUSIC for dancing on Milwaukee Road recreation car was provided by a wind-up Victrola (left) or a six-piece band (right).

Rocking while rolling

ACL.

A GOLD BELL overlooked festivities held in the recreation car of the Florida Special on the first run of its 50th season from New York City to Florida's east coast on January 2, 1937.

CB&Q.

"IS everybody happy?" This gal imitated Ted E. Lewis with a song and dance on the CB&Q (at least until Naperville curve).

ACL.

PART of the crew of musicians who furnished entertainment on both the Florida Special and the Miamian received instructions.

83

EARPHONE MAGIC creates a pleasant surprise for these girls aboard Chicago, Milwaukee & St. Paul's Pioneer Limited in the 1920's.

Mr. Edison and Mr. Marconi on board

"**FDR is the new President!**" On November 8, 1932, election results were broadcast on the Broadway Limited.

(**ABOVE RIGHT**) On October 12, 1922, this experimental new wireless apparatus on the Broadway received messages.

A YOUNG LADY tunes in the Majestic console on the Columbine in 1930.

(**RIGHT**) Electric dynamo in the baggage end of an Overland Route club car furnished power for lights in 1913.

Both photos, Pullman Company.

PULLMAN entertainment-recreation car Coliseum had a radio and a Victrola in 1926. Radio antennas were on roof of car.

PRR.

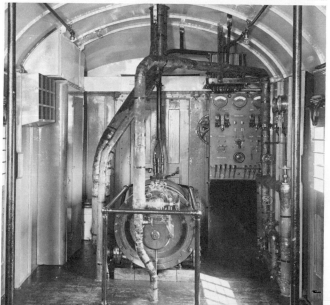

Pullman-Standard.

GN.

RADIO was enjoyed by all in the lounge of Empire Builder of 1930.

CM&StP.

CAR attached to Pioneer Limited broadcast a radio show in 1927.

CRI&P.

THE antics of these moppets as they inspect radio equipment in the lounge of the Rock Island-Southern Pacific Golden State Limited in 1929 seem to delight the passengers.

GREAT NORTHERN, New York Central, Pennsylvania, and Richmond, Fredericksburg & Potomac were once Greyhound stockholders.

SANTA FE TRAIL offered sleeper buses.

THE automobile as taxi, rail transfer coach, such as Chicago's Parmelee (above), and "Drivurself" car played an important role in the history of rail passenger service. John Hertz's "Drivurself" auto rental service was described by Railway Age in 1928 as "a new ally of passenger trains . . . helping railways regain [lost] passenger traffic."

CM&StP.

MOTOR COACH replaced "St. Paul Road" trains from Racine to Sturtevant, Wis., in 1926.

UP.

STEEL springs had replaced thoroughbraces and gasoline engines had replaced horses, but out West buses hadn't yet replaced stages.

90

GREYHOUND by day, PRR by night in 1930.

Your Own Chauffeur—

HE could not be more courteous, more attentive to your wants, more carefully trained in every detail, this uniformed North Shore Line motor coach driver, if he were your own private chauffeur. He, and all his brother drivers, operating North Shore motor coaches on schedule time over hundreds of miles of Illinois and Wisconsin highways, were chosen by a railroad famous for the excellence of its personnel.

He must pass a rigid examination. The North Shore driver comes to a dead stop before crossing a railroad, and does not shift gears while crossing. He respects the rights of other motorists, giving them assistance when necessary. He reports highway hazards to the authorities, including wilfully careless drivers.

North Shore Line motor coaches, by the way, consisting of the best types available with all the safety provisions known to engineering, are given a complete daily inspection by skilled mechanics.

On the occasion of a recent trip in a North Shore motor coach, General Pershing said, "This was the finest ride I ever had in a motor vehicle."

His comment is worth remembering when you have occasion to use this service we are proud of—or when you plan a few days' tour by North Shore motor coach this summer.

North Shore Merchandise Despatch

Over-night service for shippers between all important points on the North Shore Line. Through service to Sheboygan, Burlington, Watertown and all points on the Milwaukee Northern R. R. and T. M. E. R. & L. For rates, deliveries, etc., write or telephone local North Shore Agent, or Traffic Department: Chicago office, 79 West Monroe Street, 'phones State 5723 and Central 8280; Milwaukee office, 403 Security Building, 'phones Grand 990 and Grand 2762.

Chicago North Shore and Milwaukee Railroad Company

NORTH SHORE LINE ad emphasized the driver's dependability.

TWO sleeping coaches were built for Great Lakes Stages in 1929. Pullman-like berths were on each side of the aisle; jump seats accommodated passengers while the berths were being made down.

PICKWICK
Nite Coach

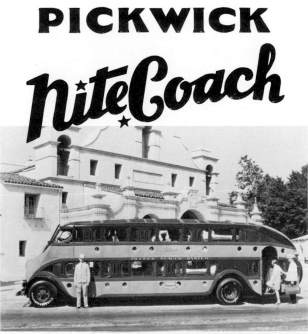

THE Pickwick Night Coach, a product of the firm that was famous for buses, hotels, and airplanes, was invented in 1928 by noted industrial designer Dwight E. Austin. The sleeper coaches ran overnight between Los Angeles and San Francisco, were later acquired by Southern Pacific's Pacific Greyhound. In 1948 Austin remodeled Chessie dome cars for C&O (page 481).

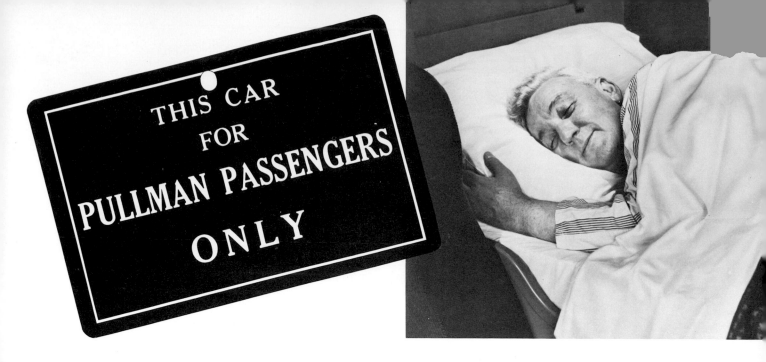

THIS CAR FOR PULLMAN PASSENGERS ONLY

✍ A PULLMAN

December 31, 1968: "The World's Greatest Hotel" closes its doors

CLEAN, crisp linens, brown wool blankets were Pullman hallmarks (above left). A master room with shower awaited 1938 Broadway and Century ticket holders (above right). Comfort was the keynote in section 2 of 12-section, 1-drawing-room McFord in 1935 (above far right).

FULLER E. CALLAWAY, a 1939 rebuild, graced Southern Railway's *Crescent Limited*.

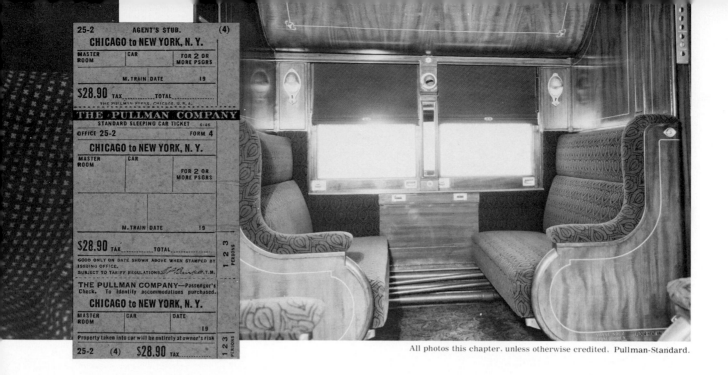

All photos this chapter, unless otherwise credited. Pullman-Standard.

POSTSCRIPT ～

AT MIDNIGHT on December 31, 1968, Pullman Company operation of sleeping cars in the United States ceased. In subsequent months that unique organization, founded a century earlier by George Mortimer Pullman, was liquidated. Thousands of employees were discharged, giant repair shops were closed, millions of dollars of inventory was sold — and a great enterprise vanished.

At the height of its operation during the 1920's the Pullman Company was termed "The World's Greatest Hotel." Every night 100,000 guests slept in Pullman berths. Every year 36 million customers paid 92 million dollars for their accommodations. Producing and maintaining such an operation was an enormous task.

In part, the Pullman name did survive. Pullman, *Incorporated*, onetime car-building affiliate of the sleeping-car company, remained. It continued as a diversified manufacturing complex after antitrust action of the Federal government completely separated it from the sleeping-car company in 1947. Following the court action, the Pullman Company sleeping-car operation was sold to the "buying group" of 57 (later 59) railroads on whose lines the cars served. From 1947 until the end of service in 1968, all newly built Pullman cars were owned by individual railroads and leased to Pullman for operation.

As the territory of the United States expanded during the "Railway Age" in the 19th century, railroads multiplied and the sleeping-car business grew rapidly. When the Pullman Company was chartered on August 1, 1867, it received 48 cars that it had purchased from George Pullman personally. The new venture was capitalized at $100,000. By 1899, Pullman Company owned almost 2000 cars and was capitalized at 74 million dollars. Thirty years later, during the peak year of 1930, it operated 9860 cars and capitalization was 120 million dollars.

After World War II ended in 1945, Pullman Company business declined rapidly, mostly because of competition from trunk airlines and a marked increase in the number of hotels and motels. In 1950 Pullman and domestic scheduled airlines each carried about 16 million passengers. By 1953 Pullman passengers had declined to 13 million while the domestic airlines could boast of 26 million passengers. Moreover, during 1953, 82 major Pullman "lines" in the United States and Canada were discontinued. The trend continued unabated until 1968, when the owning railroads finally decreed the liquidation of the company and individually assumed the operation of sleeping cars.

It was the end of an era.

GEORGE M. PULLMAN entertained presidents and royal visitors aboard his private car, which displayed a reed organ and fern plant.

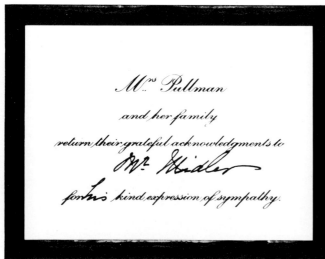

Author's collection.

PULLMAN'S WIDOW acknowledged expressions of sympathy.

George M. Pullman

GEORGE MORTIMER PULLMAN was born in Brockton, N. Y., on March 3, 1831. With experience as a cabinetmaker, contractor, and storekeeper, he turned his attention to sleeping cars. Although Mr. Pullman did not invent or build the first sleeping car in history, he did conceive of a program for an organized system of comfortable railroad transportation.* In the era of American history termed the "Railway Age," Pullman provided luxurious cars of uniform construction, adapted to both day and night use over connecting lines of railways without change of cars. Moreover, George Pullman conceived a gospel of service to the passenger that approached perfection in the realm of travel hospitality. For this he will long be remembered; in dictionaries of 20 languages throughout the world the word Pullman appears as a noun connoting luxury, comfort, and safety in overland transportation.

Fame and enormous wealth came to the sleeping-car magnate. Pullman Palace cars operated on both sides of the Atlantic — in England and Italy as well as throughout North America. But the labor unrest at the Pullman plant broke the spirit of George Pullman, and the great strike of 1894 was a blow from which he never recovered. He died suddenly of a heart attack in Chicago on October 19, 1897, at the age of 66 years. Four days after his death George Pullman was laid to rest in Graceland Cemetery in Chicago, and a bereaved widow acknowledged expressions of sympathy.

*The first American sleeping car is generally believed to have been built in 1837 for the Cumberland Valley (later Penn Central).

THE administration building (above) housed the steam power plant for the factory and town at Pullman. Hotel, water tower, workers' homes, and gardens appear in the photo below, while the artist's drawing at the left depicts Chicago's 1884 Pullman Building, which yielded to wrecking crews in 1956.

1894 started when 4000 workers were laid off and wages were cut during the depression of 1893. Soon the strike spread to all railroads that hauled Pullman cars. After 3 months of rioting, President Grover Cleveland sent Federal troops to Chicago to enforce an injunction ordering Eugene V. Debs, president of the American Railway Union, and all other persons to refrain from obstructing the business of the railroads entering Chicago. The strike was broken by the troops during this first use of Federal force in a labor dispute.

Pullman's town

THE town of Pullman, Ill., has been termed America's first planned industrial community. It was created by George M. Pullman as a great social experiment in connection with his new car works, which was the first mass-production industrial plant and heralded the advent of the assembly line. The town was built in 1880 on 3600 acres of land at Lake Calumet, 14 miles south of Chicago. The chief architect was Solon Spencer Beman, who also designed the Pullman Building headquarters and Grand Central Station, both in Chicago.

Strictly enforced rules governed life in the town of beautiful parks and broad streets. For example, such "criminally debasing influences" as saloons and idlers were barred. A rigid plan determined one's residence in Pullman: The location, type, and size of the company-owned dwelling were determined by one's station — worker, foreman, manager — in the hierarchy of the company.

It was at Pullman that the bitter and bloody railroad strike of

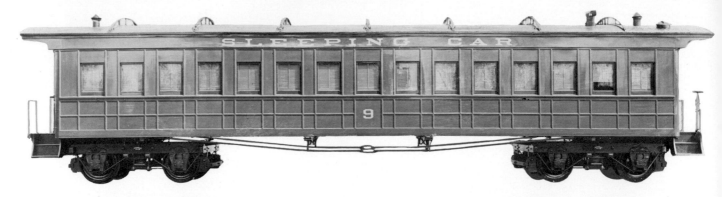

SEATS ready for daytime occupancy were reversed to "make down" beds (below) in Chicago, Alton & St. Louis Railroad car No. 9. The former day coach was remodeled without plans or blueprints into a primitive sleeping car in 1859 at a cost of $2000. The 44-foot-long car was destroyed by fire in 1897, and a facsimile was built by remodeling tourist car No. 402.

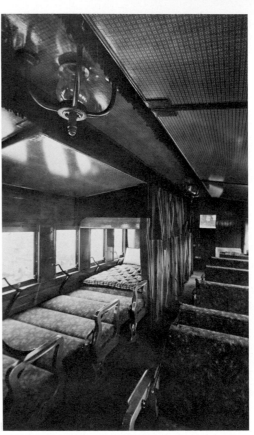

In the beginning . . . No. 9 and the Pioneer

THE first two Pullman cars were day coaches 9 and 19 of the Chicago, Alton & St. Louis Railroad which George Pullman remodeled into primitive sleeping cars in 1859. The work cost $2000 per car and was done without plans or blueprints. No. 9 was 44 feet long and contained a box stove, oil lamps, and 10 sections upholstered with plush. The wood trim was cherry.

Conductor J. L. Barnes, describing the first run on September 1, 1859, from Bloomington, Ill., to Chicago, noted that "on that first night I had to compel the passengers to take off their boots before they got into the berths. . . . I remarked to Mr. Pullman that it was a fine car, and he replied briefly, for he was a silent man: 'It ought to be. It cost enough.'" Barnes continued, "The three cash passengers, men, were from Bloomington. There was no crowd at the station, and the car, lighted by candles, moved away in solitary grandeur, if such it might be called."

Car No. 9 was destroyed by fire in 1897. In the same year, a facsimile was constructed by remodeling tourist car No. 402, which had been built by Barney & Smith and purchased from the Santa Fe.

Pullman's first all-new sleeping car was the *Pioneer*, outshopped at Chicago in 1865. First known as car "A," the *Pioneer*

cost an extravagant $20,170 to build — considerably more than the $4000 cost of contemporary cars. It had 12 sections and the interior finish included polished black walnut, crimson French plush, pure linens, chandeliers with candles, mirrors, and marble washstands.

The *Pioneer* was 58 feet long over end sills and 10½ feet high from the rail. Weight was 60,850 pounds. Patrons boarding the car admired an exterior of poplar wood panels with battens and plate-glass windows with glass "Gothics" embossed and silver plated. The body color was umber (black-brown) touched off with lavish gold-leaf ornamentation. The edges of the battens were painted black. Originally there were two reddish-brown four-wheel trucks under each end — a total of 16 wheels. The roof was wood covered with tin.

When the *Pioneer* appeared it was so large and expensive that no railroad would operate it. Following the assassination of President Abraham Lincoln, State of Illinois officials ordered the car attached to the funeral train for the trip over the Chicago & Alton line to Springfield on May 2, 1865. Platforms and bridges hurriedly were altered and the future of the Pullman car was assured.

J. L. BARNES, photographed in 1922 at the age of 85, was the conductor on the first trip of George Pullman's new sleeping car, the Pioneer.

ABRAHAM LINCOLN'S funeral train reposed under an arch erected at Michigan City, Ind., en route to Springfield, Ill. At Chicago, officials of the State of Illinois transferred the funeral party to the large and luxurious Pioneer.

THE Pioneer was only a shell of the ornamental car of 1865 when photographed inside and out in 1891. It was destroyed at Pullman in 1903. This car cost $20,170 to build at a time when no other car cost more than $4000.

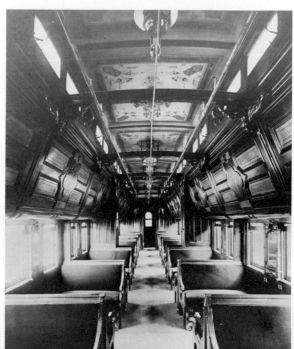

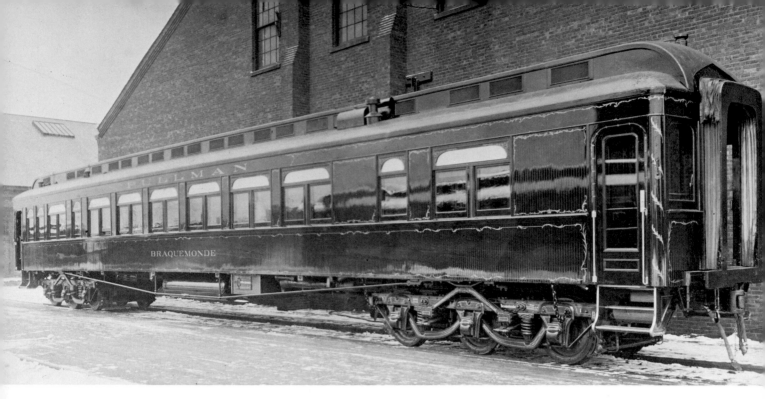

BRAQUEMONDE, a 12-section, 1-drawing-room example of the Wagner Palace cars, came to Pullman in the 1899 Wagner acquisition.

Competition, then consolidation

AS the sleeping-car business expanded rapidly after 1867, Pullman Company conducted a major part of the trade. However, a number of other sleeping-car companies were organized. Two of Pullman's early competitors were the New York Central Sleeping Car Company, organized in 1865 by Webster Wagner and the Vanderbilt interests, and the Gates Sleeping Car Company, which operated from Buffalo to Chicago over the Lake Shore & Michigan Southern. Gates was absorbed into the New York Central Sleeping Car Company in 1869. In 1882, after the death of Webster Wagner, the Vanderbilt company became the Wagner Palace Car Company.

A number of railroads established their own sleeping-car service: Chicago, Milwaukee & St. Paul; New Haven; Great Northern; Soo Line; Wisconsin Central; and Central of Georgia. On 14 additional railroads the first sleeping-car services were organized under an association arrangement by which Pullman and the railroads held the cars in joint ownership and divided the profit from operations. Among these roads were the Grand Trunk, Missouri Pacific, Northern Pacific, Lackawanna, Atlantic Coast Line, Santa Fe, and Spokane, Portland & Seattle.

One by one the competing sleeping-car companies were brought under the control of the Pullman Company: Erie & Atlantic; Central Transportation Company; Mann & Woodruff (combined as the Union Palace Car Company); Crescent City; and Rip Van Winkle. The last of the acquisitions — the Wagner company — took place in 1899. The last association contract, with the SP&S, ended in 1922.

Major railroad-owned sleeping-car services replaced by Pullman operation were New Haven (1913); Great Northern (1922); Central of Georgia (1923); and most of the Chicago, Milwaukee & St. Paul (1927). Except for local lines of the Soo and CMStP&P, sleeping-car service in the U. S. was virtually monopolized by the Pullman Company prior to the outbreak of World War II.

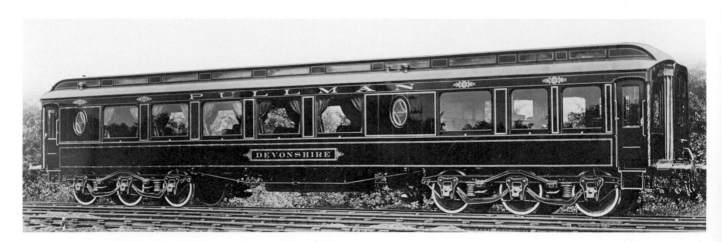

PULLMAN operated parlor cars in England from 1874 to 1907. Devonshire, built at Chicago in 1900, served on the Brighton Limited.

ACF

CENTRAL PACIFIC operated Silver Palace cars built by AC&F-predecessor Jackson & Sharp. The cars were sold to Pullman in 1883.

Author's collection.

Author's collection.

SPLENDOR of late 19th century train travel is apparent in these views of the Manila, used on the NYC's crack Lake Shore Limited between Chicago and New York.

Author's collection.

IN 1868 — before Pullman erected its own plant — CB&Q built the 16-wheel Burlington for George M. Pullman at Aurora, Ill.

PULLMAN

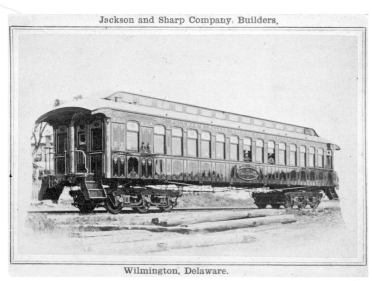

Jackson and Sharp Company, Builders,

Wilmington, Delaware.

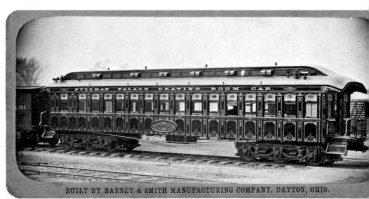

BUILT BY BARNEY & SMITH MANUFACTURING COMPANY, DAYTON, OHIO.

THE post-Civil War boom in railroad construction resulted in rapid expansion of the Pullman fleet, with decorative Pullman Palace cars. Shown in rare builder cards are Baltimore, built by the Jackson & Sharp Company of Wilmington, Del. (above), and Dayton, outshopped by the Barney & Smith Manufacturing Company of Dayton, O. (left).

When Pullman outpaced itself

THE first Pullman cars were built for George Pullman personally, either for his private ownership or in partnership with the railroad using the cars. Forty-eight of these cars were constructed between 1859 and 1867, usually in railroad shops. After the Pullman Company was incorporated in 1867, cars were purchased from carbuilders until 1870 when the company established its first manufacturing plant at Detroit, Mich. (see photo above). With demand for Pullman cars increasing, the

Detroit plant's capacity proved inadequate, and Pullman decided to build a large works in Chicago, which opened in 1881. From 1867 until 1881, Pullman found it necessary to purchase 283 cars from outside carbuilders and railroad shops. All of these were completed under the supervision of the company representative, Aaron Longstreet. Additional cars were acquired from predecessors and railroad companies during the period of expansion from 1867 to 1927, when Pullman absorbed all competing car companies and railroad-owned sleeping cars in the U.S. During this period, Pullman acquired 2271 cars owned by 58 separate companies.

When Pullman went to the fairs

GEORGE PULLMAN was an avid supporter of world fairs and expositions, both in the United States and abroad, and the Pullman Palace cars frequently won awards and prizes. The famous six-car World's Fair Train of 1893 won a gold medal at the Chicago Columbian Exposition. In the photo at the top, the train's observation car, Isabella, rests alongside the precursor — Pullman's first sleeping car, No. 9 — inside the transportation building designed by Louis Sullivan. Two trains exhibited at the 1904 Louisiana Purchase Exposition in St. Louis — shown in the lower photo — were awarded the Grand Prize. The Pullman Company's exhibit trains stimulated travel and influenced railway car architecture and design.

Pullmans . . . only the name remained the same

IN a century-plus of operation from 1859 to 1968, hundreds of changes and improvements in Pullman cars reflected the public's evolution in taste and increased standard of living. One of the major innovations pioneered or invented by Pullman engineers was the vestibule, a covered passageway between cars with an anti-telescoping device that was patented in 1887 and first applied to *Pennsylvania Limited* cars (right).

Another step forward in railroad equipment construction came in 1907 when Pullman rolled out the first all-steel Pullman sleeping car, briefly named *Jamestown* in honor of the 1907 Jamestown Exposition. Construction of the 12-1 car, which *Railway Gazette* described "as near all-metal construction as is now practical to make it," was prompted by fire-prevention laws passed in New York City to protect the tunnels into Pennsylvania Station and the new Grand Central terminal then being built. The new laws precluded the operation of wooden railway equipment into the stations. The conversion of the Pullman Car Works from wood to steel construction methods in 3 years (1907-1910) was a herculean task.

The first mechanical air conditioning for railroad trains was tested in Pullman cars in 1927-1929. Yet another breakthrough flashed across America in 1934 in the form of *M-10000*, the country's first streamlined, lightweight, air-conditioned train. Built at the Chicago plant of Pullman-Standard Car Manufacturing Company, Union Pacific's three-car aluminum speedster was a bold and successful bid to stir the gloom of the depression and restore dwindling passenger volume. Pullman's leadership continued as it placed in service the first lightweight sleeping cars on the *City of Portland* in 1934. Until World War II interfered in 1941, over 600 lightweight Pullmans were produced for assignment to the crack trains of the land. One of the less successful innovations was the sleeper coach (far right), which provided three bunks in a vertical row on opposite walls of the section. During the postwar era until 1956, more than 2000 additional lightweight Pullman-operated, railroad-owned cars were added to the Pullman Company fleet, replacing outmoded and war-weary heavyweight sleepers. As a result of the anti-trust action, the roster contained hundreds of cars built by the Budd Company (Philadelphia, Pa.) and by American Car & Foundry (St. Charles, Mo., and Berwick, Pa.).

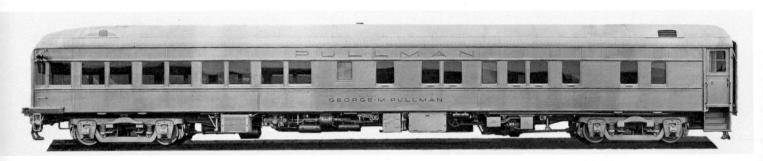

THE all-aluminum observation-lounge-sleeper George M. Pullman, exhibited at the 1933 Chicago World's Fair, marked the transition from heavyweight to lightweight sleepers.

NYC.

UP'S M-10001 (seen in New York's Grand Central) helped to ignite the streamliner era that revived interest in rail passenger service.

IN THE WAKE of antitrust action, Budd built cars for NYC's New England States (left) and AC&F supplied Pullmans to the GM&O (below).

AC&F.

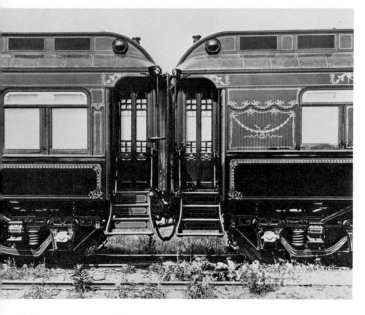

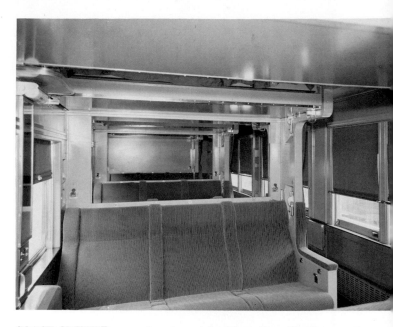

THE Pennsylvania Limited was the first to receive vestibuled cars.

COACH-SLEEPER compartments contained three tiers of berths.

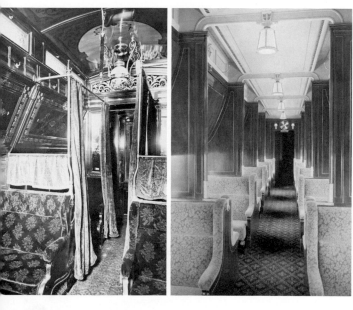

LUSH decor of 1885 Reinz gave way to utilitarian stock of 1920's.

TAIL CARS of the 1927 Pioneer Limited and the 1938 Century.

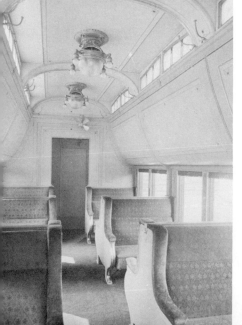

PULLMAN

JAMESTOWN, the first all-steel Pullman, had an unusual light-colored modern interior.

All photos, Pullman Company.

THIS IS TO CERTIFY THAT

Mr. GEORGE A. KELLY

OF CHICAGO, ILLINOIS

IS A MEMBER IN GOOD STANDING OF THE

SOCIETY FOR THE PREVENTION OF CALLING

SLEEPING-CAR PORTERS

"GEORGE"

ATTESTED BY *George W. Dulany Jr.*

MEMBER S.P.C.S.P.G

YEARS AGO Conductor H. G. Kettle and Porter Edward Brodie reviewed the "calls" (times to waken each passenger in the morning) and "shorts" (passengers getting off short of the train's destination). One-time Pullman President Carroll Harding stated, "Our porters are this company's greatest asset." (Left) Some 33,000 membership cards were issued for SPCSCPG.

SUCH Hollywood stars as Ingrid Bergm[an] alighting from the Broadway in New Yo[rk] used Pullman service from coast to coa[st]

Above all, Pullman meant service

SERVING the 36 million people who traveled overnight in Pullman berths in an average year in the 1920's and 1930's demanded the utmost in human courtesy and mechanical proficiency. Pullman porters — and there were 9000 of them at the peak of business — had to operate 38 different air-conditioning systems, "make down" 43 types of berths, and memorize an elaborate book of instructions. Pullman developed a standard method or regulation for almost everything that could occur aboard a Pullman car. Every aspect of hospitality to the passenger was covered in minute detail. Books of instructions and rules also were issued for conductors, attendants, maids, barbers, and bus boys. It was little wonder that for decades former Pullman employees were sought for service in the White House and in the finest metropolitan clubs and hotels.

All Pullman porters belonged to the powerful Brotherhood of Sleeping Car Porters, which was the first important Negro union in America. In the early days of sleeping-car service, berths were made up by the Pullman conductor or brakeman. The first Negro porter was hired in 1870, and although a few Filipinos were hired in the ensuing years, most porters came from the black race. Porters frequently were called "George" (probably after George M. Pullman), which prompted a wealthy lumberman from Clinton, Ia., George W. Dulany Jr., to found the SPCSCPG (Society for the Prevention of Calling Sleeping-Car Porters "George"). Dulany spent his adult lifetime and a fortune of money on the project. He enrolled 33,000 card-carrying members, including King George V of England, George Herman "Babe" Ruth, and Georges Clemenceau of France — all of whom were pledged to discourage the practice.

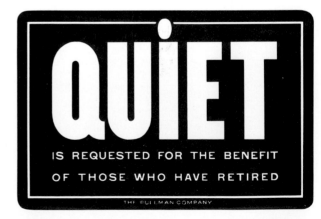

QUIET

IS REQUESTED FOR THE BENEFIT OF THOSE WHO HAVE RETIRED

THE PULLMAN COMPANY

QUIET was requested of millions of Pullman passengers.

The Pullman Company was easily the world's greatest housekeeper. The linen inventory contained over 4 million towels and nearly 3½ million sheets. One year's purchase of supplies included 98 million sanitary drinking cups and over 4 million

EAVYWEIGHTS answered the call to war.   **PULLMAN SHOPS refurbished the Century.**   **FIRM was world's greatest housekeeper.**

CARSHOPS at such cities as Wilmington, Del., and Atlanta, Ga., kept the Pullmans rolling.

cakes of soap. In order to be assured of a steady supply of specialty items, Pullman operated its own shops to produce everything from leaded glass to upholstered furniture to toilet seats to brass hardware. Pullman even established its own printing plant, The Pullman Press, to publish the enormous quantities of rulebooks, instruction manuals, car rosters, plans and specifications, material catalogs, printed forms, tickets, and advertising folders that were part of its everyday operation.

The Pullman service manual devoted two pages to the following 12-step discourse on the simple act of serving a bottle of beer:

1. Ascertain from passenger what kind of Beer is desired. 2. Arrange set-up on bar tray in buffet: one cold bottle of Beer, which has been wiped, standing upright; *glass (No. 11) 2/3 full of finely chopped ice (for chilling purpose — making it a distinctive service);* glass (No. 12); bottle opener; and paper cocktail napkin. Attendant should carry clean glass towel on his arm with fold pointing toward his hand while rendering service. 3. Proceed to passenger with above set-up. 4. Place bar tray with set-up on table (or etc.). 5. Place paper cocktail napkin on table in front of passenger. 6. Present bottle of Beer to passenger displaying label and cap. Return bottle to bar tray. 7. Pour ice from chilled glass (No. 11) into glass (No. 12). 8. Open bottle of Beer with bottle opener in presence of passenger (holding bottle at an angle), pointing neck of bottle away from passenger; wipe top of bottle with clean glass towel. 9. Pour Beer into glass (No. 11) by placing top of bottle into glass, and slide the beer down the side until beer reaches about 2 inches from top — then put a collar on the

beer by dropping a little in the glass which now should be upright. 10. Place glass containing Beer on paper cocktail napkin. 11. Place bottle containing remainder of Beer on table before passenger, with label facing him. 12. Remove bar tray with equipment not needed by passenger and return to buffet.

Cars were maintained not only to handle normal and seasonal traffic, but to accommodate numerous special movements. During a 2-month period in the summer of 1926, Pullman handled a total of 3956 extra car movements, including 2140 cars supplied for the Eucharistic Congress at Chicago in June.

Minor car servicing was performed in 275 different railroad yards. For major work, Pullman had these shops located throughout the country (with year of acquisition): St. Louis, Mo. (1880); Wilmington, Del. (1886); Buffalo, N. Y. (1899); Calumet, Ill. (1901); Richmond, Calif. (1909); Atlanta, Ga. (1926); Detroit, Mich. (1870, sold 1902); and Elmira, N. Y. (1873, abandoned 1883). Pullman's payroll included 5000 car cleaners, 4700 mechanics, 432 electricians, 353 commissary workers, and 400 employees in 10 company-owned laundries (the laundry bill often was more than 3 million dollars a year).

On June 30, 1947, Pullman obeyed a Federal court decree and elected to retain ownership of its car-building subsidiary, Pullman-Standard Car Manufacturing Company, and to sell its sleeping-car operating subsidiary to 57 railroads. Sale price of the 731,350 shares of capital stock in the Pullman Company was over 75 million dollars.

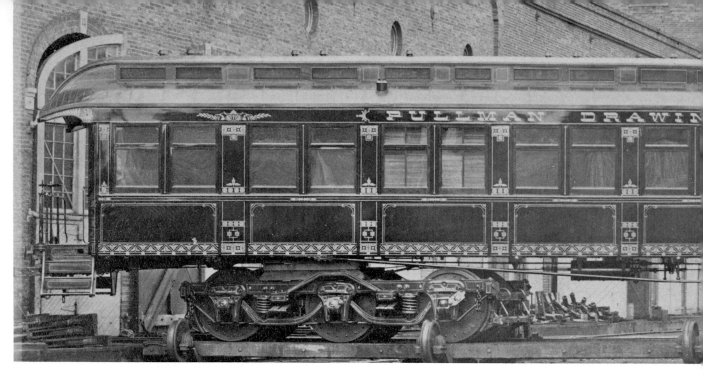

PULLMAN drawing-room sleeping car Herkimer (above), shown on the transfer track at the Detroit shops in May 1883, was heavily ornamented with gold leaf. The umber-brown car was built for service on the newly completed New York, West Shore & Buffalo (later NYC). Construction included steel-rim wheels. Sister car Mimas (below) was furnished with imported carpeting and up-holstery, brass oil lamps, and magnificent inlaid upper-berth fronts in a pineapple pattern. The seven species of wood used in marquetry work delighted George M. Pullman, an ex-cabinetmaker.

PULLMAN

Evolution of the Pullman car

THE eminent Swiss architectural historian, Sigfried Giedion, in his definitive book *Mechanization Takes Command* [Oxford University Press, 1948], related the creation of the sleeping car with the granting of the first American patent for a reversible, adjustable railway seat to Thomas Woodruff in 1856. The aim of Woodruff's patent was to convert a seat into a couch. This principle was retained by Woodruff, Wagner, and Pullman throughout the history of their sleeping cars.

The following pages contain photographs showing the interior and exterior design of Pullman cars dating from the earliest open vestibule cars by George Pullman in Detroit until the last Pullman sleeper was repaired at the Pullman Company's Calumet shops in Chicago, Ill.

INTERIOR of an early all-steel Pullman shows how open section was converted into upper and lower berths at nighttime.

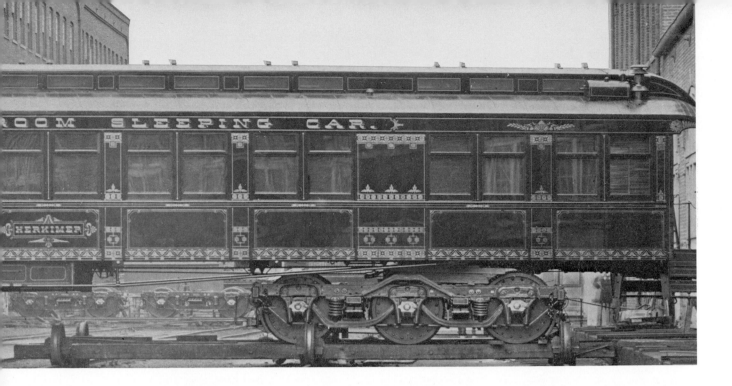

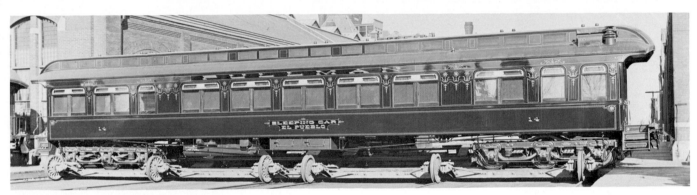

EL PUEBLO (above), constructed for service on the Southern Pacific, stands at the Pullman Car works in Chicago upon completion in November 1888. A type of car similar to El Pueblo was one (left) of six cars outshopped in 1892 for operation on the Rock Island. Note the semi-flat ceiling, carved wood trim, and Brussels carpet.

AN EARLY EXAMPLE of the narrow vestibule car was the Shoshone, built in 1889 for service on Union Pacific. The invention of the vestibule in 1887 brought the entire train under one roof, and encouraged development of cars for dining and lounging. The elaborate brass grillwork (right) gave a car a touch of elegance.

SCANDIA, a wide-vestibule 12-section, 1-drawing-room car completed in 1899, was assigned to the Colorado & Southern Railway.

PULLMAN

LARAMIE, built during the peak of the ornate period that was flourishing when this photograph was taken in 1896, displays full Empire ceiling, and flat berth front with inlaid medallion.

BELGRAVIA, also a product of the ornate period, was turned out in 1898 for the Erie. Interior decor included a groin-arch ceiling, plain curved berth fronts, and tapestry upholstery.

THE Boston was outshopped in 1903 for Boston-Springfield-New York service via the Boston & Albany-New Haven, and boasted wood sheathing painted standard Pullman green.

The opposite side of the line was operated by New Haven-owned sleeping car No. 2032 (below), which was identical to the Boston except that it was painted New Haven forest green.

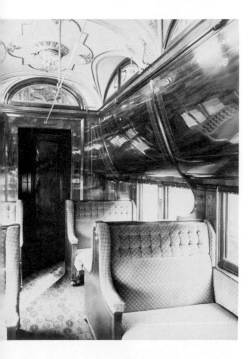

NORMANIA (left), built in 1901 for Chicago-Twin Cities service on the Chicago Great Western, possessed an interior decor consisting of groined ceiling, round upper berth with mirrorlike polished finish, leaded art glass, and of course, mahogany paneling with inlaid work. Electric lighting was supplemented by Pintsch gas lamps.

THE last wooden Pullman car was the Percivale, built in March 1910 for service on the Pennsylvania. The simply ornamented wood sheathing was painted tuscan red. The interior featured full Empire ceiling, curved mahogany berth fronts, electric lighting, and electric fans at each end of car. This was the first use of green plush with a tulip pattern.

109

PULLMAN

SANDERSON was an early all-steel car turned out in February 1911 for New York Central service. Steel sheathing which had the appearance of wood was used until 1916. The car was painted Pullman green with plain gold lining, and had a rectangular upper sash with pressed prism glass. The roomy interior had a flat ceiling with electric lighting, electric fans, painted and grained berth fronts, tulip-pattern green plush upholstery, green carpet.

NEW FARNUM (above), outshopped in 1929 for CB&Q's Chicago-Omaha-Lincoln Ak-Sar-Ben, had a flat ceiling with electric lighting and mica lampshades, semi-private sections with headboards and arches, gray-and-pastel color scheme with painted, jeweled ornamentation, and blue or green plush with small figures. Southern's renowned green and gold distinguished the William Wyatt Bibb (below), a 1932 rebuild for the Crescent Limited.

APTHORPE HOUSE, constructed in August 1930 for New York Central's Twentieth Century Limited, was an early all-room car with all-steel construction. The 13-double-bedroom sleeper was painted standard Pullman green with gold lettering.

VILLA PALATIAL, one of several Villa-series cars, was a modernized all-steel 10-section, 3-double-bedroom Pullman rebuilt from plan 3411 at the Calumet shops in 1939 for the Pennsylvania Railroad's General and later the Golden Triangle. Styling by designer Raymond Loewy included two tones of tuscan red with gold "stream lines," skirts, and rounded roof.

Everett L. DeGoyler, Jr.

SILVER MOON and twin Silver Slipper were built in 1939 by Budd for the Denver Zephyr (and reassigned in 1957 to the Texas Zephyr). Resistance by the Pullman Company to the contracting for these cars, owned by Burlington and not by Pullman, triggered the fatal Federal antitrust suit against Pullman in 1940. The Denver Zephyrs were the first Zephyrs to carry sleeping cars.

D&RGW.

ROOMETTES no longer were a novelty in 1950, when Rio Grande received Brigham Young and three other 10-6's for the Denver-Salt Lake City Prospector. However, many businesses were reimbursing traveling employees for only a lower berth, so D&RGW had 5 roomettes in each car replaced by sections. In 1955 and 1956 Union Pacific and Wabash received the last cars built with open sections (right): 6-section, 4-double-bedroom, 6-roomette National-series cars. UP intended to name them for Las Vegas hotels.

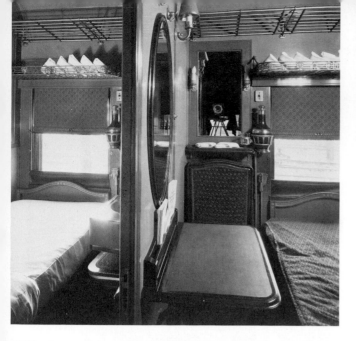

THIS photo, taken aboard the Milwaukee Road's 1927 Pioneer Limited, shows en suite single bedrooms for both day and night use. Among the features of these comfortable surroundings were box spring, mattress, full-length mirror, drop shelf for writing.

MODERNIZED, pastel-colored interior from 1940 shows Loch Doon for Baltimore & Ohio's New York-St. Louis National Limited.

PULLMAN

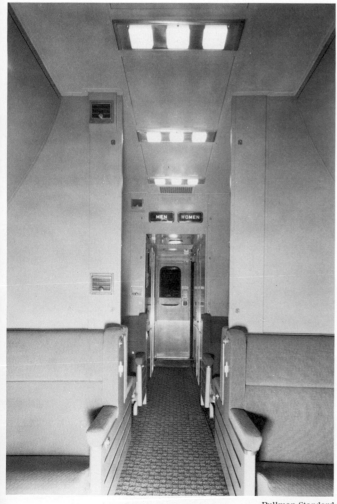

Pullman-Standard.

CB&Q.

SILVER MOON and Silver Slipper had an unusual configuration: 4 double bedrooms, 4 chambrettes (single rooms), 4 roomettes, 1 drawing room, and 1 compartment. Designer Paul Cret combined rare wood veneers and colorful upholstery fabrics to create an interior for the Denver Zephyr that was modern in the utmost. Furnishings in the drawing rooms included a wall-mounted radio.

THE White Mountains Day Express pauses at New Haven, Conn., about 1886. The locomotive is NH 4-4-0 No. 82, built in NH's Hartford shops in 1871. The second car is the Monarch Palace Car Company's side-platform observation Ymir.

Author's collection.

Author's collection.

OLD COLONY timetable of February 4, 1884, advertised the Fall River Line steamboats.

IN THE NORTHEAST CORRIDOR

From the Ghost Train to the Metroliners

HURRYING to New York, a Metroliner crosses the Susquehanna River at Perryville, Md. The electric cars are capable of 160 mph.

Don Phillips.

DE LUXE intercity passenger service in the United States was first conceived in the Northeast Corridor between Boston, New York, Philadelphia, and Washington. Many of the most notable luxury trains in the history of American railroading traversed this 460-mile passage, which contains the Hub of the Universe, the Empire City, the City of Brotherly Love, and the Federal City.

The _Fall River Line Steamboat Express_ entered service on May 19, 1847. The train, generally considered to be the first express in the United States, operated from Boston to the wharf at Fall River, Mass., where passengers transferred to the night boat for New York. The importance of the Fall River train diminished in 1876 with the completion of the all-rail Air Line route to New York. In 1891 the legendary "Ghost Train," the white-and-gold _New England Limited_, began operating on the rails of the Air Line on a 6-hour schedule between Boston and New York City.

A second all-rail route between Boston and New York, the Shore Line, was created in 1889 with the completion of the Thames River bridge at New London, Conn. The picturesque line offered service to more southern New England cities and soon became the favored route. Over the Shore Line operated such famous trains as New Haven's _Gilt Edge, Merchants' Limited,_* _Owl,_ and _Yankee Clipper,_ and the _TurboTrain._ A third Boston-New York line via Springfield, Mass., was operated jointly for many years by the Boston & Albany and the New Haven.

Construction of a through rail route between New York and the national capital was prompted by the Civil War. Completion of the line was hindered not only by the natural water barriers, the Hudson, Delaware, and Susquehanna rivers, but also by political factions in Philadelphia and Baltimore which saw local advantages in the continued transfer of passengers and goods. An efficient through rail line was finally completed in 1873.

*For the story of the _Merchants' Limited_ see _Some Classic Trains,_ pp. 44-55.

115

Speed . . . with Traction Motors and Turbines

THE Federal government passed the United States High Speed Ground Transportation Act of 1965 to stimulate research and development of alternate modes of transportation in densely populated regions. The act included two demonstration projects in the Northeast Corridor.

Demonstration I, New York-Washington, started in April 1966. The Federal government contributed 11.5 million dollars and the Pennsylvania Railroad contributed 45 million dollars toward the improvement of track and the purchase of high-speed multiple-unit cars, to make New York-Washington rail travel competitive with air travel. The demonstration included ancillary projects for employee training, park-and-ride stations, grade crossing protection, and on-train telephones. Completion was scheduled for October 1967. After many delays in the program, the first *Metroliner* train ran on January 15, 1969. During that year the *Metroliners* carried 605,000 passengers; in 1970 the number grew to 1,252,000; and in 1971 the count was 1,625,000, a total increase of 40 per cent in 2 years.

Demonstration II, Boston-New York, involved the leasing by the Government of two new trains for New Haven (later Penn Central) to operate over the Shore Line route. The trains, designed and owned by United Aircraft, were built in Chicago by Pullman-Standard and powered with aircraft-type gas-turbine engines plus two traction motors for electric operation through the tunnels in New York. The Government accepted the trains on October 21, 1968, and began equipment testing and crew training.

On April 8, 1969, service was introduced between Boston and New York. The trains originally were called *Turboliners* but were hastily renamed *TurboTrains* for legal reasons. The *Turbos* were successful on the Shore Line, although they operated without the publicity and advertising that built up business for the *Metroliners*. Ridership increased somewhat from 1969 to 1970, but fell off in 1971 because of cutbacks in the frequency of service.

The success of both demonstrations was a contributing factor in the Federal government's decision to pass the Rail Passenger Service Act of 1970, which created the National Railroad Passenger Corporation (Amtrak).

Budd.

Don Phillips.

BUDD built 31 coaches like No. 829 (above), 20 snack-bar coaches, and 10 Metroclub parlor cars (left, below, and plan) for operation by the Pennsylvania (later Penn Central, then Amtrak). Metroclub seats 34 passengers in single rotating, reclining chairs; has an airliner-type food-service galley.

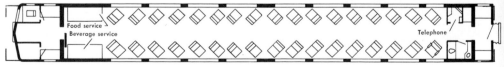

Food service
Beverage service
Telephone

Don Phillips.

United Aircraft.

THE FAST ONES: A Metroliner (left) displays the PRR Keystone emblem during testing prior to the Penn Central merger in 1968 and regular service in 1969. A TurboTrain (above) speeds past Princeton Junction, N. J., during a December 20, 1967, test run on which it reached 170.8 mph. After extensive testing on PC's electrified New York-Philadelphia main line, TurboTrain entered service on the Shore Line between Boston and New York.

Budd.

Sikorsky Aircraft Division of United Aircraft.

AN UNCOMMON view of the TurboTrain's suspension.

Sikorsky Aircraft Division of United Aircraft.

TURBOTRAIN introduced domes to the tight-clearanced Northeast Corridor.

Goodyear-Zeppelin, collection of George Krambles.

HISTORY repeats itself. Both TurboTrain and NH's Comet of 1935 are three-car articulated trains of almost equal size; both are

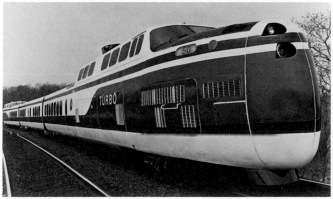

United Aircraft.

the products of aircraft companies. Ironically, TurboTrain betters Comet's Boston-Providence time by only a minute or two.

THE
American Flyer
CARS

"De Luxe Travel in Streamlined Coaches at No Extra Cost"

DURING January 1935, 50 handsome partially stream-lined passenger cars were placed in service by the New York, New Haven & Hartford Railroad. They were hailed by *Railway Age* for their maximum comfort and their improved appearance, which was advertised by the New Haven as "modernistic yet sane."

The new design represented a transition from conventional heavyweight rolling stock of the era to radical lightweight construction that was later to become the standard for all car building in the economy-minded postdepression period.

The flush, tubular exterior and the striking interior presented such a pleasing appearance that additional orders were placed for similar cars by six other railroads throughout the country: Boston & Maine; Seaboard Air Line; Kansas City Southern; Bangor & Aroostook; St. Louis Southwestern; and Lehigh Valley.

The A. C. Gilbert Company, well-known toy manufacturers of New Haven, Conn., produced a model of the car for its newly acquired American Flyer line of plastic and tinplate electric trains. Thereafter the prototype cars were referred to as "The American Flyer Cars."

Philip R. Hastings.

Author's collection.

TWO reproductions from the American Flyer catalog for 1938 featured scale models of a New Haven baggage-and-mail car and a passenger coach (above). Boston & Maine train 72 (right) leaves Bradford, Vt., in 1946.

THE GREAT STEEL FLEET an

IAT is so rare as a day in June? A rare day indeed
s June 15, 1938, as the streamlined, all-room Twen-
h Century Limited departed from Chicago's La Salle
eet Station on its maiden voyage to New York City.

I IN the early 1930's, the United States was suffering a severe economic depression. Businesses and industries — including the railroads — were at a standstill. To restore their dwindling passenger volume, the railroads and the carbuilders searched for radically different types of trains.

Lightweight air-conditioned streamliners proved to be a significant solution to the problem. In 1933 the railroads ordered 27 lightweight passenger cars; by 1937 there were 902 in service or on order. Most of these cars were assigned to the new streamlined trains that operated on railroads west of Chicago.

THE FLEET OF MODERNISM

The Twentieth Century Limited and the Broadway Limited of 1938

E same sunny June day saw the Century's foremost
npetitor, the PRR Broadway Limited, on its first run
h streamlined equipment, accelerating through
uth Chicago on its way toward the same destination.

At first, neither New York Central nor Pennsylvania, the two giants of passenger railroading, did much more than experiment with lightweight trains. Both of these Eastern railroads were managed by conservative men who considered the question of streamlined equipment with careful deliberation before making their judgments.

Finally, on March 9, 1937, after several months of conferences and negotiations, the long-awaited announcement came. In a joint statement New York Central, Pennsylvania, and Pullman Company announced new streamlined equipment for NYC's "Great Steel Fleet" and PRR's "Fleet of Modernism," primarily for the premier train of each railroad, NYC's *Twentieth Century Limited* and PRR's *Broadway Limited*, rivals for the cream of the passenger trade between the nation's two largest cities, New York and Chicago.

D. W. Yungmeyer.

THE second section of the first eastbound streamlined Century pauses at Englewood (above left). NYC bought four complete trains

PRR.

because two sections usually were required. PRR streamlined K4 No. 3768 has a rake of lightweight Pullmans in tow (above right).

America's first all-room trains

DURING 1936 and 1937 New York Central and Pennsylvania placed orders for new equipment for the two trains. The American Locomotive Company received a contract for 10 streamlined J-3a Hudsons from NYC; motive power for the *Broadway* was to be remodeled K4 Pacifics west of Harrisburg and GG1 electrics between Harrisburg and New York. Pullman-Standard was commissioned to build 114 streamlined cars: 52 sleeping cars for each railroad plus head-end and dining cars for NYC. PRR head-end and dining cars were to be remodeled at the Altoona (Pa.) shops from existing cars. The Pullman sleeping cars were designed with private rooms only. The new *Broadway* and *Century* would be the first de luxe American sleeping-car trains without the curtained berths that had been a part of rail travel for nearly a century.

Staff engineers of the two railroads and the Pullman Company collaborated with two prominent industrial designers to produce entirely new equipment for the two crack limiteds.

The New York Central chose Henry Dreyfuss, a founder of the American Society of Industrial Designers, and at the age of 32 already a pioneer in the profession of industrial design. Dreyfuss (1904-1972) was a leader in applying to American manufacturing the maxim that form follows function. Later he taught at both the University of California at Los Angeles and the California Institute of Technology.

The Pennsylvania selected Raymond Loewy, an internationally known industrial designer. Born in Paris in 1893, Loewy had served as art director for Westinghouse Electric Corpora-

tion and had styled the GG1 and other equipment for PRR. Later he formed his own design firm, Raymond Loewy/William Snaith, Inc.

On June 15, 1938, with great fanfare, the new New York Central and Pennsylvania trains entered service between New York and Chicago. For the new trains, running time was reduced from 16½ to 16 hours over both NYC's 961.2-mile Water Level Route and PRR's 907.7-mile line across the Alleghenies. Typical consists for the first sections of the two trains were: for the *Twentieth Century Limited*, a mail-baggage car, a bar-lounge car, two 17-roomette cars, three 4-compartment, 4-double-bedroom, 2-drawing-room cars, two dining cars, two 10-roomette, 5-double-bedroom cars, one 13-double-bedroom car, and an observation car with a master bedroom; for the *Broadway Limited* (a shorter train), a baggage-mail car, a bar-lounge car, two 18-roomette cars, one 4-4-2 car, one 13-double-bedroom car, one dining car, and an observation car with a master bedroom.

The simultaneous introduction of the two streamliners provided an unusual opportunity for comparison. Both trains competed for the same passengers; both offered identical Pullman accommodations; both charged the same fares and ran on the same schedules.

The differences that existed between the two trains — and there were indeed differences, even within the limits imposed by railroad standards — were attributable to the differing styles of Henry Dreyfuss and Raymond Loewy and the special requests of their clients. The immediate and outstanding success of both trains showed that even in so restricted a situation there was room for a designer's imagination and inventiveness.

American Locomotive Company, author's collection.

FROM Grand Central Terminal, New York, north along the Hudson River to Harmon, 33 miles, the Century was pulled by electric locomotives such as Class T-2a No. 1158. It was one of 26 T-2a's built by American Locomotive Company and General Electric between 1914 and 1926. No. 1158 drew direct current from a third

rail, except through complicated switchwork, where short sections of overhead third rail were mounted so contact could be made by the small pantographs at each end of the locomotive. The T-2a, which was painted black and lettered in gold, was the prototype of American Flyer's "Presidents Special" toy train.

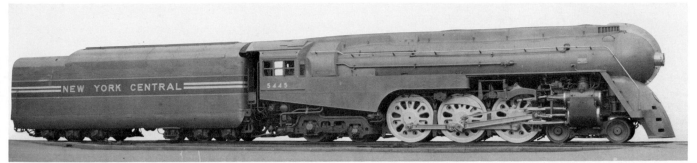

American Locomotive Company.

HUDSONS and New York Central were practically synonymous. NYC's 1938 J-3a's were the final version of a design introduced in 1927. No. 5445 and nine sisters emerged from Alco with Henry Dreyfuss's styling. Highlights of the design were 79-inch drivers accented with aluminum paint and a satin-finished aluminum fin on the boiler front. Locomotive and tender were painted light gray; the tender was contoured to the shape of the cars and was trimmed with the blue-edged dark gray band that ran the length of the train. NYC advertised that the J-3a's mechanical contrivances would "insure not only peace and pleasure to thousands of discriminating Twentieth Century lovers but undisputed dominance of American rails for this wonder train of a wonder age."

PRR, collection of the Altoona Public Library.

PACIFIC No. 3768, built in June 1920, was rebuilt at Altoona shops in March 1936, becoming the Pennsylvania's first streamlined steam locomotive. Raymond Loewy styled the K4 in co-operation with the railroad's engineering department after tests in the aerodynamics laboratory of New York University. The streamlined shroud almost completely covered the locomotive, including the running gear. Locomotive and tender were painted in dark gunmetal color with gold striping and lettering. A stainless-steel winged keystone dominated the nose. No. 3768 hauled the first eastbound run of the 1938 Broadway Limited. It was not assigned exclusively to the Broadway, so it graced other trains with streamlined power; the Broadway often received an unadorned K4.

PRR, collection of the Altoona Public Library.

STANDARD passenger power east of Harrisburg on the Standard Railroad of the World was the 139 electric locomotives of the GG1 class. (Pennsy used the letter G for its 4-6-0's; the 2-C+C-2 wheel arrangement essentially was two Ten-Wheeler's back to back.) It was designed as a co-operative effort by the Pennsylvania, Westinghouse, General Electric, Baldwin, and Gibbs & Hill, consulting engineers. Raymond Loewy's styling has proven to be one of the most durable items of the railroads' streamlined era: the GG1 remains a handsome engine, whether wearing Brunswick green and five gold stripes or the solid black livery of Penn Central.

Pullman-Standard.

DINING CAR 680 was one of six such cars built by Pullman in May 1938. Radio antenna and six-wheel trucks were distinctive features.

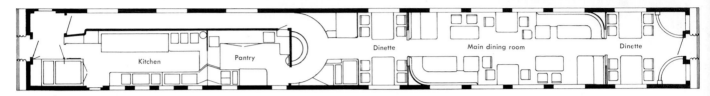

Kitchen   Pantry   Dinette   Main dining room   Dinette

Both photos, NYC.

THE interior of the Century's dining car was designed in the manner of a smart, modern restaurant. To break the "tunnel" effect of the usual dining car, Dreyfuss divided the dining section of the car into three parts. The main dining room seated 22 persons at tables of varying shapes and sizes; at each end was a small, intimate area seating 8. In the main room, the walls were gray leather with mirrored panels between the windows, and the ceiling was light gray. The banquettes were upholstered in leather that matched the walls in color but differed in texture, and the chairs were upholstered in rust leather. The two small rooms had walls paneled in walnut, rust ceiling, and gray leather upholstery. Carpet throughout the car was in shades of rust with a pattern evocative of the train's emblem. At the end of the car were two quarter-circular cabinets filled with flowering plants. The train normally carried two diners, dining-room ends together. In their end bulkheads the diners had windows, which created the impression of a continuous series of dining rooms. Mirrors covered the end windows when the cars operated singly. A distinctive feature of dining-car operation on the Century was the transformation of the car into a night club or cafe after dinner. The lighting was dimmed to a soft rose hue, rust-colored table linen replaced white, and recorded swing music created an informal atmosphere. The table setting had special Twentieth Century china; the train's emblem appeared even on such small details as the matchbooks. Among the specialties listed on the menu were clam bouillon, planked Peconic Bay Weakfish, orange pecan sticks, apricot pie, and a New York Central tradition, spiced melon rind. A complete five-course "New 20th Century Dinner" cost $1.75.

NEW YORK
CENTRAL
SYSTEM

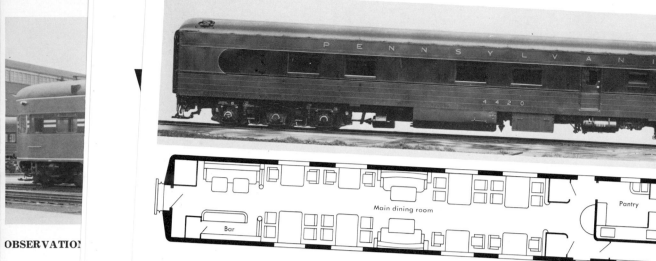

Both photos, PRR, collection of the Altoona Public Library.

RAYMOND LOEWY planned a bright, colorful interior which was divided into two dining compartments each seating 12, a lounge section seating 4, and a tavern nook at the end of the car with a bar and seats for 2. The upper walls and ceiling of the dining compartments were finished in gold and cafe au lait; the gold frames of the chairs and the light tan of the linens echoed these colors. Carpet, shades, and drapes were burgundy; the leather upholstery of the chairs was light blue. In the lounge area the walls were squares of beige polished steel separated by brass strips. The lounge sofas were upholstered in yellow leather and the ceiling was pale blue. The narrow bulkheads separating the sections were lacewood Flexwood. At the kitchen end of the car was a bulkhead with rose-colored mirror squares; the bulkhead at the tavern end was similar but with clear glass. Loewy included even the waiters' uniforms — "beige with gold buttons and a snappy-looking short apron [in] burgundy color" — in the decor. He reported only mild resistance from management to this departure from tradition. The epicurean menu listed such Broadway Limited traditions as roast prime ribs of beef, muffins hot from a copper server, grilled shad, and Pennsylvania cheesecake.

DINING CARS No. 4420-4423, built in 1910, returned to their birthplace, PRR's shops at Altoona, Pa., in 1938 to be completely refinished and refitted for service on the streamlined Broadway. Modifications included air conditioning, roller bearings, replacement of the clerestory roof with a contoured roof that matched the streamlined Pullmans, and new livery: two shades of PRR's tuscan red.

A TWIST ON TUSCAN RED

Q: Were all Pennsy Pullmans
tuscan red? A: No

Q: Were all tuscan-red Pullmans
Pennsy? A: No

ꡲ WITH the prosperity and optimism that prevailed at the end of World War II, American railroads organized extensive networks of special through-Pullman car routes. One of the leading proponents was the Pennsylvania Railroad.

Shown here are examples of the many liveries applied to Pennsylvania-owned or -operated sleepers assigned to these through-car lines. Keeping tab on the operation of these cars was enough to produce headaches and gray hairs for railroad and Pullman Company personnel.

Pullman-Standard.

Pullman-Standard.

Luce Studio, courtesy of Pullman-Standard.

KEYSTONE BANKS, a 12-roomette, 2-single-bedroom, 3-double-bedroom car, is shown in typical postwar livery for heavyweight **PRR** Pullmans. The Keystone Banks was an experimental car rebuilt from standard 12-section, 1-drawing-room sleeper Oaks in 1949 at Pullman-Standard's Osgood Bradley plant in Worcester, Mass., for Pittsburgh-Boston service on the PRR-New York, New Haven & Hartford New Englander-Quaker.

BEDFORD INN — a Budd-built 21-roomette car originally painted tuscan red and assigned to New York-Detroit Red Arrow — was refurbished and repainted in 1956 with Union Pacific yellow-red-gray for Slumbercoach service on the Milwaukee Road-UP City of Denver. Colors were also applied to three **PRR** owned Rapids cars for New York-California service in 1955.

Kaufman & Fabry.

CATAWISSA RAPIDS (left), built by Pullman in 1949, contained 10 roomettes and 6 double bedrooms, bore traditional Pennsylvania livery — tuscan-red letterboard, pier panels, and girder sheet; gold striping and lettering; and black roof and trucks. Identical livery and a like style of lettering was also applied to similar 10-roomette, 6-double-bedroom sleepers built by Pullman for three other roads and operated in joint service with the Pennsy. Three Louisville & Nashville cars named for rivers ran New York-Louisville, New York-Memphis, and New York-Nashville; three County cars operated between New York and Roanoke in joint service with Norfolk & Western; and three King cars ran New York-Richmond and Philadelphia-Richmond for Richmond, Fredericksburg & Potomac. Below left is RF&P King William; below is N&W McDowell County.

Pullman-Standard.

159

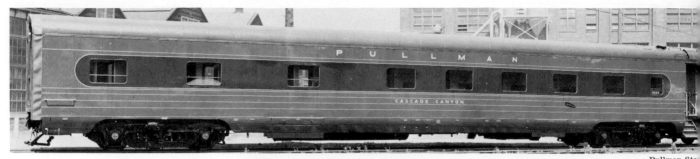

CASCADE CANYON was built by Pullman prior to World War II. The 10-roomette, 5-double-bedroom lightweight is depicted in PRR "streamlined" colors — two shades of tuscan red, with gold lining and letters — designed for the Fleet of Modernism in 1938.

CASCADE RANGE is shown as repainted in 1948 at Pullman's Buffalo (ex-Wagner) shops to match the Frisco-MKT stainless-steel Texas Special. The flat-side car had simulated stainless fluting; red roof, pier panels, and skirting; aluminum trucks; and letterboard with "Texas Special" red script. The car operated New York-San Antonio via PRR's Penn Texas to St. Louis.

BLUE RAPIDS was another oddity. ACF built this 10-roomette, 6-double-bedroom car in 1950. The livery consisted of black roof and trucks, two-tone gray sides, and silver letters. Blue Rapids operated in New York-San Francisco service via the Overland Route. During a 1955 shopping the car was repainted in tuscan red and renamed Fairless Hills for service on the Pittsburgher. Three PRR Imperial cars, in the same grays, ran on the Super Chief.

EAGLE OAK was ordered by PRR from ACF in 1947 for service on the Sunshine Eagle. When the 10-6 car was completed in 1950 the train had been renamed Texas Eagle. Eagle Oak was painted in MoPac blue and gray, with white and yellow striping, gray roof, black trucks. After the end of New York-Texas service, the car was repainted in tuscan red, renamed Brandywine Rapids.

ANACOSTIA RIVER, with 14 roomettes and 2 drawing rooms, was built by ACF for service on Atlantic Coast Line's Florida Special. Purple nameboards with gray letters, favorites of ACL's late president, Champion McDowell Davis, have been replaced with black lettering on a stainless panel in the latest ACL design. The black roof and trucks remain. A similar livery with stainless roof and sides, black lettering, and gray trucks is used on Pennsylvania cars in Southern Railway joint lines service.

160

Hare Photographs, Inc.

CADE RAVINE, with PRR nameboard, carried similar colors for New York-Tulsa service aboard American (PRR)-Meteor (Frisco).

Hare Photographs, Inc.

Budd Company.

SILVER RAPIDS, one-of-a-kind 10-6 built for PRR by Budd in 1948 for the California Zephyr, is shown in a rare view. Reporting marks near the door indicate Pennsy ownership. Car name was a compromise of Zephyr "Silver" and Pennsylvania "Rapids." "California Zephyr" black lettering was removed in 1958 after the end of transcontinental service. Stainless-steel livery with black lettering is also used for Pennsy cars operating in joint services with Seaboard Air Line, in which Silver Rapids later ran.

Budd Company.

MILES STANDISH, a 29-seat, 1-drawing-room parlor car built by Budd in 1952 for Washington-New York-Boston Congressional and Senator service, was one of the last parlor cars operated by Pullman. The car was stainless steel with tuscan red nameboards and stripe below the windows, tuscan red emblem, gold lettering, and black trucks. Tuscan red was later changed to bright red.

Author's collection.

LOW DOME CAR would have introduced still another livery consideration; but unhappily, the idea never got past the drawing-board stage. This uncommon view of the unusual Congressional-style car portrays the type of equipment proposed by American Car & Foundry engineers in 1955 for dome service on the Pennsylvania. Clearances on the railroad restricted car height.

The Black Diamond Express

The Handsomest Train In The World

ON APRIL 21, 1846, the Delaware, Lehigh, Schuylkill & Susquehanna Railroad, renamed the Lehigh Valley in 1853, was incorporated in the Commonwealth of Pennsylvania. The 45-mile line between Easton and Mauch Chunk, Pa., was extended through some of the most beautiful scenery in the East to become a strategic route between the Great Lakes and the Atlantic Ocean.

On May 18, 1896, during its golden anniversary year, the Lehigh Valley introduced a fast and luxurious express train over its 450-mile main line between New York (Jersey City) and Buffalo. It was planned to be "The Handsomest Train in the World," contrived in part to compete with the famed *Empire State Express*, pride of

the New York Central & Hudson River since October 1891. The third contender on the New York-Buffalo route, the *Lackawanna Limited*, predecessor of the *Phoebe Snow*, began running in December 1899.

To obtain a distinctive name for its new train, the Lehigh Valley held a contest. Of the 35,000 entries, the one from Charles M. Montgomery, a clerk in the Toledo, O., Merchants Hotel, was deemed the most appropriate and was awarded the $25 prize. His name, *The Black Diamond Express*, symbolized the wealth of anthracite, which was the railroad's principal source of revenue. To celebrate the new train, H. A. Lyon of Sayre, Pa., composed "The *Black Diamond* March and Two-Step."

Scheduled time for the *Black Diamond*, including the Hudson River ferry between Manhattan and Jersey City, was 9 hours and 50 minutes westbound; 9 hours 55 minutes eastbound. (Running time for the *Empire State Express* over a shorter, easier route was 9 hours westbound and 8 hours and 15 minutes eastbound.)

The *Black Diamond* offered Philadelphia-Buffalo service via a through car interchanged with the Philadelphia & Reading at South Bethlehem, Pa. Noontime departures from New York, Philadelphia, and Buffalo ensured a daylight ride through the beautiful "Switzerland of America," and the *Black Diamond* soon became a favorite of honeymooners en route to Niagara Falls.

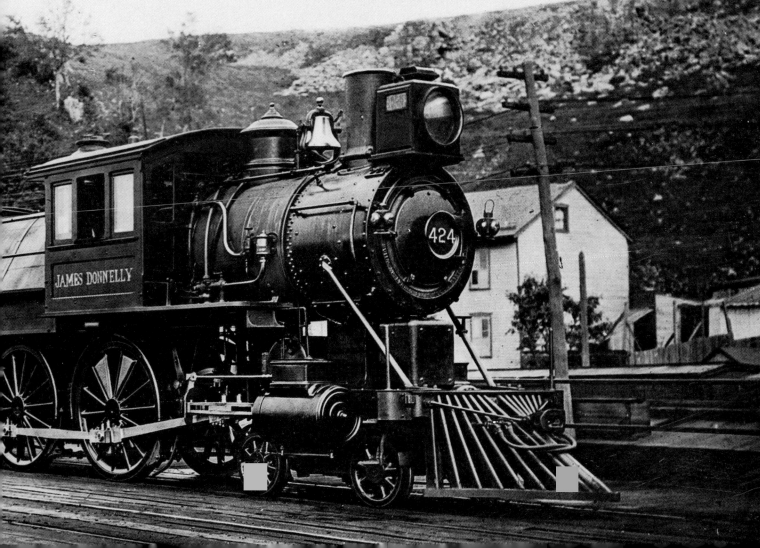

CAMELBACK 4-4-0, with wide anthracite-burning firebox and cab placed over the boiler, powered first Black Diamond Express. Collection of Everett L. DeGolyer Jr.

From Camelbacks to streamstyling to PA's

DURING its lifetime the *Black Diamond*, trains 9 and 10, appeared in four versions. Three were powered by steam, from Camelbacks to bullet-nosed Pacifics; the last was pulled by Alco-GE PA-1 diesels.

The original *Black Diamond* of 1896, "The Handsomest Train In The World," consisted of a 4-4-0 Camelback locomotive and four elegant Pullman-built cars: a baggage-smoking-cafe car, two day coaches, and a Pullman Palace observation-parlor car, all lighted with Pintsch gas and vestibuled throughout. George Pullman no doubt accepted with delight the opportunity to compete with the *Empire State Express*, built by his rival, the Wagner Palace Car Company.

The *Black Diamond* was discontinued for 4 months in 1908. The reasons stated in *Railroad Gazette* included "state and Federal orders, increasing costs, and dull business." Soon after it was restored, however, it became an all-parlor-car train, a

status it enjoyed for several years. Shortly after all-steel cars were introduced, Pullman was called upon again to re-equip the *Black Diamond*. During 1911 and 1912, railroad-owned club and dining cars were completed along with the Pullman-operated parlor and observation cars. Newly built Pacifics powered the train over Pennsylvania's Appalachian Mountains.

While the railroads were under Federal control in September 1918, the *Black Diamond* began operating into New York's Pennsylvania Station behind Pennsylvania Railroad electric locomotives, eliminating the ferry ride across the Hudson. This practice continued to the end of LV passenger service.

The third generation of Pullman-built equipment for the *Black Diamond* arrived in 1927 and 1928. Included were sun-room-lounge-parlor cars with enclosed rear platforms, an innovation from the West that extended the utility of the observation platform through the winter. New dining cars and club-

THE Black Diamond of 1938 rolls along the Susquehanna River in Pennsylvania behind a glistening 4-6-2.

ALCO-GE PA-1's, train's last new motive power, were fueled with black gold rather than black diamonds.

(ABOVE LEFT) The Black Diamond shows off its 1940 styling, the work of Otto Kuhler, at Ox Bow Curve along the Lehigh River west of Mauch Chunk, Pa. The foreground track belongs to the Central of New Jersey.

diners were built by Pullman; the coaches acquired during the USRA era continued in service on the train, which was featured by Warner Bros. in a motion picture, *Black Diamond*.

For years the train carried Pullmans variously originating in the East at New York and Philadelphia and in the West at Chicago, Detroit, and Toronto (connecting with LV at Buffalo off the Michigan Central and Canadian National-Grand Trunk).

Designer Otto Kuhler was responsible for the styling of the fourth *Black Diamond*, which was introduced in April 1940. Class K-6-S Pacifics and 16 cars — 10 conventional cars and 6 of the 10 new lightweight "American Flyer" coaches (see page 137) — were streamstyled and remodeled. The interior of the train was given a bright color scheme and fluorescent lighting. The exterior was painted Cornell (carmine) red, black, and white. Alco diesels purchased in 1948 were the only further change to the train until its last run on May 11, 1959.

BLACK DIAMOND

Gil Hutton, Photo Art Studio.

MONON President John W. Barriger III (left) helps noted cartoonist John T. McCutcheon christen the streamlined Hoosier on August 17, 1947.

The Hoosier Line

ON THE MONON

Ⅰ THE MONON was truly Indiana's own railroad. It served Indiana, Kentucky, and Illinois, and it linked the Ohio River with the Grand Calumet River, but its own trackage — 512 miles — was entirely within the state of Indiana (the railroad had operating rights over an additional 28 route miles).

The Monon's predecessor, the New Albany and Salem Railroad, was organized during 1847 by men of the New

Albany (Ind.) area. New Albany, situated on the Ohio River directly across from Louisville, Ky., was Indiana's largest city at the time. Construction work proceeded north to Salem, Bloomington, and Lafayette. Michigan City, on the shore of Lake Michigan, was reached on July 3, 1854. The road was reorganized following the panic of 1857, and on October 24, 1859, it emerged as the Louisville, New Albany & Chicago Railroad.

THE trains of summer: Business car No. 1 and Pullmans at French Lick, Ind., capture the mood of the era when all America went by rail.

MONON ROUTE
Chicago·Indianapolis & Louisville Railway

During the 1880's, the railroad entered into various consolidations and trackage arrangements which provided access to Chicago, Indianapolis, Louisville, and Cincinnati. A branch line to the watering place and spa at French Lick Springs was completed in 1887. It was also during the Eighties that the railroad became known as the Monon Route, named for the Big Monon and Little Monon creeks that flow into the Wabash River. "Monon" is a Pottawattomi Indian word meaning "swift running."

In 1897 the LNA&C was reorganized as the Chicago, Indianapolis & Louisville Railway. In 1902, more than 87 per cent of the company's stock was acquired jointly by the Louisville & Nashville and the Southern railroads.

An era of relative prosperity ended in 1933, when the Monon entered a period of bankruptcy that lasted until 1946. At that time, John Walker Barriger III, the highly regarded advocate of "super railroads," took command as president and launched a thorough modernization program. In 1956, 3 years after Barriger had resigned to become vice-president of the New Haven, the name of the road officially was shortened to Monon Railroad. In 1971 the Monon was merged into the Louisville & Nashville Railroad.

Although The Hoosier Line was a small railroad, it was widely renowned for its excellent passenger trains — *The Velvet Train, The Electric, Red Devil, Hoosier, Tippecanoe, Bluegrass,* and *Thoroughbred.*

HANDSOME 4-4-0 and peaked roof of the Dearborn Station clock tower highlight a 1900-era ad illustration for the all-Pullman Florida Flyer, which ran Chicago-Cincinnati-Chattanooga-Jacksonville via Monon-CH&D, Queen & Crescent, Southern, Plant System.

The trains of Hoosierland

THE HOOSIER LINE played an important and honored role throughout the Civil War. On May 1, 1865, in a final event of the conflict, the funeral train bearing the body of martyred President Abraham Lincoln passed over the line between Lafayette and Michigan City on its journey to Chicago and the burial ceremony in Springfield, Ill.

Luxury service on the Monon dated from May 1882, when the company entered into its first sleeping-car contract. Seven years later, during 1889, Pullman delivered *The Velvet Train*, the famed "Monon 5-Car Train," for day service between Chicago-Indianapolis-Cincinnati, in conjunction with the Cincinnati, Hamilton & Dayton Railroad. The companion train on the overnight run was *The Electric*, named after the newest form of illumination.

At the turn of the century, Monon participated in the operation of *The Florida Flyer*, "a sumptuous all-Pullman limited train" between Chicago and Jacksonville, Fla. The train was routed via Cincinnati, and was a joint operation with the Queen & Crescent Route, Southern, and the Plant System.

In July 1911, under the direction of Fairfax Harrison who later became president of the Southern, Monon introduced the *Hoosier Limited* between Indianapolis and Chicago. The following year it created the *Red Devil*, an all-sleeping-car train from Chicago to French Lick Springs, which was advertised as "The Carlsbad of America." The *Red Devil* name was derived from the trademark of Pluto Water, a well-known cathartic ("America's Laxative") bottled at French Lick. The trademark showed a red devil who represented the mythological ruler of Hades. New Yorkers journeyed via New York Central lines to French Lick aboard Pullmans that ran semi-weekly during the spring and fall seasons.

A YEAR for trains: In 1947 Pullman passengers (above left) walked to the enormous yellow brick French Lick Springs Hotel and health spa, while Lafayette residents (left) viewed return of testing Hoosier equipment during July 27 Monon centennial celebration.

"THE RED DEVIL"

A NEW THROUGH SLEEPING CAR TRAIN

NOW RUNNING BETWEEN CHICAGO
AND
FRENCH LICK AND WEST BADEN SPRINGS

TRAIN NAME and drum-sign illustration for The Red Devil (left), all-Pullman Chicago-French Lick Springs train introduced in 1912, were derived from trademark (above) of Pluto Water, bottled at the Springs. "Alligator" map (below) promoted Florida service in 1887 brochures, posters.

The prosperous years after World War I were popular ones for Monon's Indianapolis-Chicago service — the day trains *Hoosier* and *Tippecanoe*, and the overnight *Mid-Night Special*, which carried four sleepers from Indianapolis and one from Cincinnati. On the other side of the railroad, at Thomas D. Taggert's French Lick Springs Hotel, the Pullman tracks always were filled with cars. In 1925 and 1926 through New York sleepers on the Monon-Pennsylvania's crack *French Lick-New Yorker* arrived at the spa via PRR's Vandalia line at Gosport Junction. During this era the Monon was immortalized by two world-famous Hoosiers: writer George Ade and cartoonist John T. McCutcheon.

The presidency of John Walker Barriger III that began in May 1946 became noted for a complete rehabilitation of the railroad and improvement of its passenger service, which had declined during bankruptcy. In 1946, when carbuilders were swamped with orders for streamlined equipment, Barriger purchased 28 nearly new Government-surplus hospital cars for $16,500 each, a fraction of their original cost. The streamlined cars, featuring smooth-riding six-wheel trucks, wide-vision windows, and air conditioning, had been built by American Car & Foundry for the U. S. Army in 1945. Raymond Loewy, internationally known designer of Pennsylvania's "Fleet of Modernism," and E. E. Kauffman, Monon mechanical officer, directed the rebuilding of the cars at the railroad's Lafayette shops. Colorful and comfortable streamlined equipment for the *Hoosier*, *Tippecanoe*, and the new Chicago-Louisville *Thoroughbred* debuted in 1947. The cars, along with Monon's four conventional Pullmans and new EMD F3 diesels, were brightly painted "Monon Royal Red," gray, and white — a livery honoring the "cream and crimson" school colors of Indiana University at Bloomington. Freight diesels were painted the black and old gold of Purdue University at Lafayette. Years later the black and gold gradually was applied to all passenger equipment.

Hoosiers supported John Barriger's Monon: more than 84,000 persons rode the Indianapolis-Chicago trains during their first year of operation. Eventually, however, the predominance of the automobile — coupled with the advent of the Interstate Highway System in the 1960's — doomed Monon passenger business. In 1959 the Indianapolis trains came off. When the Post Office Department canceled its mail contract, the end came quickly. In 1967, after offering Hoosier hospitality for 120 years, the last passenger train on the Monon — the *Thoroughbred* — rolled to a halt.

MONON ROUTE

LOUISVILLE, NEW ALBANY & CHICAGO RY.

Pullman Palace Car Route

TO FLORIDA

THE SHORT & DIRECT LINE to all Points South.

CHICAGO
MICHIGAN CITY

LAFAYETTE
INDIANAPOLIS
CINCINNATI

MEMPHIS

Pullman Sleepers to LAFAYETTE Indianapolis Cincinnati Louisville.

ATLANTA

MONTGOMERY

MOBILE

PENSACOLA

THOMASVILLE

NEW ORLEANS
TALLAHASSEE JACKSONVILLE

For full information, Descriptive Books, Rates, etc., Address

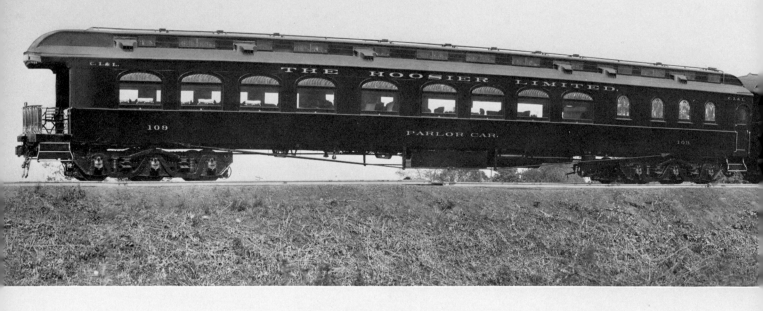

HOOSIER LIMITED, with newly built Barney & Smith observation and diner, pauses near Indianapolis for photo on August 21, 1911.

TOO LITTLE noted in its own time, the Monon of these photos revels in bucolic storyland settings. Here in 1947, No. 5, the Chicago-Louisville Day Express, stops amidst Gosport's 1850-vintage hole-in-the-wall station, a water tower, and switch stand. PRR's Vincennes (Ind.) branch is visible behind the depot.

MONON ROUTE
CHICAGO, INDIANAPOLIS & LOUISVILLE RAILWAY

JOHN T. McCUTCHEON'S cartoons and George Ade's comments embellished elaborate Monon menus in the 1920's.

My first dream as a Hoosier boy was to ride away on the Monon toward the Heaven-piercing spires of Lafayette or Michigan City. The Monon is "catty-cornered" to the whole State of Indiana, and all its trains are "Hoosiers."

George Ade

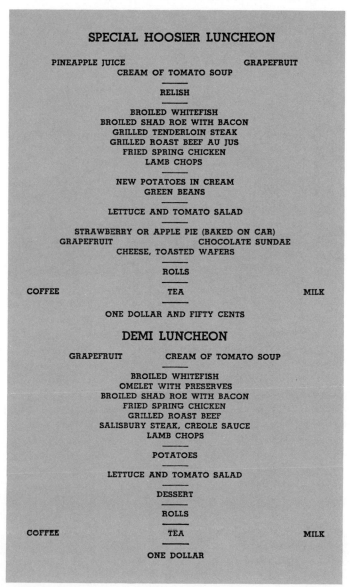

SPECIAL HOOSIER LUNCHEON

PINEAPPLE JUICE   GRAPEFRUIT
CREAM OF TOMATO SOUP

RELISH

BROILED WHITEFISH
BROILED SHAD ROE WITH BACON
GRILLED TENDERLOIN STEAK
GRILLED ROAST BEEF AU JUS
FRIED SPRING CHICKEN
LAMB CHOPS

NEW POTATOES IN CREAM
GREEN BEANS

LETTUCE AND TOMATO SALAD

STRAWBERRY OR APPLE PIE (BAKED ON CAR)
GRAPEFRUIT   CHOCOLATE SUNDAE
CHEESE, TOASTED WAFERS

ROLLS

COFFEE   TEA   MILK

ONE DOLLAR AND FIFTY CENTS

DEMI LUNCHEON

GRAPEFRUIT   CREAM OF TOMATO SOUP

BROILED WHITEFISH
OMELET WITH PRESERVES
BROILED SHAD ROE WITH BACON
FRIED SPRING CHICKEN
GRILLED ROAST BEEF
SALISBURY STEAK, CREOLE SAUCE
LAMB CHOPS

POTATOES

LETTUCE AND TOMATO SALAD

DESSERT

ROLLS

COFFEE   TEA   MILK

ONE DOLLAR

MENU from the 1930 era was inserted into a four-page cover booklet that contained prose and poetry describing Hoosierland.

EARLY in the 20th century Monon went to the Brooks Works of American Locomotive Company at Dunkirk, N. Y., for larger passenger power (Brooks had delivered 72-inch-drivered 4-4-0's to CI&L as late as 1897). The result was No. 301 (right) and sister 4-4-2 Atlantics with 73-inch-diameter drive wheels and a 26,700-pound tractive-effort rating.

Alco, author's collection.

LOCOMOTIVES came from New York, but RPO car No. 83 was built right in Indiana — at the Ohio Falls Car Manufacturing Company at Jeffersonville. The firm was one of 13 that formed American Car & Foundry in 1899.

Author's collection.

Author's collection.

ELABORATE lettering and striping that characterized late 19th-century railroading appeared on Louisville, New Albany & Chicago parlor-dining car No. 102, built by Ohio Falls Manufacturing Company.

Both photos, Pullman-Standard.

THE Velvet Train, which Monon operated with the Cincinnati, Hamilton & Dayton, carried the first dining car between Chicago and Cincinnati. Diner-parlor-observation No. 100 was outshopped by Pullman in 1889. Inside (left) were Pintsch gas lamps and carved oak seats with embossed green leather.

178

CI&L embraced the 4-6-2 Pacific-type early — within the first decade after the turn of the century. Although the 69-inch drivers and 28,250 pounds of tractive effort of Alco-built No. 351 later were surpassed by larger Pacifics, Monon load limits precluded truly powerful passenger engines — until the agile F3 diesels came in 1947.

IN 1903 and again in 1907, the AC&F shops at Jeffersonville, Ind. (formerly the Ohio Falls Car Manufacturing Company) delivered wide-vestibule cars for CI&L-CH&D Chicago-Cincinnati day service. Resplendent in standard green with gold trim, the RPO (right), baggage and express, parlor-buffet, and parlor-observation (below, top to bottom) were advertised by The Hoosier Line as equipment for the "Solid Vestibule Train."

ALCO, Monon's favorite steam-age builder, outshopped K-5-A-class Pacific No. 443 in 1923. The locomotive had 73-inch drivers, developed 34,500 pounds of tractive force. The railroad owned 13 Pacifics as late as 1947, but all steam was gone in 1949.

Alco, author's collection.

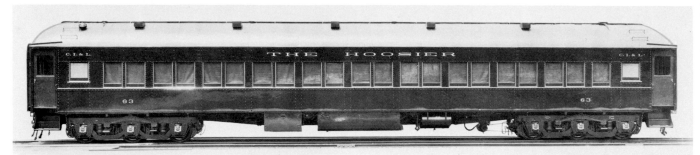

Both photos, Pullman-Standard.

MONON passengers rode in the austere as well as the ornate. In 1923 Pullman delivered four coaches, Nos. 61-64, that had walkover seats — upholstered with figured green plush — for 84 persons, and enameled arched ceilings. Lettering for the Hoosier appeared on the nameboard; the roofs were silver.

Both photos, Pullman-Standard.

ON February 13, 1913, Pullman Company inaugurated parlor-car operation on the Monon with four cars — West Baden, Delphi, French Lick, and Tippecanoe. Wicker seats at the observation end (above) accommodated 24 people, while another 12 persons sat in chairs. Electric lights hung from the groined ceiling.

180

Collection of John W. Barriger III.

IN 1948 Monon purchased four 10-section, 1-drawing-room, 2-compartment sleepers of 1920-1921 vintage from Pullman. Monon renamed the cars with such appropriate titles as Mononland, Hoosier-land, and Spring Mill Park. The Sir Henry W. Thornton (ex-Fort Gaines), shown at French Lick (above), was named by President Barriger to honor an Indiana-born international rail executive.

Collection of E. E. Kauffman.

WHEN John Barriger became CI&L president in 1946, the road had not purchased a new passenger car since coaches 61-64 had been delivered in 1923. Barriger bought 28 virtually new U. S. Army hospital cars — including No. 89388 (above) — that AC&F had built in 1945. They were remodeled into passenger equipment, such as 51-seat coach No. 21 (left), at the railroad's Lafayette carshops during 1947.

MONON
THE HOOSIER LINE

Collection of E. E. Kauffman.

RAYMOND LOEWY styled Monon's new cars. Decor of the dining-bar-lounge cars featured Kentucky Derby and Indianapolis "500" artifacts. The exterior livery: black roof, light gray letterboard, red pier panels, and gray girdersheet.

Collection of R. A. Fontaine, D.D.S.

OBSERVATION-PARLOR car No. 71 had a cast bronze tailboard sign infilled with black enamel. Cars' lettering and striping were white.

181

PHYSICAL SIZE, and even corporate longevity, were never criteria for judging the interesting and endearing qualities of a railroad or its passenger service. The Pere Marquette provides an excellent example of a small yet fascinating railroad: it was one of few roads named after a person; it briefly was involved in a little-known but intriguing alliance of three railroads; it complemented its rail operation with lake steamship service; it became one of the chips in the stack of railroad chips accumulated by the legendary Van Sweringen brothers; and, despite a life span of only 47 years, it operated luxurious trains in both the eras of the wooden cars and the stainless-steel streamliners.

The Pere Marquette was organized in late 1899 as a

consolidation of three railroads: the Flint & Pere Marquette Railroad and Steamship Lines, the Detroit, Grand Rapids & Western, and the Chicago & West Michigan. The new line took its name from the 17th century French missionary, *Pere* (Father) Jacques Marquette, a beloved Jesuit who explored the Great Lakes region. He died in 1675 and was buried near what today is Ludington, Mich.

The railroad owned more than 2000 miles of line (including 34 miles of narrow gauge), primarily in the lower peninsula of Michigan, and linked many of the state's towns with the city of Detroit, as well as with Toledo, O., and Chicago, Ill. PM steamships and car ferries plied Lake Michigan, connecting the railroad at Ludington with the Wisconsin ports of Milwaukee and Manitowoc.

ALFRED W. JOHNSON, the dean of Chicago railroad photographers, captured on film Pere Marquette No. 5, the Furniture City Special, departing Chicago at noon on September 4, 1929, for Grand Rapids, Mich. Doubleheading Alco Pacifics 721 and 720 are crossing the temporary piling erected for the straightening of the Chicago River.

JUNE 1892 timetable of F&PM pictured Pere (Father) Marquette and steamer No. 1; 1905 folder featured the Great Central Route.

On the
Pere Marquette

Resort country trains and boats

In 1904 Pere Marquette penetrated into Canada by acquiring the Lake Erie & Detroit River Railway to St. Thomas, Ont., where trackage rights were secured over the Michigan Central to Buffalo, N. Y.

From 1905 until 1907, Pere Marquette was part of the "Great Central Route," a consolidation of the PM, the Cincinnati, Hamilton & Dayton, and the Chicago, Cincinnati & Louisville into a 3661-mile system that stretched from Buffalo west to Springfield, Ill., and from Michigan south to Cincinnati, O. The short-lived venture ended in receivership.

Except for the period of Federal control of railroads during World War I, Pere Marquette functioned as an independent line until 1929, when it became part of the system created by Oris Paxton and Mantis James Van Sweringen. The brothers built a railroad empire comprising 25,000 miles of lines valued at 3 billion dollars. By pyramiding their interests in the Nickel Plate Road and the Chesapeake & Ohio, they eventually took control of the Erie, Chicago & Eastern Illinois, Wheeling & Lake Erie, Missouri Pacific, and half of the Denver & Rio Grande Western. Through the medium of the Alleghany Corporation, they used the C&O to obtain control of the PM. C&O control continued after the deaths of Mantis James in 1935 and Oris Paxton in 1936. In June 1947, the C&O, under Robert R. Young, formally acquired the Pere Marquette and gradually absorbed the small railroad until the Pere Marquette name all but disappeared.

THE Resort Special wheels along the shores of Grand Traverse Bay near Traverse City, Mich., in 1910 behind PM Ten-Wheeler 190.

"Summer only" and "Dream trains come true"

Pere Marquette

QUALITY passenger service was offered by the Pere Marquette when it commenced operations on January 1, 1900. Early PM timetables advertised parlor and sleeping-car service throughout the railroad. Integrated rail-steamship schedules featured Milwaukee, Wis., as an "on-line" city via the Michigan ports of Ottawa Beach, Muskegon, and Ludington. Summer-season folders advertised "Everyday service between Detroit and Milwaukee via Ottawa Beach with Fast Vestibuled Trains, Cafe Parlor Cars, and Fine Steamers."

THE Pere Marquette, introduced between Detroit-Lansing-Grand Rapids in 1946, was U. S.'s first all-new postwar streamliner.

PM.

IN 1949 the Pere Marquette name also was adopted for Chicago-Grand Rapids trains using domes from C&O's stillborn Chessie.

C&O.

Pullman-Standard.

SEVEN-CAR consist of the 1946 Pere Marquette included RPO-baggage, baggage, two coaches, two observation-coaches, and diner.

Pride of the Pere Marquette was the "summer-only" service operated from June until September to the resorts of northern Michigan. Initially, the train traveled overnight between Chicago and the vacationland. With the formation of the Great Central Route in 1905, a network of through Pullmans was instituted from St. Louis (via C&EI), Cincinnati (via CH&D), and Detroit (via PM). For the 1909 season, the St. Louis car was rerouted over the Chicago & Alton, and the PM train (Nos. 9-10) was named the *Michigan Resort Special.* In 1910 Nos. 9-10 were redesignated the *Resort Special,* a name they carried for years as the "Premier Train to the Holiday-Land of Michigan." Interline operation of connecting Pullmans ceased temporarily in the depression; the *Resort Special* was discontinued during World War II.

Author's collection.

Pere Marquette, planning for the return of peacetime, placed one of the first orders for postwar streamlined equipment. In March 1944 the road contracted for 14 lightweight cars from Pullman-Standard. The diesel-powered coach trains, advertised as the country's first all-new postwar streamliners, were completed in 1946 and placed in Detroit-Lansing-Grand Rapids service. They were named the *Pere Marquettes* and described as "dream trains come true." Their 14 cars, plus 2 coaches ordered in 1947 (and delivered in 1950), were the last passenger cars lettered for the Pere Marquette Railroad.

In June 1947, Pere Marquette became the Pere Marquette District — Chesapeake & Ohio Railway. The *Resort Special,* reactivated for the summer of 1946, was continued by C&O. In 1949 the "dream train" *Pere Marquettes* were supplemented by a Chicago-Muskegon-Grand Rapids *Pere Marquette,* equipped with stainless-steel dome cars from the ill-fated C&O *Chessie* (page 480). By 1951 the *Resort Special* was operating with new lightweight cars built for C&O.

The state of Michigan, home of the U. S. automobile industry, was one of the leaders in the development of Interstate highways. The ribbons of concrete took their toll of the passenger trains in the Wolverine State. Slowly but surely, the train-off petitions appeared. On September 7, 1963, the last sleeping car departed Traverse City, Mich., for Chicago. Three years later, on October 30, 1966, the last Traverse City-Grand Rapids coach ground to a halt, and service to the Michigan resorts became a memory. Only the Chicago-Grand Rapids service — often a single coach — remained, and this was discontinued with the advent of Amtrak on May 1, 1971.

CURVED GLASS of platform windows distinguished observation-parlor car No. 25, an AC&F product described in a 1902 PM timetable as "the embodiment of the modern carbuilder's skill."

BELPAIRE-BOILERED No. 389 had the lines and 72-inch drivers of a high-stepper. She emerged from the American Locomotive (Brooks) foundry at Dunkirk, N. Y., in 1901. The 4-4-2 exerted 19,900 pounds tractive force.

LETTERBOARD of No. 366, a wood RPO built by Pullman in 1905, refers to the Cincinnati, Hamilton & Dayton and Pere Marquette System. From 1905 to 1907, PM was leased by the CH&D, and both roads jointly owned the Chicago, Cincinnati & Louisville.

PM-CH&D-CC&L were known as the Great Central Route, which operated PM Nos. 1008-1010, cafe cars built by Pullman in 1905.

LUDINGTON and Charlevoix were 16-section "all-electric lighted" Pullmans completed in 1904 for Chicago-Grand Rapids service.

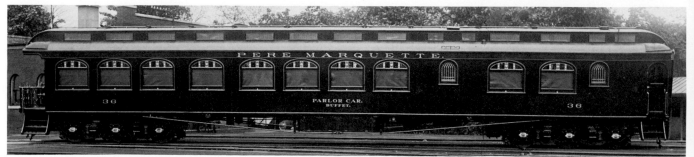

WOOD observation-parlor cars Nos. 34-37 were outshopped by Pullman in 1904 for the Pere Marquette; food was served from a buffet.

Alco, collection of *Railroad* magazine.

LOW tenders complemented the lean, racy appearance of 12 Class SP-3 4-6-2's, Nos. 711-722. They were built by Alco at Dunkirk, N. Y., in 1920. Tractive effort of each was 31,050 pounds.

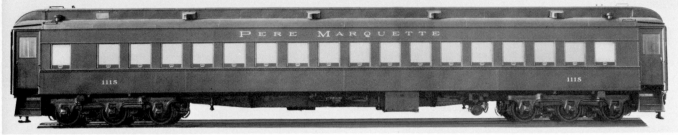

Pullman-Standard.

RARE 2-1 seating at coach fare was the attraction of eight Imperial Salon cars PM bought in 1931. C&O owned 30 such cars.

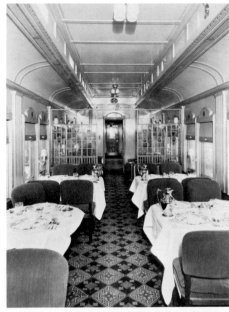

Both photos, Pullman Company.

PERE MARQUETTE

DURING the depression some railroads discontinued their dining-car departments and turned instead to the Pullman Company Commissary. In 1932 Pullman remodeled five parlor cars for Pere Marquette as restaurant-lounge cars and then operated the dining facilities. Mariner (below) and the others had marine-like names to honor the railroad's operations on the Great Lakes. They seated 14 people in the lounge section and 34 in the dining sections (above).

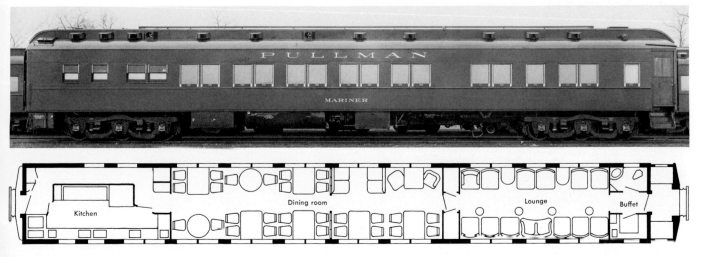

Kitchen   Dining room   Lounge   Buffet

PERE MARQUETTE No. 101 was one of the first of 510 2000-h.p. E7 diesel units mass-produced by Electro-Motive for America's streamliner fleets after World War II. The livery matched the stainless steel, maize, and blue of the new Detroit-Lansing-Grand Rapids Pere Marquettes.

PM re-established dining-car service in 1946 with 44-seat diners No. 10 (above) and No. 11. Under Robert R. Young and C&O ownership, waitresses (below left) replaced waiters and a no-tip policy was instituted. Menu (below) pictured Chessie, C&O's feline symbol.

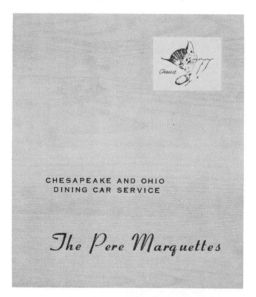

CHESAPEAKE AND OHIO
DINING CAR SERVICE

The Pere Marquettes

COACHES Nos. 135-136 of 1950 were last cars built with Pere Marquette identification. Colors honored the University of Michigan.

SISTER cars of the City of Newport News — one of 75 10-roomette 6-double-bedroom sleepers ordered by C&O (35 ultimately were sold to ACL, B&O, D&RGW, IC) — were named after such on-line cities as Benton Harbor, Grand Rapids, Ludington, Muskegon, and Traverse City when they went into overnight service on the Pere Marquette District in 1950.

All photos, Pullman-Standard.

FOUR parlor cars, including Elk Lake, were delivered in 1950. They had 30 revolving chairs (below) and were named after lakes in northern Michigan. Missouri Pacific bought the cars in 1959.

Pere Marquette

TWO coaches in each consist of the 1946 Pere Marquette were built to permit bi-directional operation of the passenger-carrying cars and eliminate turning at terminals. The four 56-seat blunt-end observation-coaches were purchased by C&EI in 1950.

The GM&O *Rebel*

The first streamlined trains in the South

GM&O.

GM&N PRESIDENT I. B. Tigrett and Rebel engineer.

Route

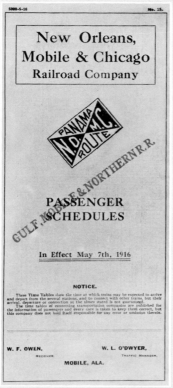

LAST NOM&C public timetable.

1 THE Gulf, Mobile & Ohio Railroad was formed on September 13, 1940, by a consolidation of the Gulf, Mobile & Northern and the Mobile & Ohio railroads. The new line formed "The Rebel Route Through Dixie" by connecting the Gulf of Mexico with East St. Louis, Ill., on the Mississippi River, opposite "The Gateway City to the West."

The new railroad was a tribute to I. B. Tigrett, banker-turned-railroad president, and his executive team of Frank M. Hicks and Glen P. Brock, men who later succeeded him as president of the GM&O. These men transformed the Gulf, Mobile & Northern from a nearly defunct short-line lumber road into a first-class rail system.

Two other men who served as directors of the Gulf, Mobile & Northern during its crucial formative period also made significant contributions to the development of the new system: W. H. Coverdale, a distinguished consulting engineer and a partner in the firm of Coverdale & Colpitts, specialists in railroad reorganizations; and Ralph E. Budd, president of the Burlington Railroad. Budd, an early exponent of the diesel-electric train, served for many years on both the GM&N board of directors and the executive committee, representing Burlington's 30 per cent stock interest in GM&N.

The history of Gulf, Mobile & Ohio passenger trains is an interesting but unrecorded story. The predecessor railroad, GM&N, was one of those lines which early explored the feasibility of providing special equipment and service to satisfy the particular needs of its passengers. It experimented with the internal combustion engine, receiving its first motor train in 1924. A complete gas-electric train, the *St. Tammany Special* (known locally as the "Linen Suit Train"), arrived in 1930, followed by the Railplane in 1935. Also in 1935, GM&N inaugurated "The South's First Streamlined Air-Conditioned Trains," the famous "Little Rebels." The *Gulf Coast Rebel* was placed in service in 1940.

On May 31, 1947, the GM&O acquired the venerable Alton Railroad Company, creating a 2800-mile system which extended "The Rebel Route" into St. Louis, Kansas City, and Chicago. On August 10, 1972, GM&O merged with Illinois Central, creating the Illinois Central Gulf.

THE red-and-silver "Little Rebel" posed alongside palm trees outside Terminal Station in New Orleans, La., in late 1941.

GM&O.

Everett L. DeGolyer Jr.

THE "Million Dollar Band" from the University of Alabama posed on Mobile & Ohio's 4-6-0 No. 234, a Baldwin product of 1906.

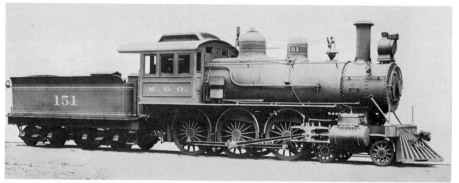

Railway & Locomotive Historical Society.

TEN-WHEELER 151 was built by Rogers Locomotive Works at Patterson, N. J., in 1898.

Baldwin collection, H. L. Broadbelt.

MOBILE & OHIO Baldwin 4-6-2 No. 268 was assigned to the Gulf Coast Special.

Author's collection.

M&O express car No. 62 came from AC&F in 1927; carried the swastika emblem of Southeastern Express Co., a Southern affiliate.

COACHES 209 and 212 were near twins: 209 was built by AC&F in 1926; 212 first saw light at Pullman in 1927.

Both photos, author's collection.

FEATU...
was the

IN 1914...

Pullman-Standard.

CAFE-lounge-observation cars Jackson, Meridian, Mobile, and Shiloh were assigned to the Mobile & Ohio for trains 1-2 and 15-16 (Gulf Coast Special). In 1935 Meridian was reassigned to Mexico as La Golondrina.

WHE...
1924,

Pullman Company.

Author's collection, from Fred Arone.

HOLIDAY DINNER: From a 1904 M&O advertisement.

GM&O.

MERRY-GO-ROUND folder publicized unique 6-day, 1423-mile tour using the Rebels, old Chicago & Southern Airline, Greyhound bus (right). GM&O-Alton's first timetable was issued in 1947.

IN a bucolic setting, the Gulf Coast Rebel nears Mobile, Ala., in post-World War II red-and-maroon colors.

Streamliners

ON September 13, 1940, the 23-year-old GM&N officially merged with the Mobile & Ohio, then in its 92nd year. The new enterprise, known as the Gulf, Mobile & Ohio, was made possible by GM&N's purchase of M&O first mortgage bonds held by the Southern Railway. Control of the 645-mile route from Mobile to East St. Louis fulfilled a long-standing dream of the GM&N executive team of Tigrett, Hicks, and Brock.

A modern passenger train between St. Louis and Mobile was placed in service over the former M&O route. The *Gulf Coast Rebel*, inaugurated on October 27, 1940, replaced the M&O steam-powered *Gulf Coast Special*. The consist included new Alco-GE 2000-h.p. diesel locomotives ordered by M&O and refurbished conventional equipment: baggage-mail; coaches; luxury coach lounges; and Pullman sleeping cars. Equipment for the new trains, known as the "Big Rebels," was restyled at the former M&O Iselin Shops in Jackson, Tenn. Twin heavy-weight Pullmans were streamlined at Pullman's Calumet (Ill.) shops. The red-and-silver livery of the 1935 "Little Rebels" was retained by the first GM&O streamliner.

In order to promote the new *Gulf Coast Rebels*, GM&O developed a "Merry-Go-Round" tour in conjunction with the Chicago & Southern Air Line (later Delta) and Greyhound Bus Lines. The 6-day all-expense vacation fun trip cost $54.75, and included all hotels and meals, plus 645 miles by rail (East St. Louis-Mobile), 153 miles by bus (Mobile-New Orleans), and 625 miles by air (New Orleans-St. Louis).

Beginning in June 1941 the cars of the two original *Rebels* of 1935 and the third *Rebel* of 1938 were remodeled to form three trainsets for a new operation: New Orleans to East St. Louis. Sleeping-coach No. 380 was remodeled as a coach for New Orleans-Jackson (Miss.) swing service, and No. 381 received a lounge compartment and the name Smokeless City to join the two round-end observation cars as a third observation car. All feature cars were given names for the new service, which was implemented on April 5, 1942, using connecting buses between East St. Louis and St. Louis:

POWER-MAIL-BAGGAGE	No. 352	No. 353	No. 354
LUNCH-COUNTER-COACH	No. 372	No. 373	No. 374
	FRENCH QUARTER	BLACK GOLD	FOREST PARK
OBSERVATION-LOUNGE-	No. 395	No. 396	No. 381
SLEEPING	OL' MAN RIVER	KING COTTON	SMOKELESS CITY
SLEEPING-COACH	No. 380 (remodeled to 64-seat coach)		

To accommodate the increased traffic during World War II, two unusual Pullman cafe-coach cars were added to the *Gulf Coast Rebel*. These cars had been rebuilt in 1936 for the St. Louis Southwestern Railway (The Cotton Belt Route) *Lone Star* and served on GM&O from 1942 to 1944.

It was during World War II that the merger of the proud old Alton Railroad with the GM&O was conceived. At that time the

Alton was bankrupt, having been returned to the court by Baltimore & Ohio in 1942. The Alton possessed Chicago-St. Louis-Kansas City main lines, but little equipment. In 1945 the Interstate Commerce Commission gave its approval to consolidation of the Alton and GM&O; final legal details were completed on May 31, 1947, and the merger formally was concluded.

With acquisition of the Alton, GM&O trains entered Union Station at St. Louis for the first time. Prior to the merger all GM&O passengers for St. Louis were bused to and from East St. Louis. GM&O also acquired a fleet of renowned passenger trains operating between St. Louis and Chicago (the *Alton Limited*, the *Abraham Lincoln*, the *Midnight Special*, the *Ann Rutledge*, the *Prairie State Express*), and between St. Louis and Kansas City (the *Night Hawk*).

During the depression years, much surplus B&O passenger equipment had been transferred to the Alton, including the lightweight, steam-powered *Royal Blue* trains (built with Gov-

208

Thigpen photo, courtesy GM&O.

Author's collection.

THE first railroad-ordered passenger diesel to appear as a separate unit was Baltimore & Ohio's 1800-h.p. Class DP-1 No. 50. Built in 1935, it was sent to the Alton in April 1936; later it became Gulf, Mobile & Ohio 1200. It is now preserved on display at the National Museum of Transport in St. Louis, Mo.

Baldwin collection, Everett L. DeGolyer Jr.

GM&O bought two Baldwin DR-6-4-20 diesels in 1946. The rare units primarily ran south of St. Louis, in conjunction with Alco DL109's and PA's. Each unit housed two 8-cylinder engines.

Author's collection.

ALTON'S red-and-maroon E7 units 101A and 101, delivered in 1946, served on GM&O trains into the Amtrak era.

ernment assistance) that later served as the *Abraham Lincoln* and the *Ann Rutledge*.

The post-World War II consolidation of 1947 ushered in a new era on the Gulf, Mobile & Ohio Railroad — the Alton Route, advertised as "The Direct Route Between the Midwest and the Gulf Ports." One of the most noticeable changes was the new passenger-car livery that combined the GM&N-M&O red band at the pier panels with the darker red of the Alton on the remainder of the car. Special lettering was gold leaf.

Eleven new lightweight streamlined coaches, 4 parlor cars, and 4 sleeping cars were ordered from AC&F and received between 1947 and 1950. Gradually this new equipment replaced older cars.

With a general decline in passenger service, the "Little Rebels," Nos. 1 and 2, made their last runs on February 21, 1954. On October 14, 1958, GM&O rail passenger service was discontinued south of St. Louis. The last GM&O sleeping cars operated between St. Louis and Chicago on December 31, 1968, over the route where between Bloomington and Chicago more than a century earlier — on September 1, 1859 — George M. Pullman ran his first sleeping car.

Yet during the twilight of privately operated railroad passenger service in the United States, prior to Government subsidization of Amtrak in May 1971, GM&O maintained a high standard of service on its Chicago-St. Louis trains. Some of the last parlor cars in the country and one of the finest dining-car menus were offered by the Gulf, Mobile & Ohio.

GM&O, courtesy Everett L. DeGolyer Jr.

IN October 1940 the Gulf Coast Rebel showed off its new Alco diesel and the remodeled cars with rounded roofs and skirts.

Alco, courtesy Everett L. DeGolyer Jr.

TWO-THOUSAND-H.P. DL109 No. 270 was styled by Otto Kuhler, and was built at Alco's Schenectady (N. Y.) plant in late 1940.

GM&O.

CONVENTIONAL Mobile & Ohio coaches were remodeled at the Iselin (Tenn.) shops for the Gulf Coast Rebel in 1940. Coach-buffet-lounge cars featured attractive hostesses in red uniforms (left), intercar phones, radio, easy chairs, and refreshments. Here passengers relax and converse in the lounge.

Menu

GULF COAST REBEL

Breakfast

GM&O

GULF, MOBILE & OHIO R. R.

Author's collection.

BLUE-AND-WHITE menu from Gulf Coast Rebel.

COTTON VALLEY (above) and twin Cotton Land were cafe-coach-sleepers with 8 sections (right). Coach section (far right) was arranged for meals. Car ran on the Cotton Belt before 1942-1944 stint on the Rebel.

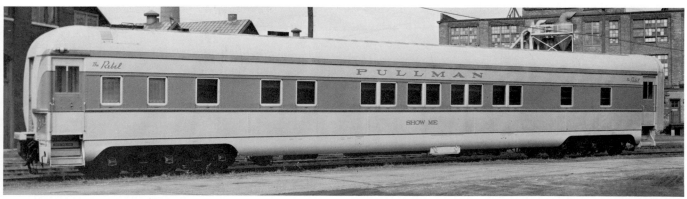

SHOW ME (ex-Leaning Tower) was a restyled Pullman sleeping car with 8 sections, 1 drawing room, 3 double bedrooms. It was completed at the Calumet shops of the Pullman Company in September 1940. Otto Kuhler styling featured red-and-silver color scheme, special lettering, rebuilt rear end (below left). Twin car Deep South (ex-Torazzo Tower) is shown in 1947 in red-and-maroon livery.

B&O CONTROL of the Alton also brought 1937 AC&F-built Royal Blue equipment to the Chicago-St. Louis route as the Ann Rutledge, named for Abraham Lincoln's boyhood love. Coaches (above) had extra sheeting beyond vestibules and painted diaphragms, giving articulated appearance. Observation-parlor (right and below) was used on the Abraham Lincoln in 1960's.

LADY BALTIMORE, a one-of-a-kind 4-4-4, was one of the original engines for the lightweight trains (far left) built by AC&F in 1935 for B&O's Royal Blue service and quickly transferred to the Alton as the Abraham Lincoln. Illinois Gov. Henry Horner and 4-6-4 Lord Baltimore appeared at May 15, 1935, dedication ceremonies (above left) at Springfield, Ill. The Lincoln tavern offered lunch counter (above right) and dining sections.

SOUVENIR STUB from the Abraham Lincoln, "World's Most Modern Train."

GM&O's frequent Chicago-St. Louis service (six trains each way in the 1950's) found heavyweight cars supplementing the lightweight trains. C&A Alton Limited diners carried names Springfield and Bloomington (bottom) when built in 1924; cars survived through Amtrak takeover and were probably last heavyweight diners running. GM&O's four AC&F parlors of 1947, with six-wheel trucks (above and below) were leased by Amtrak.

THE SEABOARD COAST LINE

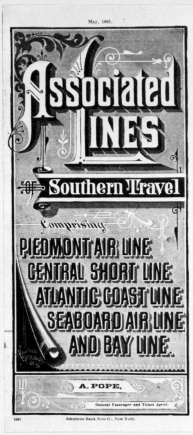

RIVALS offered joint service in 1881.

Author's collection.

"It is a pleasure to have you aboard."

I IN July 1967 two railroads, the Seaboard Air Line and the Atlantic Coast Line, were merged to form the Seaboard Coast Line Railroad. Each of the predecessor companies had histories which dated to the very beginnings of railroad construction in the United States.

ACL's earliest predecessor was the Petersburg Railroad, chartered in Virginia in 1830. SAL also had its roots in Virginia, in the form of the Portsmouth & Roanoke Railroad chartered in 1832. Both lines sought access to the

ROUTE TO THE SOUTH

rich Roanoke River Valley. From these early times, the destinies of the two companies — Seaboard and Coast Line — paralleled each other almost as closely as did their tracks across the Piedmont Region of the Southeast.

The merger was not the first instance of close association between the two railroads. A timetable from May 1881, reproduced here, publicized through train services on the two routes that later became the Seaboard Coast Line — a strong regional carrier with 9200 miles of track in the six southeastern states of Virginia, North and South Carolina, Alabama, Georgia, and Florida.

The *Atlanta Special* was a contemporary of the all-Pullman *Florida Special* of the Atlantic Coast Line Route.* Indeed, it was the inauguration of the *Florida Special* during January 1888, concurrent with the opening of the magnificent Ponce de Leon Hotel in St. Augustine, Fla., by Henry M. Flagler, that helped create the first tourist exodus to Florida.

*For the story of the *Florida Special*, see *Some Classic Trains*, pages 124-137.

BALDWIN 4-8-2 with Vanderbilt tender sported orange-and-black nameboard of the Orange Blossom Special above the drive wheels.
SCL.

The Seaboard Air Line passenger route

OFFICIAL GUIDES from the 1880's and 1890's listed the "Seaboard Air-Line Passenger Route," which consisted of an association of five separate railroads that formed a through "air-line" route between Atlanta and the North. The participants were the Seaboard & Roanoke Railroad, Raleigh & Gaston Railroad, Raleigh & Augusta Air-Line, and the Carolina Central Railroad. Later, the Georgia, Carolina & Northern Railway and the Durham & Northern Railway were added.

The crack train of the Seaboard Air-Line was the *Atlanta and Washington Special*, or *Atlanta Special* for short, and often referred to locally as "The Cyclone." It was a "solid train for Raleigh and Richmond" with special equipment built by Pullman's Palace Car Company in 1893. Connecting trains of the Richmond, Fredericksburg & Potomac took passengers from Richmond, Va., to Washington, D. C. (where they could connect again with PRR's *Congressional Limited* to New York).

The Seaboard Air-Line timetable for June 1893 promoted a friendly relationship with the Atlantic Coast Line of Railroads, another group of southeastern railroads. A notice advertised "Connections at Weldon, N. C. with the Atlantic Coast Line for Charleston, Savannah, Jacksonville, Thomasville and all Florida points." Seaboard also owned the Bay Line steamships that sailed between Norfolk and Baltimore.

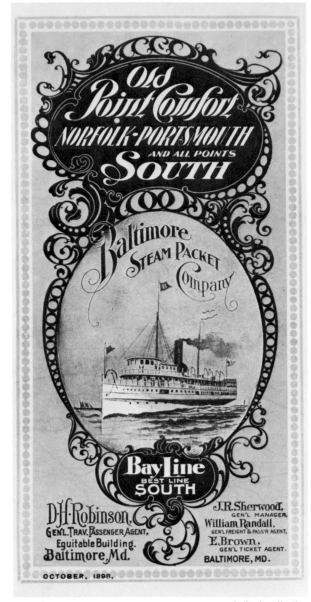

BAY LINE steamers sailed overnight, connected with rails.

BALDWIN delivered 4-4-0 No. 606 in 1900, at a time when Seaboard Air Line was promoting its Richmond to the Gulf of Mexico route as the "Florida & West India Short Line."

LUGGAGE of turn-of-the-century Eastern nabobs went south aboard the Florida Special's No. 4, a unique 1898 Pullman baggage car. The train was 10 years old when No. 4 came.

216

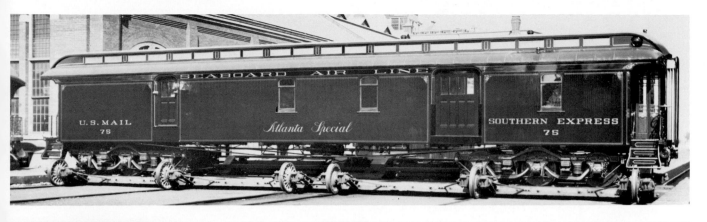

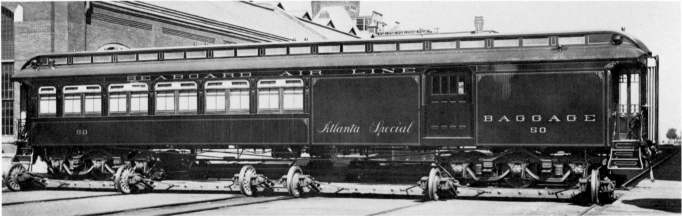

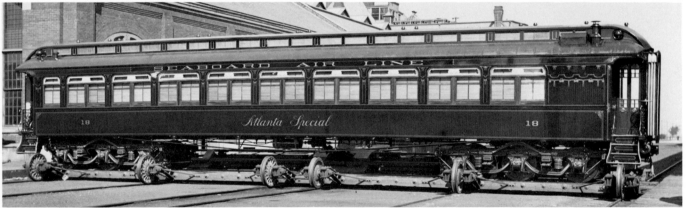

IN 1893 Pullman outshopped 12 Atlanta Special cars in three lots of 4 cars each. The cars included U. S. Mail-Southern Express No. 75 (top), combination baggage-smoking car No. 50 (above center), and coach No. 18 (above). All had six-wheel trucks and narrow vestibules.

IMMACULATE Atlantic Coast Line of South Carolina combination car of 1898 rolled south on the Florida and West Indian Limited.

BEFORE the jet-set age, the affluent of America rode FEC's Overseas Limited to Key West, Fla., where they boarded ships for Cuba.

SEABOARD'S first 4-6-2 passenger locomotives were 22 members of the P class, built by Baldwin Locomotive Works from 1911 to 1913. In 1940 two P's were streamlined to pull Silver Meteor connecting trains in Florida.

OBSERVATION platform of 10-section Delmonico (left) decorated the Seaboard Florida Limited late in 1909; Pullman Montcalm (above), a 10-section car with a lounge featuring leaded deck sash, electric fans, a bookcase, and a writing desk, joined the SAL fleet in January 1912. Atlantic Coast Line received sister cars.

218

The Seaboard Florida Limited

"A TRAIN of Quality For People of Quality — A Luxurious Electric-Lighted Train That Runs on Time."

During the early 1900's, travelers from the Northeast planning a winter stay in Florida, the Bahamas, or Cuba, had a choice of two superb seasonal trains: the *Seaboard Florida Limited* of the Seaboard Air Line and the *Florida Special* of the Atlantic Coast Line. For years a rivalry existed between the two trains. Pullman Company records show the equal division of orders for special feature cars — one half to SAL, one half to ACL. Even the purple, white, and gold brochures advertising the two trains were similar.

Announcement of the inaugural run of the *Seaboard Florida Limited* on January 4, 1903, attracted the attention of steel magnate Andrew Carnegie, who was politely advised that the special nature of the train precluded attaching his private car on the rear. Instead, he was offered — and he accepted — a drawing room-compartment suite.

The *Seaboard Florida Limited* and *Florida Special* were operated as separate trains by the PRR and RF&P between New York-Washington-Richmond. From Richmond to Jacksonville, Fla., the two trains traveled over the competing lines of the SAL and ACL in a rivalry as keen as that of the *Century* and *Broadway* between New York and Chicago. South of Jacksonville the *Limited* and the *Special* ran as separate trains on Henry Flagler's Florida East Coast line as far as West Palm Beach and Miami. After a 128-mile sea-going extension was completed on January 22, 1912, the trains were consolidated into FEC's *Overseas Limited* at West Palm Beach for the run to Key West, where passengers boarded steamships *Governor Cobb* and *Halifax* for the cruise to Havana, Cuba. At the time, Miami was a village of 5000 and the *Overseas* passed through what became Florida's "Magic City" in the small hours of the morning.

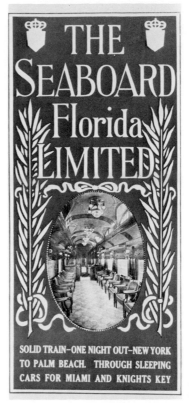

Author's collection.
PURPLE folder sold 1911 service.

TREONTA was one of five 7-compartment, 2-drawing-room cars built by Pullman in December 1911 for assignment to SAL. Five similar cars in the lot went into ACL service.

Three photos, Pullman-Standard.

SIX 1913 steel diners with "Gothic" upper window sash served "celebrated Harris Lithia Springs Table Water" from Harris Springs, S. C.

PASSENGERS and townspeople could personally deposit mail through brass mail slot at the end of RPO No. 171, delivered in June 1911.

With permission of Otto Kuhler.

FAMED artist and locomotive stylist Otto Kuhler employed water colors to recreate the heyday of the Orange Blossom Special.

The Orange Blossom Special

PASSENGER train travel to Florida increased greatly after World War I, particularly during the Florida "boom" of the 1920's. Most traveling occurred in the winter season between December and March. *Railway Age* reported an enormous growth in traffic — from 415,000 passengers in the 1922-1923 season to 752,000 in the 1924-1925 season. Most tourists arrived in regularly scheduled Pullmans that originated from points as far away as Denver and Kansas City. Others filled trains from St. Louis, Chicago, Detroit, Cleveland, and Buffalo. Canadians from Toronto, Montreal, Ottawa, and Quebec joined throngs from New England and the eastern states. It was estimated that 58 per cent of the traffic originated in the Northeast and 42 per cent in the remaining areas. Only because of the logistics of the Pullman "pool" were such seasonal movements possible. Thousands of Pullman cars that operated to the Southland in the winter were transferred to northern and western resort service in the summer.

The rush of tourists during the Florida boom led to the November 21, 1925, introduction of the *Orange Blossom Special* by the Seaboard Air Line. SAL track extensions to Miami on the east coast, and Fort Myers and Naples on the west coast, were completed in January 1927. These new lines made it possible for Seaboard to advertise the only service from the North to *both* Florida coasts over one railroad. The *Orange*

Blossom was a special train, indeed. From the inaugural ceremonies in 1925 (at Winter Haven, Fla., six bathing beauties christened the train with a bottle of orange blossom perfume) until its last run from Miami on April 12, 1953, the *Orange Blossom* earned a reputation as one of America's most distinguished trains.

Every refinement of the train's equipment emphasized an atmosphere of luxury: there was a club car with a barber shop, gentlemen's shower, and valet service; another car had a ladies' shower, a boudoir and lounge, and maid-manicure service. Special dining cars served exquisite meals. As an extra touch, Pullman and dining-car employees wore armbands with the train name embroidered in orange silk. For the season that began on January 5, 1934, the *Special* was advertised as the "first and only Air-conditioned train to Florida . . . travel-

ORANGE
BLOSSOM
SPECIAL
New York~Florida

SEABOARD
AIR LINE RAILWAY

ALL·FLORIDA·ROUTE

Author's collection.
FOLDER described services, schedule.

Pullman-Standard.
BAFFIN BAY, built in 1926, had 3 compartments, 2 drawing rooms, lounge, and ladies' bath.

Pullman Company.
OAK CITY — with 12 roomettes, 1 single room, and 4 bedrooms — was a 1949 rebuild.

Pullman Company.

SEAVIEW and 6-section sisters Seaboard, Seabreeze, and Seaside were remodeled in 1930.

Bruce D. Fales.

Author's collection.
ORANGE BLOSSOM twins wave good-bye to winter at New York in late 1936.

BRRRR! Returning vacationists encounter 13-degree weather on RF&P.

ing the longest distance of any Air-conditioned train in the world." All of this was offered without an extra fare.

The era of diesel-electric locomotives on the Seaboard began on October 31, 1938. An SAL exhibition at Washington's Union Station presented the *Orange Blossom Special* headed by three 2000-h.p. Electro-Motive units. The triple E4 units were brightly painted in a green, yellow, and orange livery that today is considered as one of the all-time classic diesel color schemes. The new diesels — the first in the Southeast — were placed in service on December 15, 1938, to power the *Orange Blossom* during its greatest years, when twin sections — one for the east coast and one for the west coast of Florida — hurtled through the night with 15 or 16 steel Pullmans and dining cars, leader and follower only 15 minutes apart.

World War II brought a temporary halt to the *Orange Blos-*

som; it did not operate from March 1942 until December 12, 1946. In 1949 it was still advertised as "leading the Seaboard fleet . . . the premier train between New York and Florida." In 1951 it was re-equipped with 35 conventional steel Pullmans, specially painted light gray and maroon. The four regularly assigned sets of equipment included *Oak-* and *Fir-*series conventional Pullmans that had been remodeled in 1949 to provide streamlined-type roomettes and bedrooms. The seasonal deployment of these cars, which were assigned to the famed *Bar Harbor Express** during the summers, climaxed the era of the great Pullman pool. The *Orange Blossom* was withdrawn after the 1952-1953 season, perhaps because it was one of the few classic American trains that never was streamlined.

*For the story of the *Bar Harbor Express,* see *Some Classic Trains,* pages 42-43.

221

BALDWIN built 36 72-inch-drivered M2's in 1924-1926; 15 were modernized in the 1930's for through Richmond-Jacksonville runs.

DECEMBER was a brisk month in 1926 for deliveries of Railway Express cars to the Seaboard: SAL received 32 from Pullman-Standard.

1925 CURRENCY bought a shave (30 cents), bath (50 cents), and suit pressing ($1.50) aboard club-smoking-baggage car Eagle Bay.

IN time for winter was Orange Farm, a 12-1 Pullman assigned to SAL in December 1925; others in lot went to SP-UP-C&NW's Overland.

CLOVER MILL, an 8-section, 5-double-bedroom 1937 rebuild of 12-1-1 Wellford, ran on SAL in winters and on NP in summers in late 1930's.

NINETEEN "special" dining cars, named for Lakes, came to SAL in 1925-1926. Lake Magdalene had 36 seats, mosaic tile floor; was air-conditioned in 1933.

ORANGE BLOSSOM SPECIAL

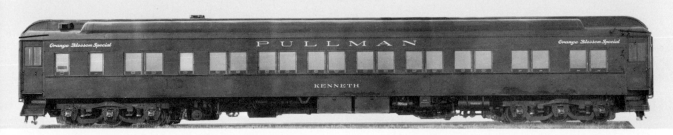

FOR service during the 1934 winter season, Seaboard sent 32 Pullmans and 2 diners to Pullman, Ill., to have air conditioning installed. Modified with early roof "bubbles" that served as ducts were the 6-compartment, 3-drawing-room Glen Elm, the 10-section, 2-drawing-room Point St. Joseph, and the 12-section, 1-drawing-room Kenneth. All were lettered Orange Blossom Special.

FAMOUS triple crossing at 16th and Dock streets in Richmond, Va., was the scene of a 1949 publicity photo involving a 6000-h.p. set of Seaboard E7 diesels, Chesapeake & Ohio 2-8-2 No. 2327 (Alco 1926), and a 1500-h.p. Alco RS2 roadswitcher of the Southern Railway.

MOUNTAIN NO. 224 (Alco 1922) has a 12-car Orange Blossom Special in tow at Auburndale, Fla., in 1935. Around the corner: diesels.

ONE of the most widely acclaimed of all diesel color schemes came to railroading on the point of the Orange Blossom Special in 1938. The orange, yellow, and green EMD E4's had a retractable walk-through nose (below).

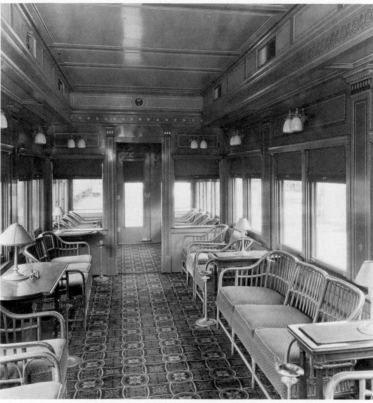

SUNBURST (above and below), built in 1927 for MP's Sunshine Special (see page 462) and modified in 1934, had 2 compartments, 1 drawing room, buffet, and a lounge, while Dixie Land (bottom), built in 1928 for C&EI's Dixie Flyer, had one additional compartment. They joined the Pullman pool in the 1930's, and both were assigned to the first Orange Blossom trips in 1937.

Streamliners to the South

SEABOARD scored a "first" in north-south transportation history on February 2, 1939, with the introduction of the *Silver Meteor*, a seven-car, Budd-built, stainless-steel train that operated every third day between New York in the North and Miami and St. Petersburg in the South. The name *Silver Meteor* was selected from among 76,366 entries in a $500 prize contest (30 persons submitted the winning name and shared the prize).

Seaboard's new train was such a success that by December 1939 Atlantic Coast Line and Florida East Coast had placed in service three similar Budd-built seven-car Florida streamliners which had been named *Champions* in a prize contest. Also in December 1939, capacity of each *Meteor* was increased by adding more cars.

By 1941, enough equipment was available to provide daily service to both coasts of Florida via the SAL and ACL. In May of that year, conventional steel Pullman sleeping cars were added to the consists of the *Silver Meteors* and *Champions*. The Seaboard cars were painted aluminum and "shadowlined" to simulate fluted stainless steel. Coast Line sleepers were painted to match the stainless-steel and purple *Champions*. The rival trains featured beautiful interiors, radio entertainment, stewardess-nurse or hostess service, low-cost meals, diesel power, and "one-night-out" schedules. During World War II,

IN the 1960's Seaboard promoted en route fashion shows and movies and TV to attract and entertain passengers on Florida runs.

SILVER METEOR 1940's publicity pose (left) featured oranges and a 1947 observation car; the train retained its handsome appearance (below) after the Seaboard Coast Line merger.

FLORIDA SPECIAL
THE RELAXING WAY TO TRAVEL

IF YOU WANT TO GO TO MIAMI WITHOUT A STOPOVER IN HAVANA, CALL US.

SCL
SEABOARD
COAST LINE
RAILROAD

Our trains to Miami are the safest, most relaxing way to go. Lots of room to move around. Courteous service. Your choice of coach or Pullman. Round-trip reserved seat only $83.93. Phone: (212) 245-7380 • Address: 12 West 51st Street • New York, New York 10020

SCL boosted trains with brochures, ads (that capitalized on contemporary plane hijackings), and train TV.

when SAL's *Orange Blossom Special* and ACL's *Florida Special* were withdrawn, the *Silver Meteor* and *Champion* trains provided the finest service from New York to Florida.

Following the war, lightweight equipment was ordered by SAL, ACL, and the three other railroads — Pennsylvania, Florida East Coast, and the Richmond, Fredericksburg & Potomac — that participated in the Florida service. Some of the last post-World War II sleeping cars built by Budd and Pullman-Standard were delivered to Seaboard in 1955 and 1956.

On the Seaboard Coast Line merger date of July 1, 1967, full-page newspaper advertisements announced that "The New Railroad is here," and invited passengers to come aboard SCL's great streamliners: the *East Coast Champion, West Coast Champion, Silver Meteor,* and *Silver Star* between

New York and Florida; the *City of Miami* and *South Wind* between the Midwest and Florida; and the *Silver Comet* between New York and Birmingham. During the winter seasons the *Florida Special* served as the flagship of the new fleet.

SCL's *Florida Special* was a unique train. It was promoted as a "resort on wheels" and the "champagne train." Passengers were pampered by a friendly crew, including pretty hostesses. Patrons feasted at candlelight dinners which included complimentary champagne, were entertained by fashion shows, and could watch television or participate in songfests and bingo games. Although Amtrak temporarily dropped *Florida Special* services after the 1971-1972 season, the Seaboard Coast Line routes remained prominent in the plans of the National Railroad Passenger Corporation. **I**

ACF.

RED MOUNTAIN and two sisters built by AC&F in 1949 had 6 double bedrooms and a lounge; car became SCL Palm Beach in 1967.

Both photos, Pullman-Standard.

PULLMAN construction in 1949 included one lot of 15 sleeping cars, each containing 10 roomettes and 6 double bedrooms, for Seaboard

Air Line. Norfolk (above left) was one of 12 for SAL while Lancaster (above right) was one of 3 to be furnished by RF&P.

Budd.

SOUTHERN PINES was a 1955 Budd Sleeper named for a famous North Carolina resort.

Budd.

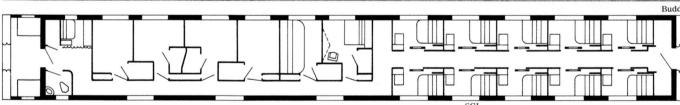

SCL.

TWO orders to Budd in 1949 produced 12 10-roomette, 6-bedroom sleepers — 6 for Seaboard and 6 for Pennsylvania. Photo (above) of West Palm Beach shows original appearance; view (left) of sister car Lake Wales was taken after the SCL merger in 1967.

228

Both photos, SCL.

COACH-TAVERN car (above) is original 1939 Silver Meteor equipment. Hostess conducts bingo games in Florida Special diner (below) after the dinner hours.

Both photos, Pullman-Standard.

IN 1956 Seaboard's Silver Meteor introduced three Sun Lounge cars. Miami Beach had 5 double bedrooms and a lounge with sun roof, became SCL Sun View.

Both photos, Pullman-Standard.

DE LUXE accommodations were specified for nine sleepers delivered in 1956. Boca Grande (above) was one of three luxurious all-room cars with 5 double bedrooms, 2 compartments, and 2 drawing rooms. Ocala (below) and six roster mates had 11 double bedrooms.

229

PATRONS enjoyed North Carolina Country Ham and Eggs with hominy grits aboard SCL 5903 (ex-SAL 6103), a 1939 Budd 48-seat diner shown on the Silver Meteor in 1951 (right).

IN 1950 the Florida Special, a rival to Seaboard's trains, was equipped with 13 diners from Pullman. Ten went to ACL, 2 to FEC, and 1 to RF&P. SAL entered the picture when it bought 36-seat Fort Drum (above) from FEC. Inside (left) were de luxe tables on the bias.

ACL President Champion McDowell Davis favored purple letterboards on such cars as Tampa, a 1947 48-seat diner built by Budd.

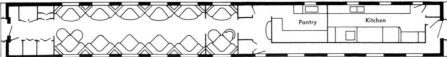

INTRODUCED on the 1939 Champion, 36-seat-diner Newark became SCL 5907 (left).

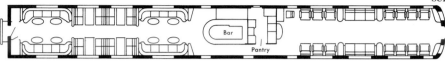

SCL.

THE CHAMPION

All photos, unless otherwise credited, Budd.

FUNCTION had outpaced form when blunt-end observation car Lake Okeechobee (left and above) entered ACL-FEC Champion service. The 85-foot Budd-built tavern-lounge was sold to LIRR; sisters were sold to SAL but finally emerged in SCL livery with black roofs (top).

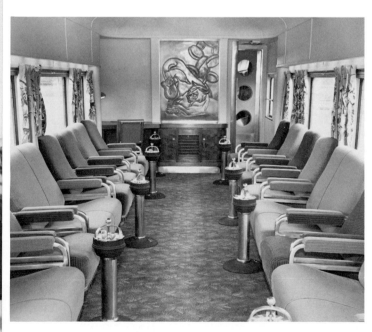

SYMBOLIZING the streamliner era was No. 6600, a 1947 round-end tavern-observation from Budd that seated 58 persons in two lounges.

I TH
in
1850.
busine
River
of the
sparse
in Ma
Fro
one o
and t
agric
and t
from
conti
and
Lo
of ur
year
the

231

JAMES LANE ALLEN, named for a Southern author and displaying diaphragm stay rods (above right), was rebuilt in 1938 with 10 sections (above), 2 double bedrooms, 1 drawing room. The rooms were done in pastels with contemporary upholstery.

IN 1934 the Empress cars (below right) were replaced by rebuilt 3-compartment, 1-drawing-room lounge cars Alabama, Kentucky, and Tennessee, originally built in 1929 for CN as the Montreal, Quebec, and Toronto.

The **Pan-American**
ALL-PULLMAN

Pullman-Standard.

PARLOR CARS Calla Lily (below) and Easter Lily operated between Cincinnati, Louisville, and Memphis. The 34 revolving chairs (left) were upholstered in plush; walls and ceiling were shades of gray and gold.

Pullman-Standard.

DINER 2722, delivered by American Car & Foundry in 1929, seated 36 for famous L&N meals. Car later was named Globe Coffee House.

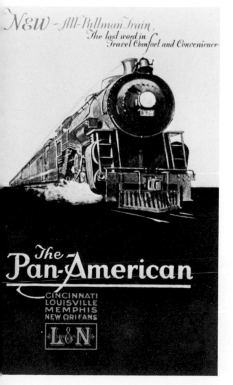

PARLOR-OBSERVATION cars Empress(es) Josephine (above), Catherine, and Victoria were built in 1925. (Below) Their appointments included a women's shower and a radio.

THE second Alabama, Kentucky, and Tennessee were 10-section lounge cars. Pullman rebuilt them in 1938 from 10-section-lounge-open platform observation cars, giving them closed ends (below left) for midtrain service and a modernized interior, with chromium chairs and continuous strip lighting (below right). L&N purchased the three cars in 1948 and completely rebuilt them again in 1954 into tavern-lounge cars named Alabama Club, Kentucky Club, and Tennessee Club (above). Outside, the L&N-owned cars were dark blue, with a gray roof and gold script lettering. Inside were a lounge seating 14 and a cheerful tavern section seating 24 (top). The tavern was separated from the bar by etched glass with the car name and the corresponding state capitol.

Pullman-Standard.

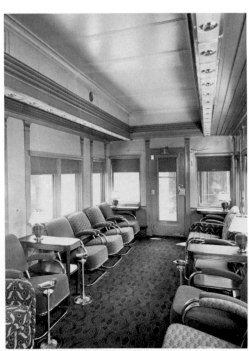

Pullman-Standard.

K. C. McDaniel, courtesy of L&N.
BY 1940, the Pan had lost its sun-room observation car, but its drumhead remained.

THE Pan cruises south through Hubers, Ky., in 1948. Locomotive numbers on the headlight glass were an L&N practice, even for diesels.

L&N

TIME TABLES

LOUISVILLE AND NASHVILLE RAILROAD

No. 461

DIESELS came to the head end of Louisville & Nashville passenger trains on May 18, 1942. Electro-Motive E6 No. 450 (above right), in a livery of royal blue, cream, and red, made its first run by taking the Pan-American south out of Louisville Union Station. Almost 29 years later, on April 28, 1971, E7 No. 791 (right) led a seven-car Pan-American north from New Orleans to Cincinnati. The advent of Amtrak — and the demise of the Pan — was 3 days away.

ONLY the six-wheel trucks, riveted ends, and clerestory roof betray coach 2561's heavyweight ancestry. L&N's South Louisville shops rebuilt it in 1948 with wide windows, welded sides, skirting, and folding steps.

DINER-LOUNGES Dixie Traveler (left and above) and Dixie Journey were Pullman-built in 1947 as Maine Central's Merrymeeting (below) and Arundel. They came to L&N in 1959 from the Chicago & Eastern Illinois, which bought them from MEC in 1951.

NO. 3253 was one of 13 streamlined coaches built for L&N in 1955 by ACF Industries. Coupled to it in Louisville Union Station was a wooden combine that normally accompanied the General, of Civil War fame.

GREEN RIVER (right), Barren River, and Kentucky River were 10-roomette, 6-double-bedroom sleepers built in 1949 by Pullman-Standard to Pennsylvania Railroad specifications for through service to New York via the Pan-American and PRR's Cincinnati Limited. Originally painted tuscan red, they later wore L&N blue and gold.

L&N.

CURLY PINE was one of 29 6-roomette, 4-double-bedroom, 6-section "Beauty Sleepers — the very latest in travel comfort," built in 1953 for L&N, Chicago & Eastern Illinois, and Nashville, Chattanooga & St. Louis for the Pan, Georgian, Gulf Wind, and Humming Bird. Some cars of the series were sold to the National Railways of Mexico in 1970. Monte Aconcagua (below) displays new livery at William Kratville's Auto-Liner shops in Omaha before heading south.

Pullman-Standard.

Author's collection.

The Pan-American
ALL-PULLMAN

Charles B. Castner, courtesy of L&N.

PASSENGERS board the combined Pan-American and Gulf Wind in New Orleans on April 27, 1971.

243

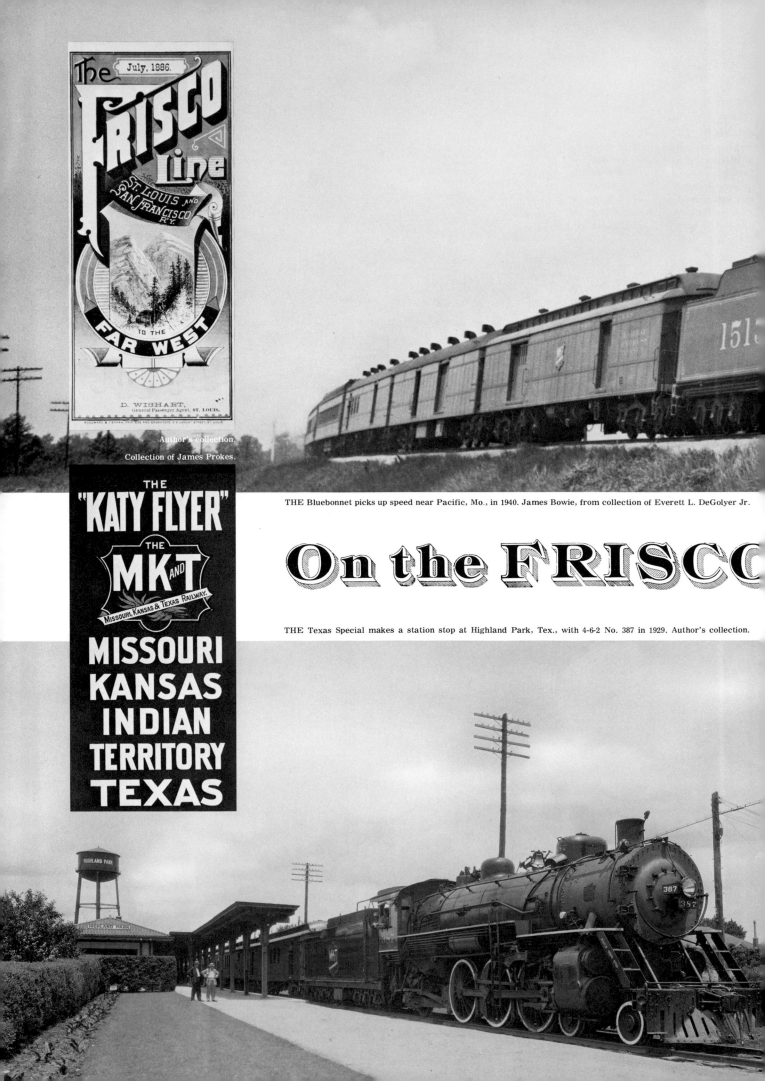

The July, 1886.

FRISCO Line

ST. LOUIS AND SAN FRANCISCO R'Y.

TO THE FAR WEST

D. WISHART,
General Passenger Agent, ST. LOUIS.

WOODWARD & TIERNAN, PRINTERS AND ENGRAVERS, 2 & 4 LOCUST STREET, ST. LOUIS.

Author's collection.

Collection of James Prokes.

THE Bluebonnet picks up speed near Pacific, Mo., in 1940. James Bowie, from collection of Everett L. DeGolyer Jr.

On the FRISCO

THE Texas Special makes a station stop at Highland Park, Tex., with 4-6-2 No. 387 in 1929. Author's collection.

THE "KATY FLYER"

THE MKT AND

MISSOURI, KANSAS & TEXAS RAILWAY.

MISSOURI
KANSAS
INDIAN
TERRITORY
TEXAS

nd KATY Limiteds in the Last Frontier

TWO RAILROADS are closely identified with the area south and west of the Gateway City of St. Louis: the Missouri-Kansas-Texas Railroad, called the Katy; and the older and larger St. Louis-San Francisco Railway, known as the Frisco. Both railroads were chartered during the middle of the 19th century as pioneers in the Last Frontier.

During their early years, the two roads competed for the passenger traffic from St. Louis and Kansas City to the Southwest. Later, a spirit of co-operation developed between them, and for many years some of their premier trains were jointly operated.

Frisco timetables listed such featured trains as the *Meteor, Hustler, Texas Limited, Texas Special, Kansas City-Florida Special, Sunnyland, Bluebonnet, Will Rogers, Firefly,* and *Black Gold.* The Katy boasted of the *Katy Flyer, Katy Limited, Texas Special, Sooner, Alamo Special,* and *Bluebonnet.*

In 1915 Katy announced the inauguration of the *Texas Special* from St. Louis to Texas. Two years later, Frisco and Katy entered into an agreement for joint operation of the train. This agreement later was expanded to include additional routes. Frisco-Katy limiteds were some of the most elegant and well-managed trains in America; the streamlined 1948 version of the *Texas Special* was described by Everett L. DeGolyer Jr. as "a real ornament."

Unfortunately, the passenger market in the Southwest dwindled during the 1950's. By 1965 the number of passengers on the *Texas Special* averaged only 10 per train-mile. Because of the precarious financial condition of the Katy, it became necessary for management to end all passenger service. Two years later, in December 1967, Frisco also ceased passenger operations. The Frisco-Katy partnership, which had produced some of the most famous limiteds in the land, joined the ranks of railroads listed as "freight only."

RESPLENDENT in blue-and-silver colors, Frisco's Meteor prepares for an evening departure from St. Louis Union Station behind a 4-8-4.

Competitors become co-operative

JULY 4, 1851 saw ground broken in St. Louis for the Pacific Railroad, predecessor of both the Frisco and the Missouri Pacific. It was the first steam railroad west of the Mississippi River. In 1876, after a period of control by the Atlantic & Pacific Railway, the Southwest Branch of the railroad, from Pacific, Mo., to Springfield, Mo., became the St. Louis & San Francisco Railway. It was planned to ultimately connect St. Louis with California's Golden Gate in conjunction with the Santa Fe. Early advocates of the scheme were Capt. (later General) John C. Frémont and his father-in-law, Sen. Thomas Hart Benton of Missouri. Although Frémont received a charter for a transcontinental railroad, his dream of a rail line from St. Louis to San Francisco never was realized. Difficulties with the use of Federal Indian lands, and also with the Santa Fe, caused the Frisco to lose its western franchise rights. The idea of a Frisco line to the Pacific Coast vanished. In its place emerged the development of a system to serve the Southwest and Southeast.

The second Frisco company was formed in 1896 and lasted until 1916. Cleared of all affiliation with the Santa Fe, the new Frisco road came under the influence of B. F. Yoakum, who envisioned a Mississippi Valley system composed of the St. Louis and San Francisco; Chicago & Eastern Illinois; New Orleans, Texas & Mexico; and Rock Island Lines.

The Yoakum dream also ended in disaster. On May 27, 1913, the Frisco went into a receivership that lasted until 1916, when the St. Louis-San Francisco Railway Company was formed. This third Frisco company ultimately came to operate 4880 miles (in 1970) of road in nine states of the South and Southwest: Missouri, Kansas, Arkansas, Oklahoma, Texas, Tennessee, Mississippi, Alabama, and Florida.

The Katy's ancestor, the Union Pacific, Southern Branch, was chartered in 1865 to build south from Junction City, Kan., toward New Orleans. Construction went slowly until the line found itself in a three-way race with predecessors of the Frisco and the Santa Fe for the Indian Territory, which later became Oklahoma. On March 31, 1870, the railroad changed its name

to the Missouri, Kansas & Texas Railway and reset its sights for Texas. On Christmas Day 1872, the MK&T, "the Great Texas Route," entered Texas over the Red River bridge north of Denison. Acquisition of existing lines and construction of new trackage also was in progress at the north end of the system. On August 10, 1873, the MK&T's line from Parsons, Kan., reached Hannibal, Mo., and a connection with the Burlington.

During the panic of 1873, Katy was quietly taken over by Jay Gould, who was described by the contemporary press as a master of speculation. Gould was in the process of building a railroad system which included the Union Pacific, Wabash, Denver & Rio Grande, and Missouri Pacific. In what has been termed "The Rape of the Katy," Gould leased the MK&T to Mis-

KATY Pacific No. 373 heads up the six cars of the first southbound Texas Special at Muskogee, Okla., on the morning of December 16, 1915.

souri Pacific. History has shown the many ways in which Katy was used to support the Missouri Pacific. However, it was under Gould's trusteeship in 1881 that the Katy finally reached Fort Worth and Dallas.

The Gould era on the Katy ended at the annual meeting of the road in 1888, when the MK&T was placed in receivership and the Missouri Pacific lease was terminated. By 1891 the Katy was a vastly improved property headed by John D. Rockefeller. Galveston, the Island City on the Gulf of Mexico, was reached in 1893, and entry into St. Louis on the north was achieved in 1896. By 1899 the Katy extension to San Antonio was completed. At the start of the 20th century, Katy was operating 2400 miles in four states — Missouri, Kansas, Texas, Louisiana — and the Indian Territory that became the state of Oklahoma in 1907.

The complex histories of the two railroads are reflected in the variety of passenger trains and cars they ran. George M. Pullman brought the luxury of Pullman sleeping-car service to the frontier on both the Frisco and Katy lines in the early 1870's. During the Gould era, Wagner Palace cars were operated on the MK&T lines. Dining cars first appeared on the two roads in the 1880's. Frisco offered Fred Harvey service until 1930. The MK&T also operated 12 dining stations and 3 hotels. Meals cost 50 cents; hotel rates were $2.

Passenger cars for both roads were the products of either Pullman at Chicago or American Car & Foundry at St. Charles, Mo., and Jeffersonville, Ind. In addition, the Frisco car and engine shops at Springfield, Mo. — said to be the largest of its kind west of the Mississippi River — built new or extensively rebuilt many interesting and handsome cars, including innovative dual-purpose rolling stock for use on routes with little passenger traffic.

Frisco and Katy competed for the traffic between St. Louis and the Southwest. A great rivalry developed between the *Katy Flyer*, established in 1896, and the Frisco *Meteor*, which first ran in 1902. Soon each train carried through cars to Chicago, the Katy by way of Illinois Central and the Frisco via its subsidiary Chicago & Eastern Illinois.

On December 5, 1915, the MK&T announced that the *Texas Special* would be inaugurated on December 15.

The new, fast Katy train between St. Louis, Kansas City, and San Antonio. An entirely new steel train, new equipment, new schedules; finer and faster than any train heretofore in service to or from Texas — *MK&T public timetable.*

Short-term debt caught up with an overbuilt Katy in 1915, and the road entered receivership. A reorganized and shortened Missouri-Kansas-Texas Railroad Company emerged from receivership in 1923.

Another milestone in St. Louis-Texas service occurred on March 4, 1917, when Frisco and Katy entered into an agreement for joint operation of the *Texas Special*, designated as trains 1 and 2 on both lines. The new route was via Frisco from St. Louis to Vinita, Okla., thence Katy to Dallas-Fort Worth-San Antonio — a total run of 1039 miles. Operation by way of Frisco to Vinita (361 miles) was 78 miles shorter than the MK&T line through Parsons, Kans. As part of the new arrangement, Frisco Nos. 9 and 10, the *Meteor*, ceased operation to Texas and became a St. Louis-Oklahoma train.

Additional joint services were established during 1927: the introduction of the *Bluebonnet*, named after the state flower of Texas, and the pooling of service between Tulsa and Texas points over the route later served by the *Black Gold* between Tulsa, Houston, and Galveston.

During the depression there was serious talk of a merger between the two railroads. A report prepared by the Federal government (RFC) during 1933, which was approved by the RFC chief examiner, John W. Barriger III, recommended the merger because of the savings to be effected by eliminating "parallel and almost duplicate passenger and freight services." (Years later, in 1965, John Barriger was summoned from retirement to become president of the nearly bankrupt Katy.)

Inspired by the success of streamlined trains across the country, the Frisco in 1939 created the *Firefly*, one of the earliest streamliners in the Southwest. Conventional equipment, modernized at Frisco's shops in Springfield, Mo., was placed in service between Kansas City, Tulsa, and Oklahoma City on December 10, 1939. The blue-and-silver steam-powered speedster traveled the 379-mile route at an average speed of 52.3 mph.

Author's collection.

PACIFIC No. 409 was one of five (Nos. 409-413) Class H-3d 73-inch-drivered oil burners built by Lima Locomotive Works in 1923.

Pullman-Standard.

BAGGAGE CAR No. 178, one of 10 built for MK&T by Pullman in 1913, proclaims its contents in larger lettering than it advertises its owner.

POSTAL CAR No. 30 was one of five built for MK&T by Pullman in 1913.

Pullman-Standard.

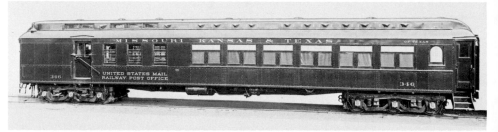

COACH-Railway Post Office combinations such as No. 346 were rare. Note the allusion to MK&T's Texas subsidiary at the right end of the car.

Pullman-Standard.

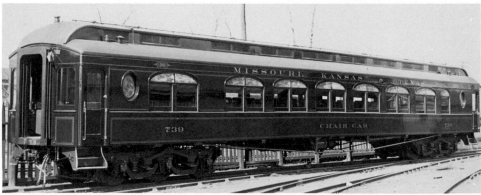

AC&F.

CHAIR CAR No. 739 was ornamented with fine gold-leaf decoration and art-glass upper sash.

FRISCO
LINES

FRISCO 4-6-2 No. 1069 was built by Baldwin in 1917 with 73-inch drivers and a total engine weight of 296,000 pounds. Oil-burn-ing 4-8-2 No. 1519, built by Baldwin in 1925, was based on a de-sign developed by the United States Railroad Administration.

MAIL-COACH 73 (left) and mail-baggage 128 (right) were built by Pullman. No. 128's steel underframe sported heavy side sills.

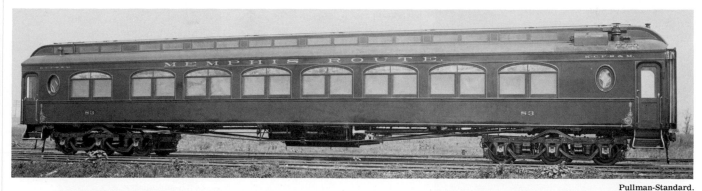

IN 1901 the Ozark Equipment Co., a Frisco subsidiary, became the owner of Memphis Route (Kansas City, Fort Scott & Memphis, another Frisco subsidiary) coach No. 83, a car that served on the Kansas City-Birmingham Southeastern Limited, trains 105 and 106.

ARCH WINDOWS, six-wheel trucks, and varnished wooden sides identified C&EI-Frisco System diners 475-476, delivered in 1903.

KATY'S Pacifics always put forth a trim appearance, the result of liberal amounts of white striping and a red-and-white herald on the tender. Roundhouse crews kept the Katy's motive power spotless and shipshape.

All photos, unless otherwise credited, author's collection.

BAGGAGE-RPO car 232 was built by American Car & Foundry in 1928.

AC&F.

MKT dining cars 434-436 were named for Texas heroes: David Crockett (above), James Bowie, and Sam Houston. They were among the first air-conditioned cars and proved so popular that they served as recreation cars between mealtimes.

DINING CARS 437-439, the last heavy-weight feature cars built in the United States, were named Alamo, Goliad, and San Jacinto (AC&F builder's photo, below, was taken before final lettering). Contemporary interior (right) had two-tone gray walls and a pale rose ceiling.

AC&F.

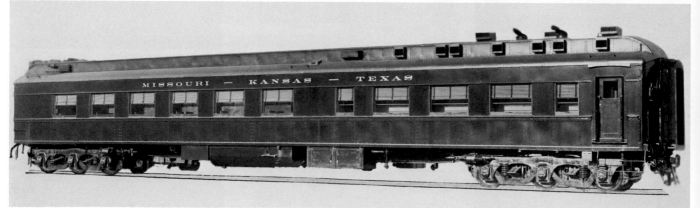

AC&F.

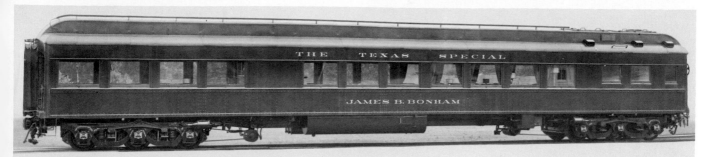

AC&F.

JAMES B. BONHAM and three similar lounge cars, plus the two Frisco lounge cars on the next page, were the only passenger cars ordered in the U. S. during 1933. Interior boasted framed tapestry, carved window valances, shower-bath.

AC&F.

FOUR Texas-series Pullman lounges were built in 1927 for the Texas Special. They had two compartments, one drawing room, buffet, and barber shop (above).

AC&F.

THE last heavyweight lounge car built in the U. S. (1937) was the William B. Travis (below), advertised by MKT as "America's Finest and Most Beautiful Railroad Equipment." The interior (above), furnished by Marshall Field, featured soda bar, radio, and shower.

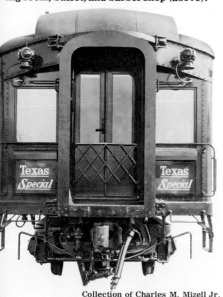

Collection of Charles M. Mizell Jr.

AC&F.

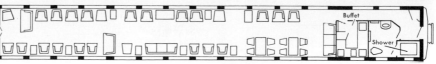

253

Arthur B. Johnson.

FRISCO 4-8-4 No. 4502 sported blue-and-silver livery and the train signature of the Meteor on the tender when it was photographed in 1945.

Collection of C. C. Roberts.

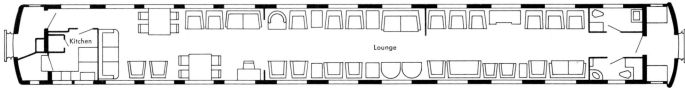

TWO of the six passenger cars ordered in the depression year of 1933 were the Tulsa and the Oklahoma City (above). In 1934 the green-and-silver lounges were extensively rebuilt from AC&F dining cars 637 (below) and 639. Frisco carshop employees carved the valances and crafted the grillwork (right).

Author's collection.

AC&F.

254

DINING CARS 641-643 were among the last heavyweights built by Pullman. They were noted for their artistic interiors decorated in Louis XVI style (far left). Walls were light sea green with moldings in a darker shade. The ceiling was ivory. The 36 oval-backed chairs were upholstered in brown floral-pattern fabric.

UNIVERSITY CITY (and twin Magic City) had 8 single bedrooms and a lounge (far left). Built in April 1930 for the Meteor, they were named for St. Louis suburbs. Later they were assigned to New York Central's Detroiter and renamed for Detroit suburbs Palmer Woods and Grosse Pointe.

NORWICH UNIVERSITY, a 12-section, 2 double-bedroom car, was assigned to Frisco in 1939 by Pullman; it was sold to Frisco in 1948.

255

FRESH from the shops, the blue-and-silver Firefly poses with a streamlined Pacific, baggage-mail-coach, full coach, and diner-lounge.

FRISCO LINES

THE *Firefly*
NEW FRISCO STREAMLINER

FRISCO'S shops streamlined several Pacifics such as No. 1026 and also applied similar skirting and paint to Hudsons and Mountains.

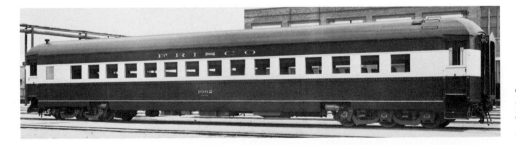

THE heavyweight cars — 1062 was rebuilt in 1942 — were advertised as "heavier than ordinary streamliners . . . resulting in smoother riding."

SNACK-LOUNGE 1605, rebuilt at Springfield shops, had a lounge and five-seat lunch counter (right).

256

Coach Buffet Sleeper

IN January 1935 the Frisco completed the conversion of two steel coaches into all-welded coach-buffet-sleepers with 6 sections. In the views at the left are the sleeping and coach accommodations. In 1949 the cars were rebuilt with 2 double bedrooms, and a lunch counter replaced the coach section.

The Sunnyland

PACIFIC 1045 shows a clean stack as it rolls the six cars of the Sunnyland north toward St. Louis on a summer in 1943.

Collection of C. C. Roberts.

UNTIL May 1, 1950, diesels powered the Texas Special only as far south as Waco, Texas (below right), where steam took the train (above) to San Antonio. In Missouri the Special sometimes encountered snow (below left). The Special and the Meteor (left) carried through Pullmans to the East via both PRR and B&O.

Collection of C. C. Roberts.

A stunning livery

DURING October 1945 the Frisco and the Katy placed orders with Electro-Motive for diesel-electric locomotives and with Pullman-Standard for passenger cars to dieselize and streamline the *Texas Special* and *Meteor* trains. The Frisco ordered six 2000-h.p. E7's, two for the *Texas Special* and four for the *Meteor*; the Katy ordered two E7 units. Of the 52 lightweight stainless-steel-sheathed cars, 38 were for the Frisco and 14 for the Katy.

Both railroads had asked passengers to fill out questionnaires toward the end of World War II. The responses were used to determine the design features of the new equipment. The questionnaires indicated that the public wanted a bright and colorful exterior appearance. Katy and Frisco managements agreed on a stunning livery for the *Texas Special* and the *Meteor*: fluted stainless-steel sides; bright red roof, pier panels, ends, and lettering; maroon underbody skirts; and aluminum-painted trucks. The *Texas Special* cars carried the train name on the letterboard in red script, and the *Meteor* equipment was lettered "Frisco" in Roman letters.

Katy and Frisco each contributed one full set of equipment

for the *Texas Special*. Because three sets were required for the St. Louis-San Antonio line, the train as operated included conventional heavyweight equipment: a 12-section, 1-drawing-room Pullman plus lounges and diners that were among the last heavyweight cars built in the U.S. At Frisco's Springfield shops the sides of the cars were repainted with shadowline striping to simulate fluted stainless-steel sheathing.

In addition to the observation-lounges, both trains catered to coach passengers with a coach-buffet-lounge — part coach and part lounge, with buffet, writing desk, and tables for refreshments. Traditionally fine dining and observation-car facilities and all-room Pullman sleepers were available on both trains. The first new *Meteor* left St. Louis on May 14, 1948, and made its first eastbound trip May 15. The new *Texas Special* service began May 16. Each of the new *Texas Special* trains cost more than 2 million dollars.

Both trains offered through sleeping cars from New York and Washington, continuing the services which had been inaugurated on July 7, 1946, with conventional Pullmans. The 1948 streamliners offered New York-San Antonio and New York-Tulsa cars that operated via the Pennsylvania Railroad east of St.

258

Philip R. Hastings.

Author's collection.

**MENU COVER was decorated with a paint-
ing of Katy's San Antonio (Tex.) station.**

es M. Mizell Jr.

Philip R. Hastings.

**TAIL SIGNS with train heralds on the observation cars brought up
the rear of both the Texas Special (above) and the Meteor (below).**

Pullman-Standard.

Louis and a Chicago-Oklahoma City car via the Gulf, Mobile
& Ohio. Within a few months Baltimore & Ohio cars entered serv-
ice on Washington-San Antonio and Jersey City-Washington-
Oklahoma City routes. In 1955 and 1956 a Chicago-San Antonio
Pullman operated via the Wabash.

For a few years the Frisco and Katy trains were successful,
but during the 1950's patronage began to decline. On January
5, 1959, the Frisco discontinued its operation of the *Texas Special*
from St. Louis to Vinita, and the Katy changed the northern
terminal of the train from St. Louis to Kansas City, replacing
the *Bluebonnet* with the rerouted *Texas Special*. The southern
terminal remained at San Antonio until 1964, when the train
was cut back to Dallas. Finally, on June 30, 1965, the *Texas
Special* made its last run.

Passenger trains survived longer on the Frisco. The *Meteor*
operated until September 17, 1965, when it was replaced by a
daytime train named the *Oklahoman*. The last passenger train
operated by the St. Louis-San Francisco Railway was the *Southland*, successor to the *Kansas City-Florida Special*. It made its
final run between Kansas City and Birmingham, Ala., on December 8, 1967.

FRISCO'S Rock Hill and MKT twin Anson B. Jones (right) carried the mail and baggage on the Texas Special.

All photos, Pullman-Standard.

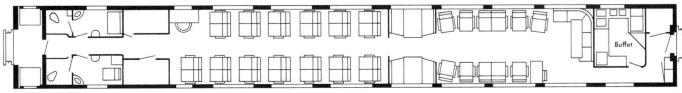

CHAIR-buffet-lounges Sterling Price (above) and Mirabeau B. Lamar furnished lounge space for coach passengers. Glass partitions with the State of Texas seal separated the lounge area from the 26 coach seats (right).

SERVICE on dining car Sam Houston "rivaled that of the finest hotels." The decor included photomurals of Southwestern cities (above).

The Texas Special

Pullman-Standard.

SLEEPING CAR George G. Vest had 14 roomettes and 4 double bedrooms.

Collection of C. C. Roberts.

CONVENTIONAL chair-lounge-buffet Glendale displayed "shadow line" livery. Girdersheets and letterboards first were painted

stainless-steel color, then masked with tape and airbrushed with dark gray to create a shadow effect, simulating fluted sheathing.

Hare Photographs, Inc., courtesy of Pullman Company.

CASCADE RANGE, a PRR 10-roomette, 5-double-bedroom car built in 1940, was repainted in 1948 at Pullman's Buffalo (N. Y.) shops with simulated stainless-steel fluting, red trim, and red Texas Special script lettering for New York-San Antonio service. This car also appears on page 160.

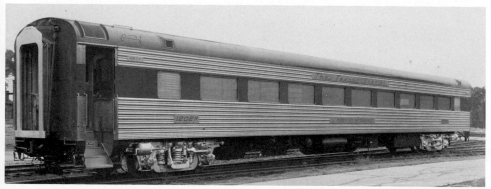

Pullman-Standard.

PULLMAN built an experimental coach in 1954 using stainless steel for the entire superstructure, instead of high-tensile carbon steel or aluminum alloy. Katy purchased the car to replace one that had been wrecked; hence the number 1202R. Northern Pacific purchased it in 1965. The car became Amtrak No. 7200.

Both photos, Pullman-Standard.

STEPHEN F. AUSTIN and Joseph Pulitzer were observation cars with 1 drawing room, 2 double bedrooms. Lounge (right) seated 21 people.

FRISCO restyled (complete with racehorse names) its E7's to match newer E8 fleet. Roof line and louver betray the masquerade.

VALLEY PARK and Normandy were lettered "Frisco," served on Meteor.

SLEEPING quarters for crew were in dormitory-coaches Maplewood and Manchester, named for on-line towns.

OUTSHOPPED by Pullman in 1947, chair-buffet-lounge Huntleigh, No. 1652 (above), was 85 feet long, had red and stainless-steel exterior. The lounge (right) was furnished with red and blue club chairs. The glass partition between sections was etched with the seal of the State of Texas.

COACH Ferguson carried 56 persons in Sleepy Hollow reclining seats.

All photos, unless otherwise credited, Pullman-Standard.

Hare Photographs, Inc.

SLEEPER Cascade Ravine was owned by Pennsylvania. The 10-roomette, 5-double-bedroom car posed in 1948 at Pullman shops in

Buffalo, N. Y., after shadow-line painting for New York (N. Y.)-Tulsa (Okla.) service on Pennsy's American and Frisco's Meteor.

MERAMAC RIVER was one of 10 sleeping cars with 14 roomettes, 4 double bedrooms named for on-line rivers. Red and stainless-steel car was sold to Canadian National in 1965, and renamed Reversing Falls.

OKLAHOMA CITY was a diner-lounge-observation built for the Meteor in 1948. The car was rebuilt for midtrain operation in 1959. The lounge (above right) had light blue ceiling, frosted walnut paneling, burgundy chairs, dark blue carpet. Beyond the bulkhead with photomurals (above) was a dining section that seated 24 passengers for snacks and breakfast.

263

THRU THE ROCKIES···

A story of railroading in Colorado

MOUNTAINS and mountain railroading are of great fascination to travelers and railroad enthusiasts. The Rocky Mountains of Colorado and Utah, and the crest of the Continental Divide, imposed a special influence on travel in the American West. Mormon migration in 1847 and the California gold rush in 1849 established the country's two great transcontinental wagon routes. Both touched the eastern corners of Colorado, but because of the great mountain barrier, the Santa Fe Trail veered south and the Overland Trail, north. Only because of the efforts of the Colorado railroad builders — Gov. John Evans, Gen. William Palmer, David Moffat, James Hagerman, and Otto Mears — did the Centennial State develop. Significantly, the Denver & Rio Grande and other Colorado railroads brought modern transportation into Colorado and through the Rockies . . . not around them.

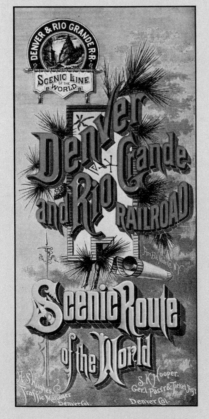

PERIOD timetables had excursion advertisements to lure travelers to the Rocky Mountains.

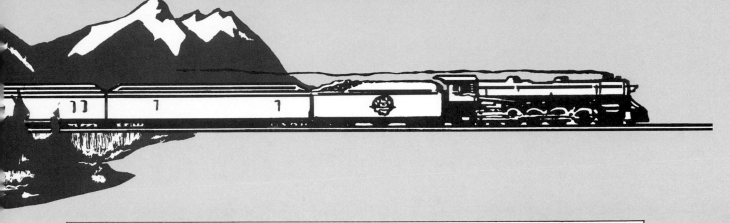

...NOT AROUND THEM

George L. Beam, courtesy Jackson C. Thode,

THE Pacific Coast Limited, train No. 1, cuts through the Royal Gorge of the Arkansas River in Colorado.

THE first Scenic Limited poses at Burnham Shops in Denver, Colo., in 1906. Brochure (below) called the limited "The Finest Train in the West," and boasted that it was "Always on Time."

In the days of the narrow gauge

THE discovery of gold in the front range of the Colorado Rockies prompted a rush of fortune hunters to the area. As communities became settled, railroads were organized.

On October 27, 1870, the Denver & Rio Grande Railway Company was incorporated by Gen. William Jackson Palmer, engineer and Civil War veteran. Initially, the road was planned to run from Denver to El Paso paralleling the Rio Grande from southern Colorado to the Mexican border.

A track gauge of 3 feet was selected as most suitable for the steep mountain grades and sharp curves. The road pushed southward to Colorado Springs and Pueblo, bound for the headwaters of the Rio Grande by way of the Royal Gorge of the Arkansas River, en route to the land of the Aztecs.

Upon reaching Pueblo, D&RG considered the route over Raton Pass as being more desirable than that through the Royal Gorge; but California-bound Atchison, Topeka & Santa Fe also was heading for Raton and was determined to build an extension through Canon City to Leadville via Royal Gorge. Intense rivalry developed between the two roads. The Santa Fe won the Pass of the Rat, but D&RG prevailed in the war for the Royal Gorge.

Strikes of gold and silver lured miners deeper into the Rockies. Timber and coal discoveries intensified the need for good transportation. The D&RG satisfied the demand by building westward from Salida, with one line into fabled Lead-

ville, and another to Gunnison via the legendary Marshall Pass.

By 1880 the D&RG had abandoned its plan for building to Mexico. Instead, a decision was made to turn westward to Salt Lake City and Ogden, Utah, "through the Rockies, not around them," constructing what was to become a major link in a transcontinental route.

In 1881 the Denver & Rio Grande Western Railway (later known as the Rio Grande Western) was formed to carry out plans of building a line from Ogden and Salt Lake City to connect with the D&RG near the Colorado-Utah border. Completion of the "Great Salt Lake Route" in 1883 created a continuous narrow-gauge line of 772 miles from Denver to Ogden.

Sleeping-car service on the slim-gauge lines commenced when Denver, South Park & Pacific signed a contract with Pullman on November 20, 1879, for service between Denver and Leadville. After intensive negotiations, a contract finally was signed with D&RG on December 26, 1879. Apparently, Palmer was not optimistic about the success of the Palace cars. He argued in vain for a 3-year contract, because George Pullman would not agree to any term less than 10 years. Mr. Pullman judged correctly; the original D&RG order for 10 cars soon was increased to 18.

The miniature sleeping cars were built by Pullman's Palace Car Company in Detroit. Each contained 10 sections with beautiful polished woods, brass lamps, and imported fabrics. Ultimately, 25 of the 42-foot 5-inch-long cars were built: 5 were assigned to the DSP&P, 18 were assigned to the D&RG, and 2 went to the Utah & Northern Railroad. Most of these cars ended their days in Mexico after the Rocky Mountain lines became standard gauge.

Denver & Rio Grande's quest for new traffic potentials resulted in the construction of a standard-gauge line west from Leadville over Tennessee Pass, as well as the rebuilding of the RGW to standard gauge. This led to the completion of a new through Denver-Ogden route in 1890.

In addition to the D&RG, other railroads and their builders have contributed to Colorado legend. Four extraordinary developers loom large in the romance of the West: John Evans and his Denver, South Park & Pacific; James J. Hagerman and the Colorado Midland; David H. Moffat and the Denver, Northwestern & Pacific (later, Denver & Salt Lake); and Otto Mears and his narrow-gauge silver roads of the San Juan.

RIO GRANDE WESTERN 4-6-0 No. 54 stands ready for departure (left) at Salt Lake City in 1890. In a glass-plate photo- graph from the 1880's (above) by **William Henry Jackson**, the Silverton train threads south through Las Animas Canyon.

PUSHING through the Rockies, Denver & Rio Grande 3-foot-gauge 2-8-0 No. 45, Mojanda, leaves the west end of the Toltec tunnel.

267

ENJOYING the scenery, travelers on this open-observation car are westbound at the Hanging Bridge in the Royal Gorge.

Railway & Locomotive Historical Society.

DENVER & RIO GRANDE No. 1, the Montezuma, was a narrow-gauge 2-4-0 built in 1871 by Baldwin.

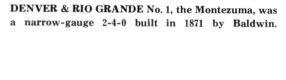

THE first double-truck passenger car built for the Denver & Rio Grande Railway was coach Denver, which came out of Jackson & Sharp's Delaware Car Works in about 1871.

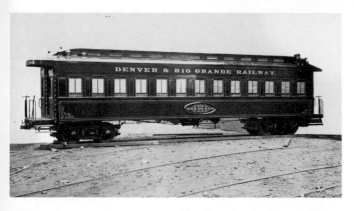

TWO early passenger cars were No. 80 and a baggage-mail car.

PULLMAN narrow-gauge tourist car No. 466 was built in Chicago, Ill., in August 1889 for service on the Denver & Rio Grande Railway.

WESTBOUND on the new Western Pacific, 4-6-0 No. 71 and train posed on the Great Salt Beds of Salduro, Utah, in 1910.

THE "Serpentine Trail" of the Colorado & Southern which was advertised on brochures (left) got its name from the twisting loop near Georgetown, Colo. Under a cloud of gray smoke, D&RGW 2-8-2 No. 477 works up Cumbres Pass near Cresco, N. Mex., with train No. 116, the San Juan, on its run between Durango and Alamosa.

IN a print from a glass plate made at the Detroit works, narrow-gauge, 8-section Pullman Toltec rode the transfer table in July 1880. The interior had inlaid berth fronts and brass lamps. The floor plan showed a ladies' dressing room at one end and a saloon at the other.

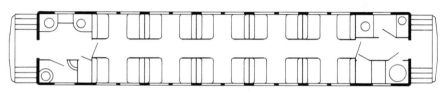

ALAMOSA was built in 1880 by Jackson & Sharp as chair car No. 25, Hidalgo. In 1937 it was renamed and rebuilt into a parlor-buffet car for service on the San Juan.

SILVERTON, GLADSTONE & NORTHERLY, a line started by a group that operated the Gold King Mine at Gladstone, Colo., was owner of this narrow-gauge combine built by AC&F. Otto Mears bought the line in 1915 and abandoned it a few years later.

IN 1909, Pullman built elegant dining car No. 704 for the Colorado & Southern, a railroad which had an early start in the famed Georgetown Loop line that opened in 1884. The 704 featured polished mahogany interior, Spanish leather upholstery, and was a twin to the FW&DC 262 (below).

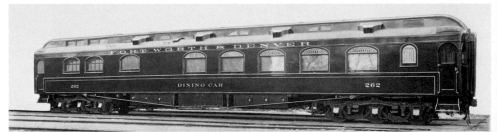

THE Colorado & Southern owned the Fort Worth & Denver City Railway, a line that operated between Texline, Tex., and Fort Worth. Together the two lines offered through service between Denver & Fort Worth. Diner No. 262, like sister 704 (above), seated 30 in mahogany splendor.

RIO GRANDE WESTERN four-wheel-truck coach 216 was built in 1898.

HANDSOME Wells Fargo & Co. express baggage car was built for the Rio Grande Western Railroad in 1899.

PULLMAN Chicosa was one of six sleepers built in 1888 for Denver & Rio Grande service. Each car contained 8 sections, a drawing room, and a buffet, and cost $13,914 to construct. The other five were named Monero, Chamita, Granite, Pinon, and Poncha.

All photos, Pullman-Standard.

BAGGAGE and express car No. 665 was one of nine such cars Pullman built in 1890 for Denver & Rio Grande.

PRIVATE CAR Ballyclare was built in 1890 for D&RG president David H. Moffat.

(LEFT) Interior view shows 1890-era D&RG coach. (Above) RGW chair car 403, built in 1898.

273

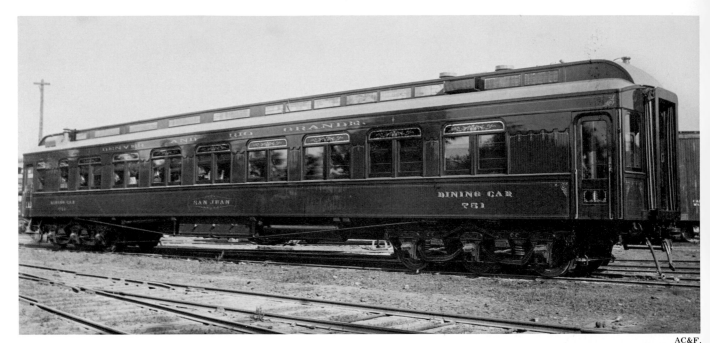

DENVER & RIO GRANDE diner San Juan was built in 1899 and was the first diner built at AC&F's St. Charles (Mo.) works. Interior (below) was ornate.

UTAH, an 1899 RGW diner from Pullman, had a less flamboyant interior (above) than the San Juan's.

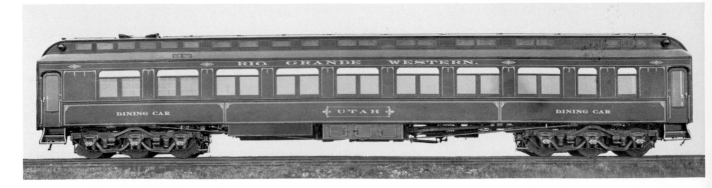

Pullman-Standard.

BUILT by Pullman in 1901, Rio Grande Western dining car Colorado was lettered "Colorado-Utah Line," the road's descriptive title.

Author's collection.

D&RG 1904 menu offered "Sirloin Steak, for two, $1.25."

D&RGW, collection of Jackson C. Thode.

INTERIOR of one of eight cars built by Barney & Smith of Dayton, O., in 1910 for D&RG's Western Pacific Railroad. Cars were returned to D&RG service in 1923. Nebo (below) was built in 1906.

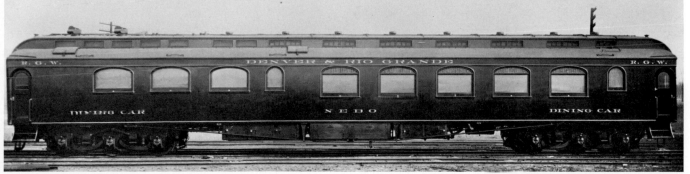

Barney & Smith, collection of Jackson C. Thode.

Author's collection.

COLORADO MIDLAND 306, one of six Baldwin 2-8-0's built for CM in 1907 (primarily for freight service), exemplified road's heaviest class of engine.

Author's collection.

TRIM Ten-Wheeler 302 of the Denver, Northwestern & Pacific was built at Alco's Schenectady plant in 1906. Engine lasted on D&RGW's roster until July 1948.

CHAIR CAR 248 was one of five such cars Pullman built in 1901 for the Colorado Midland. Walkover seats (below) featured individual armrests. In 1907, two of the cars were rebuilt into diners Idlewild and Ivanhoe according to floor plan at right.

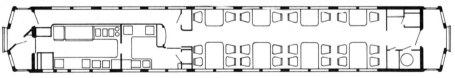

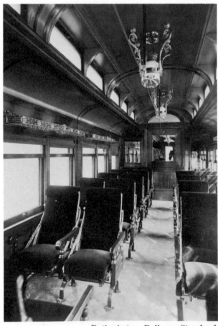

Both photos, Pullman-Standard.

FOLDERS of CM and DNW&P depicted routes and scenery.

BEAUTIFULLY lettered Wells Fargo & Co. express-baggage car was built by Pullman in 1900 for the Colorado Midland Railroad.

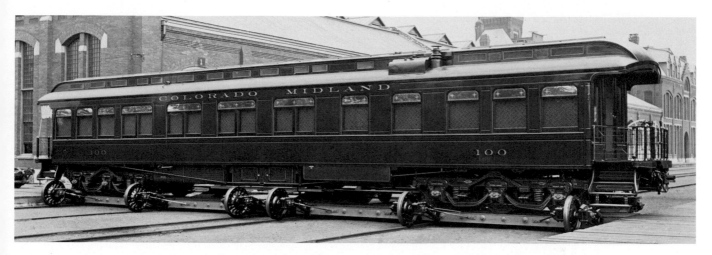

BUILT in 1898 and later renamed Cascade, private car No. 100 was used by millionaire CM president A. E. (Bert) Carlton.

DENVER & SALT LAKE 900 (later D&RGW 900), an early steel car built in 1913, was sold to the Algoma Central & Hudson Bay.

DENVER press hailed David Moffat's new (1906) private car Marcia as a "palace on wheels." Car was named for his daughter.

A New Exposition Train

All Steel

THE Scenic Limited

The only through Train between St. Louis and the Pacific Coast

Via the

MISSOURI PACIFIC

DENVER & RIO GRANDE

WESTERN PACIFIC

Author's collection.

PANAMA PACIFIC fair pamphlet promoted Scenic Limited.

The first transcontinental

railroad through Denver

THE purchase of a large interest in the Denver & Rio Grande by financier Jay Gould in 1879 marked the beginning of a new era in history for the Rio Grande.

When Jay Gould was forced to relinquish control of the Erie in 1872, he turned to the western roads. Soon he either owned or controlled the Union Pacific; Kansas Pacific; Denver Pacific; Denver, South Park & Pacific; Missouri Pacific; Central Pacific; Texas & Pacific; St. Louis-Southwestern; and the Wabash. After the senior Gould died in 1892, control of the family fortune, including the Gould railway lines, passed to his oldest son George Jay Gould. It was through the Missouri Pacific that George Gould became involved in the affairs of the Denver & Rio Grande.

The younger Gould almost succeeded in establishing a 10,000-mile transcontinental system by purchasing the Western Maryland, Wabash, and the Pittsburgh Terminal Railway (Pittsburgh & West Virginia) in the East, and by committing the D&RG to build the Western Pacific in the West. However, George Gould failed in his coast-to-coast effort and, indeed, lost control of his rail empire before World War I.

Completion of the 4-foot 8½-inch standard-gauge line between Denver and Ogden on November 14, 1890, resulted in the transformation of the D&RG from a provincial mountain railroad to an important link in a great transcontinental system. The D&RG-Rio Grande Western then entered into through car arrangements with connecting eastern and western roads. The June 1893 *Official Guide* listed two through trains in each direction: No. 1, the *California Fast Mail* and No. 3, the *Transcontinental Express*; No. 2, the *Transcontinental Limited* and No. 4, the *Atlantic Coast Express*. All four trains were equipped

with First Class and Tourist Pullmans between Denver and Los Angeles (via Sacramento) in connection with the Southern Pacific at Ogden. Between Grand Junction and Ogden, RGW trains also handled through Pullmans that came from Denver over the Colorado Midland.

During 1900 the D&RG-RGW boasted of three trains each way through the Rocky Mountains. The lines offered "Double Daily Pullman Palace Car Service" between San Francisco and Chicago via Denver and Omaha, with the Burlington and Rock Island handling one through train each between Denver and Chicago.

In 1901 George Gould bought the RGW from General Palmer and arranged for consolidation of the RGW into the D&RG. The consolidation formally took place in 1908, ending the Siamese twin arrangement which had existed since 1884.

Sponsorship by the D&RG of the construction of the Western Pacific Railroad, "The Feather River Route," between Oakland and Salt Lake City and introduction of through Denver-Oakland passenger train service on August 22, 1910, provided the final link in George Gould's D&RG-WP western transcontinental, a line which later would serve as the route for some of the most famous limiteds of the land: *Scenic Limited*, *Panoramic*, *Exposition Flyer*, and *California Zephyr*.

The name *Scenic Special* first appeared in the RGW timetable in 1900 for trains Nos. 1 and 2 between Ogden and Grand Junction. During the summer of 1906, the name *Scenic Limited* was applied to D&RG all-Pullman trains Nos. 19 and 20 between Denver and Ogden — "The Finest Train in the West." Later, in April 1915, a "New Exposition Train," the all-steel *Scenic Limited* (Nos. 19 and 20) was inaugurated by the MP-D&RG-WP as a "daylight observation train" through the Royal Gorge, operating between St. Louis and San Francisco during the Panama Pacific International Exposition. In December 1915, the *Scenic Limited* became Nos. 1 and 2 and continued to serve as one of the premier trains of the Rio Grande until 1946 when it was renamed the *Royal Gorge*.

August 1, 1921, marked the end of receivership for the D&RG and the emergence of the newly organized Denver & Rio Grande Western Railroad Company. Soon the road was negotiating with the Denver & Salt Lake for the development of a new mainline route through the Rockies utilizing the existing D&RG line between Salt Lake City, Utah, and Dotsero, Colo.,* and a proposed 38-mile cutoff between Dotsero and the D&SL line at Orestod, Colo. (Dotsero spelled backwards). From Orestod existing D&SL trackage would be used for the run into Denver through the marvelous new 18-million-dollar 6.1-mile Moffat Tunnel under James Peak (alt. 13,260 feet), 50 miles from the Mile High City.

On June 10, 1939, a new daily through train was established on the "Moffat Tunnel Route" between Chicago and San Francisco via Burlington-Rio Grande-Western Pacific. The train was christened *Exposition Flyer* in Chicago to honor the Golden Gate Exposition in California and the World's Fair in New York. A bottle containing water from San Francisco Bay; Feather River; the Great Salt Lake; the Colorado, Missouri, and Mississippi rivers; and Lake Michigan was used at the ceremony.

To publicize the train, the spectacular scenery in the Rockies and the Feather River Canyon was stressed more than the 60-hour schedule which had to compete with the 39¾-hour extra-fare streamliners of the Overland Route. (It was reported in *Railway Age* that the original schedule of 57 hours was increased by 3 hours to comply with an "understanding" that all trains between Chicago and California on schedules of less than 60 hours be extra-fare trains.)

Westbound passengers on the *Flyer* enjoyed 2 full days of spectacular scenery during the daylight hours — between Denver and Salt Lake City, and in the majestic Feather River Canyon of the Sierra Nevada mountains.

Equipment consisted of steam power and an interesting assortment of conventional rolling stock furnished by the three sponsoring railroads and the Pullman Company. The demand for space on the maiden voyage was so great that six extra Pullmans and an additional diner were operated.

*An apocryphal story translates Dotsero as "dot zero" — a surveyor's term.

SPELLBINDING vistas of the Royal Gorge of the Arkansas encompass the westbound 1925 Scenic Limited, double-headed with Ten-Wheelers 762 and 787. Trains were scheduled through scenery during daylight.
D&RGW, collection of Jackson C. Thode.

PANORAMIC SPECIAL poses handsomely (above) for a portrait prior to 6 p.m. departure from Salt Lake City on June 2, 1924. One day later and one car longer (below), the Panoramic Special awaits start of trip to Denver as patrons enjoy the "back porch."

SCENIC LIMITED of 1927 double-heads up west side of Tennessee Pass in a favorite photo of Jackson C. Thode, noted Rio Grande historian. D&RGW 2-8-0 1170 and three-cylinder 4-8-2 1604 have honors of taking Denver-bound No. 2 over the Divide.

D&RG SHOW on Soldier Summit: San Francisco and Chicago Express pounds uphill under Utah skies in September of 1913.

D&RG FOLDER featured color-tinted photos.

SCENIC LIMITED makes 10-minute stop in the Royal Gorge — observation car's namesake point — in December 1928. Patrons had time to stop off, stroll along the Arkansas.

281

CB&Q.

MEET Miss Treasure Island, Miss Feather River Canyon, Miss Salt Lake City, Miss Denver, and Miss Chicago — hostesses who christened Exposition Flyer.

DRAMATIC VIEW on the Western Pacific: Westbound Exposition Flyer eases across Spanish Creek trestle in the Feather River Canyon near Keddie, Calif.

R. H. Kindig.

SCENIC LIMITED also offered "scenery" for railfans: Witness D&RGW doubleheaded No. 2 exiting Eagle River Canyon in 1938.

D&RGW.

SUMMER OF '27 brought riding pleasure to travelers aboard observation car Glenwood Canon, here at Provo, Utah, on Rio Grande's eastbound Panoramic Special.

WP.

Collection of Harold K. Vollrath.

TWENTY-TWO minutes after leaving St. Louis on the Missouri Pacific, the westbound Royal Gorge coasts into Kirkwood, Mo., in 1948.

CLASSIC PACERS of the Rio Grande were its class M-64 4-8-4's; 1702 (above) and her nine sisters were built by Baldwin in 1929.

HEAVIER 4-8-4 power arrived on D&RGW when Baldwin delivered the class M-68's in 1938, just in time for the Exposition Flyer.

BURLINGTON S-4 Hudsons (like 3000, above) often powered the Exposition Flyer across the prairies between Chicago and Denver.

LIMA built six locomotives such as No. 485 for Western Pacific in 1943. The 73½-inch-driver engines were identical to SP's GS-6 class.

HARRIMAN-ROOF coach No. 307 of the Western Pacific (above) had spartan interior furnishings (left). Pullman built 20 cars of this design in 1923 for use on WP's Feather River Route.

Pullman-Standard.

WP COACH No. 321 (above) represented part of a 51-car order Pullman completed in 1910 for D&RG and WP. **No. 1002** (below), also from the same order, was rebuilt to a streamlined parlor-coach by D&RGW in 1939 for the Exposition Flyer. The car was scrapped in 1961.

E. B. Cooper, collection of Jackson C. Thode.

Three photos, Pullman-Standard.

INTERIORS (top, left, and right) show the coach and dining sections of WP cafe-coach No. 393 (above) that Pullman built in 1928.

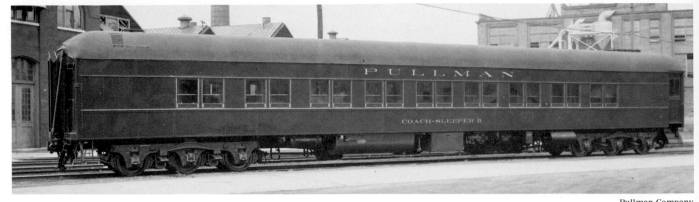

Pullman Company.

COACH-SLEEPER II was one of four unusual experimental cars that were operated on the Exposition Flyer during the summer of 1940, the same year that Pullman remodeled them. Each of the cars had accommodations for 45 persons in three tiers of berths.

Pullman-Standard.

IPSUS was a product of the Pullman Company in 1920. The standard 12-1 sleeping car was built for Denver & Rio Grande service.

Author's collection.

WINTER PARK (above) and its twin David Moffat began life as Pullman parlor cars Harrington and Clairton. In 1939, Denver & Salt Lake bought the two cars. Later, D&RGW remodeled them into chair-sleepers for use on D&SL's overnight Denver-Craig run. Winter Park interior shows the car's 4 sections (lower left). The coach portion (lower right) included a smoking section.

Bottom photos, E. B. Cooper, collection of Jackson C. Thode.

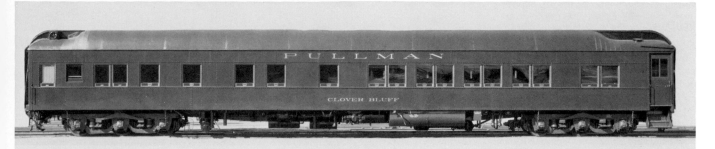

CLOVER BLUFF was an 8-section, 5-double-bedroom Exposition Flyer Pullman that was rebuilt from 12-1-1 sleeper Green Tree in 1935.

CALIFORNIA (above) was one of eight diners built by Pullman in 1923 for Western Pacific. Interior (below left) was home for "Unsurpassed dining car service" as advertised by WP, offering a 50-cent breakfast, a 65-cent luncheon, and a 75-cent dinner aboard the Exposition Flyer in 1939.

CHEYENNE MOUNTAIN (above) and twin San Isabel were diner-lounges built by Budd in 1942. The cars, with their porthole-shaped aisle windows, were clad in Missouri Pacific blue and gray and ran on the streamlined St. Louis-Denver Colorado Eagle.

287

THE open platform of the observation car was an ideal gathering place for farewell photographs of those lucky enough to be bound for distant destinations. The platform of D&RGW Royal Gorge was enlarged to accommodate 12 persons when Rio Grande rebuilt the car in 1926 for Panoramic service. The cars as remodeled in 1934 by D&RGW's Burnham Shops (below left) had a pleasing arrangement of sofas, tables, plush chairs, and even a radio.

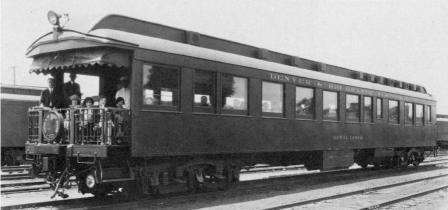

Three photos, D&RGW, collection of Jackson C. Thode.

D&RGW.

WHERE MOUNTAIN TROUT was served every day: D&RGW Twin Peak and three sister diners (Pikes Peak, Castle Peak, and Sorris Peak) arrived from AC&F in 1927. Interior furnishings (above) included Spanish leather seats, Wilton carpets, bronze trimmings.

PULLMAN-BUILT and very posh was Chicago, Burlington & Quincy lounge car Minneapolis, one of five such cars built in 1927 and named for cities on CB&Q. They saw service on the Exposition Flyer. Interiors (left) had walnut trim and parchment-shaded lamps.

SOLARIUM LOUNGE CAR No. 652 (below) of the Western Pacific was rebuilt in 1931 from the Pharsalia — a 16-section Pullman. Car was used on the Exposition Flyer and Scenic Limited. Interior (right) had leaded-glass partitions and richly upholstered chairs.

Rio Grande Prospector

ARRIVAL TIME in Denver is near as the heavyweight Prospector of 1947 (above) rolls down from the Front Range. (Below) Morning sunlight greets the 1941 Budd Prospector exiting Gore Canyon.

TRAIN M-2 Prospector (Brigham Young and Heber C. Kimball cars) stands ready at the Budd plant.

The Prospector

ON June 17, 1934, the *Panoramic* (Nos. 5 and 6) became D&RGW's first regular passenger train on the "Moffat Tunnel Route" under James Peak and over Dotsero Cutoff. The new routing of the *Panoramic* between Denver and Ogden was 175 miles shorter than the "Royal Gorge Route" and enabled D&RGW to establish overnight service between the two cities.

Eventually the *Panoramic* was cut back to Salt Lake City and combined with the Denver-Montrose *Mountaineer*. In 1939 the *Panoramic* became Nos. 19 and 20, and the numbers 5 and 6 were assigned to the *Exposition Flyer*, a new train on a daylight schedule through the Rockies. Several months later the *Panoramic* was discontinued.

On November 17, 1941, Rio Grande embarked on a bold new venture to provide overnight service between Denver and Salt Lake City when it introduced the stainless-steel *Prospectors*. The two self-propelled Budd trains contained coach, sleeping, and dining accommodations. (Operation of the railroad-owned sleeping facilities on the *Prospectors* was accepted by the Pullman Company without quibble, because the trains arrived during the height of the U. S. Government anti-trust suit against the giant sleeping-car operator.) Practically the entire floor space of the two-car trains was available for revenue passengers since the horizontal diesel-electric power plants were suspended beneath the car floors in soundproof boxes. Amenities included fluorescent lights, porter service, and free pillows. The cars of train M-1 were named for John Evans, Colorado's second territorial governor, and David Moffat, early D&RG president. Train M-2 carried the names of Brigham Young, the great Mormon leader, and Heber C. Kimball, his friend and advisor. The name *Prospector* paid tribute to one of the Rocky Mountain states' greatest industries — mining.

Unfortunately, the diesel engines and traction generators proved inadequate for Rio Grande's mountain grades, where track altitude increases from 5200 feet to 9600 feet in 39 miles. The trains were withdrawn from service in July 1942 and sold back to Budd in November 1945. Notwithstanding their mechanical failures, George Krambles, world-renowned authority on electric railroading, termed the Budd *Prospectors* an ultimate development of the classic American interurban train.

Popularity of the Budd *Prospectors* prompted Rio Grande to reinstate the train in 1945. Diesel power and heavyweight equipment were used until streamlined cars, part of an order canceled by Chesapeake & Ohio, arrived from Pullman-Standard in 1950. The *Prospector* was discontinued on May 28, 1967, ending overnight service on the Rio Grande between the Mile High City and the City of the Saints.

291

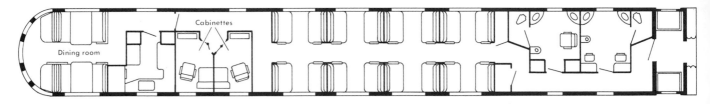

PASSENGERS spent a night in shining armor when they crossed the Rockies in Rio Grande's stainless-steel Prospectors of 1941.

D&RGW.

BUDD efficiently fit 8 sections (one of which, above, is sampled by two young ladies), 2 "cabinettes," a dinette (right), and an observation-lounge area into the rear car of the Prospectors.

Rio Grande Prospector

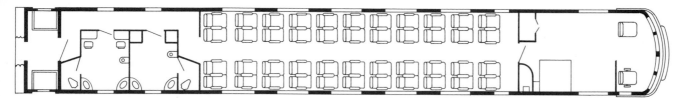

TRUCKS weighed 45,500 lbs.; had disc brakes.

PRECURSOR of the Rail Diesel Car — the Prospectors.

PULLMAN Lake Ernest, a 10-2-1 car, was repainted yellow and black at Pullman's Richmond (Calif.) shops for the second Prospector in 1945.

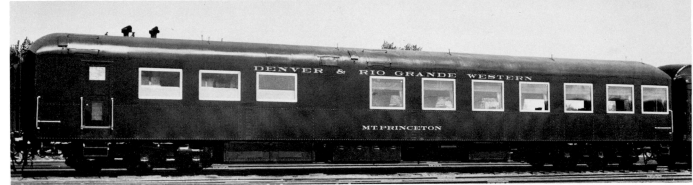

BARNEY & SMITH diner Mt. Princeton began life in 1910 as the Nevada. It was rebuilt in 1935 and saw service on the Prospector.

THE
Rio Grande
PROSPECTOR
Sez . . .

THE
PROSPECTOR FAVORITE TRAIN OF THE TRAVEL-WISE BUSINESSMAN

between **DENVER** and **SALT LAKE CITY**

OVERNIGHT *Every* NIGHT

Comfort ALL THE WAY

MAIN LINE
Rio Grande
THRU THE ROCKIES

BUFFET-LOUNGES Royal Gorge (above), Castle Gate, and Eagle Canon had wood-grained walls and serpentine seating (left). D&RGW painted Prospector cars "Grande Gold" with black striping. Roofs were silver, and the cars had stainless-steel sheathing below the windows.

TRIM-LOOKING (no doubt unlike its rugged namesake) Prospector of 1952 coasts through Plainview, Colo., 24 miles from Denver.

Rio Grande
Prospector

BAGGAGE-R.P.O. 1201 (right) was one of three. Sister 1200 was sold to D&H in 1967.

DAVID MOFFAT (above left) was one of four 10-6 Prospector sleepers. Interestingly, in 1950-1951 Pullman-Standard converted half the roomettes in each car to open sections. Sections were still popular on many Western lines, but the move was also a case of

the Government paying only lower-berth charges (versus roomette) for persons traveling at its expense. No. 1250 (above right) was one of three Budd dome coaches bought from Chesapeake & Ohio. Originally, C&O had them built for its ill-fated Chessie train.

DINER-LOUNGE Mt. Timpanogos operated on Delaware & Hudson's Laurentian in 1967.

JUPITER meets CZ on Spanish Creek trestle, Keddie, Calif., at Western Pacific's 40th anniversary celebration in November 1949.

The California Zephyr

ON March 20, 1949, an extraordinary streamliner was placed in service between Chicago and San Francisco by the Burlington, Rio Grande, and Western Pacific railroads. Twenty-one years later (and almost to the very day) on March 22, 1970, the same train made its last run. That train was Nos. 17 and 18,

the *California Zephyr*, affectionately known as the "CZ."

Because of the success of the 1939 *Exposition Flyer*, representatives of the CB&Q, D&RGW, and WP met in August of 1939 and agreed that the *Flyer* should become a permanent service and be re-equipped with modern, streamlined equipment. New cars were contemplated in 1941, but World War II interfered with plans.

In October 1945, Judge Wilson McCarthy, trustee of the D&RGW, announced that orders had been placed with the Edward G. Budd Company for a diesel-powered train to be operated jointly by the three roads under the name *California Zephyr*. A total investment of more than 10 million dollars for cars and locomotives was to be divided among Burlington, Rio Grande, and Western Pacific. The six sets of equipment necessary to protect the service consisted of 66 stainless-steel cars: 27 were owned by CB&Q, 24 by WP, and 15 by D&RGW. Pennsylvania Railroad furnished one additional sleeping car for through coast-to-coast service. The *California Zephyr* proved to be such a success that an additional 12 cars were purchased from Budd in 1952.

Timing for the 2532-mile run (including the ferry between Oakland Mole and San Francisco) was established at 50 hours 30 minutes eastbound, and 51 hours 20 minutes westbound. The schedule was carefully arranged to permit passengers in both directions to traverse the Colorado Rockies and

296

FIRST PRIZE in a Budd-sponsored California Zephyr photo contest was this scene on the Western Pacific.

MOFFAT TUNNEL was a trip highpoint in more ways than one: CZ reached its highest altitude in the bore.

California's Feather River Canyon in daylight, all year round.

In addition to the CZ's regular railroad and Pullman crews, young women known as "Zephyrettes" were employed to serve as hostesses. Five Vista-Domes (the CZ was the first transcontinental train to have them), a public-address system with recorded music, inter-car telephones, two lounges, a superb diner, and a coast-to-coast sleeping car all were available at no extra fare.

In 1960 patronage began to decline. By 1968 the number of CZ passengers had dropped 23 per cent, and out-of-pocket losses on the train rose to nearly 2 million dollars in 1969. Western Pacific, financially burdened by CZ operations, thrice petitioned the Interstate Commerce Commission to drop its portion of the run. In February 1970 WP's request was granted.

One month later the *California Zephyrs* made their final Chicago-San Francisco runs, but because of impending legislation in Congress for Federal assistance to passenger trains, the ICC ordered that a tri-weekly "California Zephyr Service" be substituted between Chicago and Oakland (San Francisco) via Burlington Northern, Rio Grande, and Southern Pacific.

The signing of the Rail Passenger Service Act of 1970 by President Nixon on October 30, 1970, authorized that Federally subsidized Amtrak operations become effective on May 1, 1971. An Amtrak-reinstated *California Zephyr* was to be operated over BN-D&RGW-SP between Chicago and Oakland, but at

VIEW from CZ domes was among the best in the West.

the last minute Rio Grande elected not to join Amtrak. Accordingly, service to Oakland was routed via Union Pacific and Southern Pacific west of Denver. By law, however, D&RGW was required to continue operating its CZ remnant, the *Rio Grande Zephyr*, between Denver and Salt Lake City.

S. L. Logue, collection of Everett L. DeGolyer Jr.

EVIDENCE of a streamliner soon to be born: CZ dome cars and new Alco PA1's are in the consist of the westbound Exposition Flyer. This 1948 scene at Fireclay siding (on the Front Range west of Denver) depicted the Flyer in its last months of service.

SPANISH explorers dubbed it "El Rio de las Plumas" — the Feather River. The CZ wound along its canyon walls for 116 miles.

WP.

Budd.

ALTHOUGH in regular service it departed from Oakland, the California Zephyr was exhibited on San Francisco's Embarcadero (above) before its first run. Here, on March 19, 1949, movie star Eleanor Parker christened the CZ with California champagne.

CHAMPION for world's longest interurban run had to be WP's Oakland-Salt Lake City Zephyrette RDC (below), sister to the CZ.

WP.

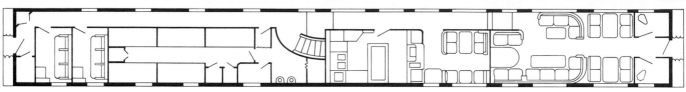

Budd.

SILVER SHOP (above) was one of six Budd dormitory-dome-buffet-lounge cars built in 1948. In 1960 they became "Cable Car" lounges (below) complete with cable-car-track carpeting.

WP.

CB&Q.

OPEN-SECTION CARS (above) operated on the California Zephyrs as late as 1962. Six 16-section sleepers, such as Silver Aspen (below), were built in 1948, rebuilt to coaches in the 1960's.

Budd.

PHOTOS and floor plan (above) reveal why Silver Bay, PRR-owned Silver Rapids, and 17 other CZ 10-6 sleepers were a unique set of cars: Unlike other Pullmans, each had aisle windows opposite every bedroom.

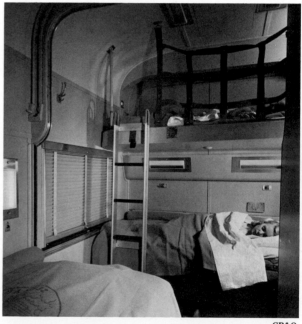

SILVER QUAIL (below) was one of six 5-compartment, 6-double-bedroom Pullmans added to California Zephyr consists in 1952. Spacious bedroom suites (right) on these CZ cars were 7 feet wide and . . . 2532 miles long!

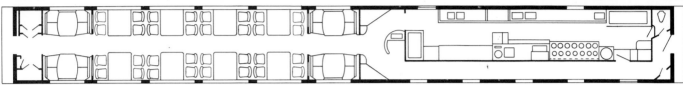

Budd.

WP DINER Silver Platter (above) seated 40. (Below) Snowy linens and china clatter were sights and sounds in Silver Platter.

CB&Q.

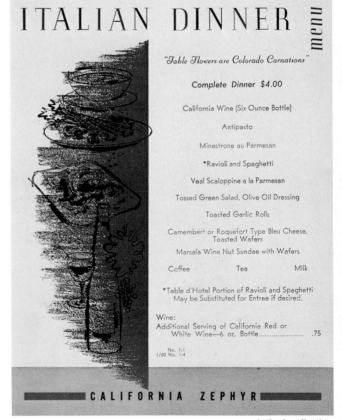

Author's collection.

ITALIAN DINNER, a celebrated CZ tradition, included wine.

THE CZ Vista-Dome sleeper-buffet-lounge-observation cars (such as Silver Lookout, below) provide a fitting finale to this chapter of Colorado railroading. Observation-lounge (left photos) seated 13, and below-dome buffet section seated 12. Forward, the car had three double bedrooms and a drawing room complete with shower. The striking cars were a favorite of passenger-car connoisseurs and were considered the epitome of travel luxury on the California Zephyr, one of America's best-liked streamliners.

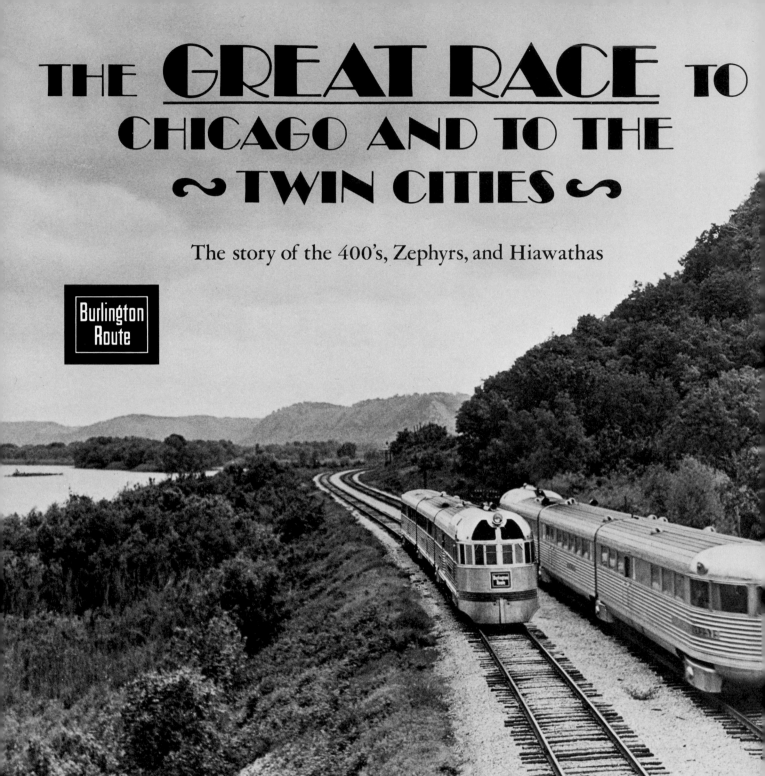

THE GREAT RACE TO CHICAGO AND TO THE ~ TWIN CITIES ~

The story of the 400's, Zephyrs, and Hiawathas

Burlington Route

ᴵ ONE of the most thrilling chapters in the chronicle of American railroading was written in the Chicago-Twin Cities corridor. Between 1934 and the post-World War II era, the Chicago & North Western, Chicago, Milwaukee, St. Paul & Pacific, and Chicago, Burlington & Quincy vied with each other for supremacy on the 400-plus-mile route.

During the summer of 1934 *Railway Age* ran a series of articles announcing the beginning of what would be an exciting drama. Of the seven competing railroads on the route,* the three major contenders for traffic — North Western, Milwaukee, and Burlington — prodded by increasing competition from the automobile and motor bus, were reported to be planning mile-a-minute or better schedules for route distances ranging from 407 to 431 miles.

On July 15, 1934, the North Western and the Milwaukee Road both reduced the running times of their major Chi-

*C&NW, CB&Q, CGW, CMStP&P, CRI&P, IC-M&StL, and Soo Line.

CMStP&P.

NorthWestern LINE

C&NW.

CB&Q.

IN the series of photographs on these pages, the original Twin Zephyrs, Nos. 9901 and 9902, meet along the Mississippi River (left); the Hiawatha strikes a pose with Alco Class A 4-4-2 No. 2 in May 1935 (top); and the 400 departs Chicago, Ill., in July 1936 (above).

cago-Milwaukee express trains from 105 minutes to 90 minutes for the 85-mile run, establishing the fastest regular service in the West.

Two weeks later the tempo increased. On July 29, 1934, the Milwaukee smashed the world's record "for sustained steam-train speed" by running its regular 9 a.m. express, the *Pacemaker*, between Chicago and Milwaukee at an average speed of 91.1 mph for 70 miles.

The next day, to confirm the feasibility of fast Chicago-

Twin Cities service, the Burlington operated its famed *Zephyr* streamliner, No. 9900, from Chicago to St. Paul, 431 miles, in 6 hours 4 minutes. The news media was having a field day!

Five days later, on August 4, 1934, the Burlington ordered two *Twin Zephyr* trains from the Edward G. Budd Manufacturing Company in Philadelphia, Pa., for high-speed day service between Chicago and the Twin Cities. The challenge was made, and the Great Race was on.

305

PHOTOGRAPHER dramatically captured E-2-A Pacific No. 2908 at speed in command of the 400, shortly after the train's first run.

400 miles in 400 minutes

DURING the fall of 1934, the Chicago & North Western cast its lot with steam-powered conventional equipment instead of experimenting with the lightweight streamliner, and hurriedly rebuilt four Class E-2 Pacific-type locomotives and 10 conventional passenger cars in its Chicago shops at 40th Street. Two Pullman solarium-parlor cars built for North Western service were refurbished at Pullman's Calumet shops. Because the new train was to travel about 400 miles between Chicago and St. Paul in slightly over 400 minutes, it was christened the *400* and became the first entrant in the Great Race to the Twin Cities.

The locomotives received 79-inch Boxpok drivers, oil-burning equipment, and new six-wheel-truck tenders. The complex rebuilding for high-speed service was completed in only 60 days at a cost of $14,000 per locomotive. All the cars were air-conditioned and the interiors redecorated in modern colors. The C&NW roadbed was reconditioned and newly ballasted.

Numerous conferences between the operating and mechanical departments resulted in a remarkable schedule that demanded the *400's* to average 60.5 mph on the 408.6-mile run to St. Paul. The schedule included four intermediate stops. Northbound and southbound *400's* met midway at Adams, Wis.

The *400* made its premier run on a cold January 2, 1935. It was the first high-speed, standard-weight, steam-driven passenger train designed to compete with lightweight, diesel-electric, streamlined equipment and was advertised as "The Fastest Train on the American Continent." Sixty-four crew members and three smartly dressed hostesses catered to the passengers. Part of the inaugural festivities included $1000 in awards for the best-written stories of a ride on the *400*. Judges were Col. R. R. McCormick, publisher, Chicago *Tribune*; Howard Vincent O'Brien, columnist, Chicago *Daily News*; and Dr. Walter Dill Scott, president, Northwestern University.

The *400* achieved instant popularity and success. More than 10,000 passengers rode the train during its first month. Day after day it broke records, bringing travelers back to the railroad. In April 1935, when the Burlington and Milwaukee streamliners arrived on the scene, the *400* schedule was reduced to 6½ hours, with frequent sustained speeds of 96 mph.

Three issues of *Railway Age* during January 1938* reported that the North Western planned to streamline the *400* and was seeking manufacturers' proposals for locomotives and cars. Three alternate locomotive bids were received: for streamlined steam power of the E-4 type (4-6-4); for diesel-electric; and for steam-turbine. Finally, in January 1939, orders were placed with Electro-Motive for two sets of diesel-electric locomotives costing $720,000, and 20 cars from Pullman-Standard at a cost of 1.6 million dollars. The exterior color scheme was to be the armour yellow and brown of the first Chicago & North Western-Union Pacific-Southern Pacific West Coast *City* streamliners.

On September 24, 1939, the beautiful new *400* streamliners began Chicago-to-St. Paul service on a 6½-hour schedule that later was reduced to 6¼ hours until World War II. Each train was 960 feet long and weighed 885 tons. Total seating capacity was 486 passengers. A yellow-and-green exterior paint scheme North Western had used earlier ultimately was selected.

Encouraged by the success of the *Twin Cities 400*, the North Western established an entire fleet of *400* trains on January 12, 1942, shortly after the outbreak of World War II. Twenty-five yellow-and-green streamlined cars entered service on new trains to Madison, Milwaukee, Green Bay, upper Michigan, and southern Minnesota.

During the 1950's, as the postwar network of superhighways and airlines expanded, the *400* fleet diminished. Even the innovative bi-level *400's* of 1958 to Green Bay, the Wisconsin North Woods, and upper Michigan (see pages 490 and 491) could not stem the tide. The last *Twin Cities 400*, trains 400 and 401, operated on July 23, 1963. On April 30, 1971 — the day before the Amtrak takeover — bi-level *400* service between Chicago and Green Bay was terminated, and a colorful era ended.

*January 8, p. 138; January 22, p. 213; January 29, p. 248.

C&NW.

C&NW.

PRIOR to delivery of the streamlined cars, EMD E3 5002 (far left) eases the 400 out of North Western Terminal, Chicago, in June 1939. Three months later the streamlined 400 departs Chicago (left). In January 1942, streamlined Pacific No. 1620 pauses at Winona, Minn., on the first run of the Minnesota 400 (above).

CONSTRUCTED by Alco in 1923, Class E-2-A No. 2908 was remodeled for 400 service with 79-inch Boxpok drivers in the fall of 1934.

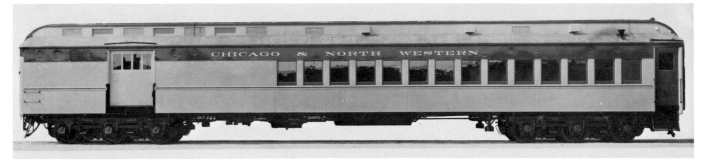

THIS builder's view of yellow-and-green baggage-and-smoking car No. 7416 was made in May 1927 at American Car & Foundry.

COACH No. 6105, a 79-foot all-steel car built in July 1914, was air-conditioned with an ice-activated system. Two 1600-pound bunkers were located under the car. Interior had oyster-gray walls, tan-and-buff floor tile, rebuilt seating upholstered in brown for 65 persons (below).

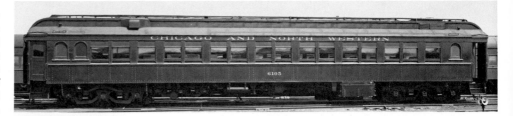

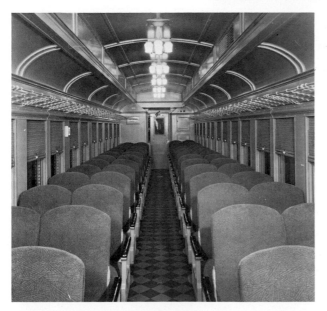

PULLMAN-BUILT (in 1914) diner 6922 was 73 feet long. The wide letterboard covered original upper sash. Thirty-six people could be seated in brown leather chairs (above). Mahogany walls were repainted pearl gray.

THE 7300-series observation-parlor cars outshopped by Pullman between 1910 and 1915 were rebuilt as lounge cars (above) for 400 service. A waiter served refreshments in car 7303 aboard the 400 in 1935 (left). Note the writing desk and freshly cut flowers.

HEAVY, easy-riding parlor car 6401 weighed 70 tons, was built by Pullman in 1912. The main room (right) seated 19 people in revolving chairs upholstered in brown plush and had convenient hat racks and coat hooks. There also was a private stateroom with a private toilet, and a large smoking room.

PULLMAN parlor cars with sunroom (above) were built in 1930 for C&NW's predecessor to the 400, the Viking. For several years the cars carried a drumhead for the Viking as well as one for C&NW-Soo-CPR's Soo-Dominion (below). A Pullman porter tunes the radio for passengers relaxing in revolving parlor chairs (right).

C&NW.

Alco.

SLANT-NOSED 2000-h.p. EMD E3A's (above) were delivered to C&NW in 1939 to pilot the 400 and the North Western Limited. (Left) Green-and-gold Class E-4 No. 4002 was one of nine C&NW streamlined Hudsons built in 1938. The E-4's were considered for 400 service, but delegated to the C&NW-UP-SP Western trains.

Both photos, Pullman-Standard.

BAGGAGE-TAPROOM car No. 7500 (above) was built in September 1939. The floor plan was divided into four parts: baggage room, Rathskeller, counter, and lounge. Rathskeller (below left) had photomurals, red leather booths, and a speedometer over the bar.

Both photos, Pullman-Standard.

COACH 3400 (below) contained 56 seats and a nurse's room. Cars for the 400 were painted apple green and English stagecoach yellow, with black striping and silver lettering. Parlor cars with drawing rooms featured photos of on-line scenes (above right).

HIGH-CAPACITY dining car No. 6950 seated 56 at 14 tables. Interior (top) was decorated in pastels: beige ceiling, peach-colored blinds, rose-colored drapes, green leather chairs, and a coral-and-burgundy carpet. Menu (below right) featured a continental dinner priced at $1.75 and included wine, whitefish or filet mignon, dessert, and cafe et cognac. The 400's diner stocked 400 items.

THE forward end of parlor-observation car No. 7200 (below) contained 12 parlor chairs; rear half was a bar-lounge seating 29 passengers. The rear of the lounge was decorated in tones of blue and apricot (above). A speedometer was mounted on the fascia.

Continental Dinner On The "400"

Fruit or Shrimp Cocktail

Red or White Wine
(as desired)

Soup Du Jour

Assorted Relish Tray

Broiled Lake Superior Whitefish, Maitre D' Hotel
Broiled Fillet Mignon or Loin Lamb Chops, Fresh Mushrooms
Broiled Half Chicken, Virginia Ham Saute in Butter
Long Branch Potatoes   Fried Tomatoes

Assorted Bread

Chilled Hearts of Head Lettuce,
Roquefort Cheese Dressing

Ice Cream and Cake

Roquefort or Brie Cheese,
Toasted Wafers

Mints

Cafe Noir   Cafe et Cognac
• $1.75 •

From The Broiler
Sirloin Steak Dinner $1.50
Includes Soup, Potatoes, Salad, Dessert and Beverage

Parents may share their portion with children without charge.
Half Portions served at half price to children under twelve years of age.
No Substitutions.

Meal service by waiter outside of dining car, 25c extra for each person served
Suggestions for betterment of the service are invited
C. H. SHIRCLIFFE, Superintendent Dining Cars, Chicago, Ill.

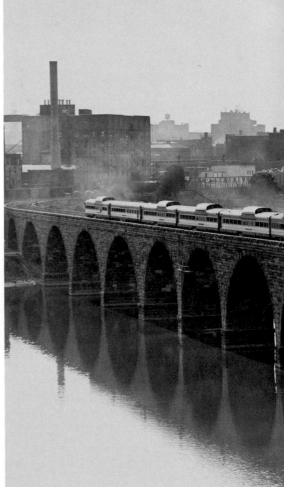

All photos, CB&Q.

IN 1935 the first Twin City Zephyrs (above) began operation between Chicago and the Twin Cities. Forty-four sets of twins attended the christening of the 197-foot-long trains (below). In 1936 larger, more luxurious Zephyrs replaced the original trains and were known as "Trains of Gods and Goddesses" because of their car names. Twin Zephyr of 1936 races along the Mississippi (top) behind power car Pegasus. (Right) A pair of Burlington's famous stainless-steel EMD E-5's glide the Morning Zephyr across Great Northern's Stone Arch Bridge in Minneapolis in July 1948. The domed third-generation Twin Zephyrs arrived in 1947.

Trains of the gods and goddesses

ON November 11, 1934, the Chicago, Burlington & Quincy introduced the first lightweight, diesel-powered, streamlined train in America. Built by the Edward G. Budd Manufacturing Company in Philadelphia, a new era in passenger travel was born with the debut of the revolutionary *Zephyr* No. 9900 between Lincoln-Omaha-Kansas City. The little three-car, stainless-steel, articulated train, named *Zephyr* by Burlington president Ralph Budd for the Greek personification of the west wind, was to be the precursor of many diesel-powered streamliners. It is now preserved at Chicago's Museum of Science and Industry.

On July 30, 1934, a test run of *Zephyr* No. 9900 between Chicago and St. Paul was completed in the record time of 6 hours 4 minutes, nearly 5 hours faster than the regular scheduled time. Five days later, the Burlington ordered *Twin Zephyrs* Nos. 9901 and 9902 from the Budd Company for regular service between Chicago and the Twin Cities.

Before the *Twin Zephyrs* began revenue service, *Zephyr* 9901 completed a 2900-mile exhibition run to Florida, during which it was visited by more than 136,000 people. Later, on April 14, 1935, a unique ceremony took place to welcome the new trains. Forty-four pairs of identical twins rode the 88 seats of *Zephyr* 9901 to Aurora, where *Zephyr* 9902 was met. The two *Zephyrs* then ran side by side back to Chicago, with each train carrying half the twins. On the following day, after a simultaneous christening in Chicago by twin sisters wielding bottles of champagne, the *Twin Zephyrs* departed side by side on a trip to the Twin Cities.

On April 17, 1935, the *Twin Zephyrs* were placed in revenue service, the second entry in the Great Race to the Twin Cities. Public acceptance of the trains was so enthusiastic that just 6 weeks later the service was doubled — by each train making a daily round trip. However, even the addition of a new Twin City schedule was inadequate to handle the demand.

On December 18, 1936, larger and more luxurious seven-car articulated *Twin Zephyrs* replaced the original *Twins*. The two new trains were known as the "Trains of the Gods and Goddesses" because of their cars' names. The second *Twins* were so popular that it was necessary to add an eighth car in 1937. In 1940 the *Morning Zephyr* introduced 6-hour scheduling between Chicago and St. Paul.

The friendly rivalry between the *Twins, 400,* and *Hiawathas* was highlighted on several ceremonious occasions when crew members of the trains were feted as guests aboard the competition. Yet railway officials were concerned about the rationality of the intense competition. In August 1938 negotiations were held to discuss the pooling of Twin Cities service and to eliminate one *Zephyr*, the *400*, and the *Pioneer Limited*, but nothing came of the matter. Soon World War II was declared and such ideas were forgotten.

In 1945 the first dome car was built in the Burlington's Aurora (Ill.) shops from designs developed by General Motors. It was tested and demonstrated on the *Twin Cities Zephyr* scenic route which traversed the Mississippi River "Where Nature Smiles 300 Miles" between Savanna, Ill., and St. Paul.

With the return of peacetime, the entire *Zephyr* fleet was upgraded with new and refurbished equipment. The first regular trains featuring the Vista-Dome, "a glass-enclosed observatory," were the nonarticulated *Twin Zephyrs* of December 17, 1947. Five cars of the train's seven-car consist were Vista-Domes built by Budd. Delivery of the 1947 equipment for the *Twins* released the "Trains of the Gods and Goddesses" for refurbishing and reassignment as the *Nebraska Zephyr*. Each train had traveled more than 2 million miles; together they had carried over 3 million passengers in 11 years of service. Other postwar additions to the *Zephyr* fleet included the fabled *California Zephyr*, the *Kansas City Zephyr*, and the *American Royal Zephyr* between Chicago-Kansas City-St. Joseph via the 1953 Brookfield cutoff.

Despite efforts by Burlington to secure passenger business, the number of passenger-train miles operated by the road between 1949 and 1963 decreased by one-third. When the incorporators of Amtrak selected the endpoints to be served by the national passenger system, the *Denver Zephyr* between Chicago and Denver was retained, but *Twin Zephyr* service between Chicago and the Twin Cities via the famous Mississippi River Scenic Line was terminated on April 30, 1971. An interesting testimonial to the *Zephyr* is the fact that 101 cars of the 1190 passenger cars initially purchased by Amtrak in 1971 were former CB&Q cars built for the *Zephyrs*.

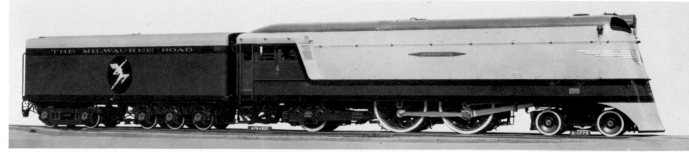

American Locomotive Company.

MILWAUKEE ROAD Class A 4-4-2 No. 4 was outshopped by Alco in April 1937. Ten-wheel tender sported the famous Hiawatha emblem.

CMStP&P.

CMStP&P.

CMStP&P.

COACH No. 4000 (ex-Barney & Smith 12-1 sleeping car Great Falls) and coach No. 4400 (above) were Nystrom-designed experimental lightweight coaches constructed in February 1934. No. 4400 was 81 feet 8 inches long and weighed 50 tons. The interior (left) had wood veneer walls and bright floral-patterned upholstery. The car was exhibited at the Chicago World's Fair in 1934.

Hiawatha
**THE FIRST OF THE
SPEEDLINERS**

CMStP&P.

ADVERTISEMENTS said Beaver Tail had a "rear end that minimizes the vacuum that . . . exists behind a fast-moving train."

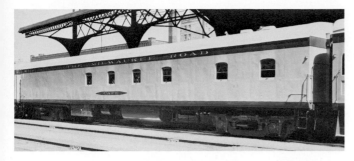

THE Tip Top Tap car (left) was part bar, part diner; it could provide both meal and beverage service. Cars of the first Hiawatha had

arch windows. Cars from the 1937 Hiawatha (right) had squared-off windows, winged nameplates, and full-width diaphragms.

OTTO KUHLER poses in front of 4-6-4 No. 100 at American Locomotive Company's Schenectady (N. Y.) plant in August of 1938.

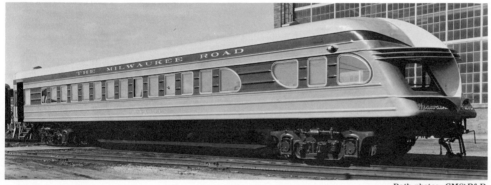

MITCHELL was one of four observation-parlor cars built for the 1939 Hiawatha. Cars of the third set of Hiawatha equipment had full-ribbed sides and underbody gear housed in a long box. Interior (right) had 24 parlor seats, plus 17 seats in the Beaver Tail's solarium-lounge section.

FOURTH version of the Hiawatha was styled by Milwaukee industrial designer Brooks Stevens. "The finishing touch to a perfect train" described the superb Skytop Lounge cars such as Cedar Rapids (above). The Skytops were part of the new 1948 Twin Cities Hiawathas produced by the Milwaukee shops. (Right) On a clear day you could see forever in the Skytop Lounge, where glass covered 90 per cent of the observation area. The car also contained 24 revolving parlor seats and a drawing room.

El Camino Real—the

The Lark and the Daylight

NEAR THE END of the 18th century, the Franciscan fathers of Mexico made an expedition north along the California coast, planting the cross as they went and establishing a chain of 21 missions a day's journey apart. Soon there was a well-traveled route through the rich Santa Clara and Salinas valleys and along the coast connecting the missions: San Diego, San Gabriel, San Fernando, Santa Barbara, San Luis Obispo, Soledad, Monterey, Santa Cruz, San Francisco, and others. The route was called El Camino Real — the royal road, the highway of the king. It was the artery of commerce and religion in California; it was also the territory's link with its government in Mexico and Spain.

The Mexican War in 1846, the discovery of gold at Sutter's Fort in 1848, and statehood in 1850 changed the destiny of California and El Camino Real. The new state needed better transportation than the slow, jolting, expensive stagecoaches; it needed an iron trail along the route of the padres.

The first link was the San Francisco & San Jose Railroad, completed in 1864 between the two cities of its name. On December 2, 1865, the Southern Pacific Railroad, formed by the builders of the SF&SJ, was incorporated in California and later authorized by Congress to build from San Jose south and east through the San Joaquin Valley to Needles, there to connect with the Atlantic & Pacific-Santa Fe line being built westward from the Missouri River.

The "Big Four" of the Central Pacific — Collis Huntington, Leland Stanford, Charles Crocker, and Mark Hopkins — soon acquired the Southern Pacific and continued its construction through the San Joaquin Valley (reaching Los Angeles in 1876) and down the coast. Building of the line along the coast progressed slowly. Heavy construction was required over the Coast Range at the south end of the Salinas Valley. A spectacular horseshoe curve brought the line down into San Luis Obispo; then came 113 miles of track along the very edge of the Pacific, skirting mountains and bridging deep ravines. In 1901 the line was completed to Santa Barbara, where it met a line completed from Los Angeles via Saugus and Santa Paula in 1887.

March 4, 1904, saw the opening of the direct line into Los Angeles via Chatsworth, 18 miles shorter than the route through Saugus, but requiring tunnels through the Santa Susana Mountains northwest of Los Angeles.

The *Coast Line Limited*, later the *Coaster*, began operating on December 6, 1901, as a daytime coach train. At the same time, the *Sunset Limited* began using the Coast Line between Los Angeles and San Francisco rather than the San Joaquin Valley Route.

The best-known trains of the Coast Line came later. The *Lark* began overnight service between San Francisco and Los Angeles in 1910, and the *Daylight* started its career as a Friday-and-Saturday-only coach train in 1922.

THE 20-car first section of the Lark rolls through Santa Susana heading for Los Angeles behind GS-5A No. 4459 in 1945.

highway of the king

EMPTY coaches and the train number (2-69) betray the Daylight's mission at Chatsworth — publicity photographs.

IN its early days, the Lark carried a drumhead with a colored portrait of its namesake bird.

In the days of Edward H. Harriman

THE *Shore Line Limited*, which commenced service on March 1, 1906, was a luxury all-parlor-car train. Scheduled time for the *Shore Line* was 13½ hours, with 8 a.m. departures from both San Francisco and Los Angeles.

The *Lark* was inaugurated on May 8, 1910, as Nos. 75 and 76, providing overnight service for first-class sleeping-car passengers on the 470-mile Coast Line. At first, the *Lark* competed with the older and better known *Owl Limited*, which had been running since December 18, 1898, over the San Joaquin Valley Route via Fresno and Bakersfield. Soon, however, the *Lark*, which departed directly from San Francisco and served the wealthy Peninsula suburbs, became the favored train of West Coast businessmen. Thick blue Southern Pacific timetables listed the *Lark* on the "Sunset Route via the Coast Line."

In 1915, during the Panama-Pacific Expositions at San Francisco and San Diego, and for years thereafter, the *Lark* carried a through Los Angeles-Seattle sleeper between Los Angeles and San Jose for handling in the prestigious *Shasta Limited* north of Oakland.

DINER No. 10069 was one of 10 built in 1906 for the Harriman lines. Southern Pacific advertised "Tastefully prepared, well-cooked, delicious meals. Gleaming silver, fresh white linen."

OBSERVATION-SMOKER No. 1728 was one of a group built for SP and UP in 1906. SP rebuilt the car with a deep rear platform for service on the Daylight. Central Pacific 1907 (below), a similar car, had overstuffed chairs and art-glass upper sash.

THROUGH CAR SERVICE

No. 78 and 77. SHORE LINE LIMITED.

Pullman Parlor Cars: Observation Parlor Car, Composite Car (lounging parlor, library and writing desk), San Francisco and Los Angeles.

Dining Cars: San Francisco and Los Angeles.

Tickets Honored: First-class tickets only with Pullman Car tickets honored on Nos. 77 and 78.

Telephone Connections in Observation Cars for thirty minutes before departure: at San Francisco, "Sutter 6280," at Los Angeles, Main 8421.

Nos. 22 and 21. THE COASTER.

Steel Chair Car and Smoker: San Francisco and Los Angeles.

Dining Car: San Francisco and Los Angeles.

Transportation Honored: All classes.

Nos. 76 and 75. THE LARK.

Electric lighted throughout.

Pullman Standard Sleepers and Observation Car, San Francisco and Los Angeles. San Jose to Los Angeles (en route from Seattle on Shasta Limited)

Dining Car: Breakfast into San Francisco and Los Angeles.

Transportation Honored: First-class tickets only, in connection with Pullman tickets. No passengers carried locally between San Francisco and Watsonville Junction, except interline tickets from or to points beyond Portland, Ogden, Albuquerque or El Paso will be honored for stops at any scheduled stopping point between San Francisco and Los Angeles. Passengers will be carried locally only when lower berth space is available.

Telephone Connections in Observation Cars for thirty minutes before departure, at San Francisco "Sutter 6280," at Los Angeles, "Main 8241."

and SEAS PRESS

THE equipment listing in the 1915 timetable advertised a Pullman observation-parlor car on the Shore Line Limited, electric lights on the Lark, and pre-departure telephones on board at the two terminals.

PALO ALTO — 10 sections, 1 drawing room, 1 compartment — was one of 20 steel cars built in 1913 for service on the Lark and the Golden State.

OBSERVATION-PARLOR cars Santa Susana (right), Santa Anita, Santa Clara, and Santa Monica were built in January 1906 and assigned to the Coaster and the Shore Line Limited.

IN the short-lived pearl-gray livery of 1930, the Daylight winds its way uphill toward the horseshoe curve north of San Luis Obispo.

SOUTHERN PACIFIC LINES

THE ROAD OF A THOUSAND WONDERS

Steam and steel on the Coast Line

THE *Daylight Limited* began service on April 28, 1922, as Nos. 71 and 72, with coaches and a dining car. It was the fastest train on the SP, covering the scenic Coast Line Route in 13 hours and making no revenue stops between its terminals. The new train operated Fridays and Saturdays only until November 25 of that year. Service was resumed on the same basis April 27, 1923. On June 10 a Sunday train was added; Thursday service began July 5. A week later, July 12, 1923, the train became a regular daily, year-round operation.

The *Daylight Limited* was assigned some of the most interesting and luxurious equipment on the railroad. Two unique observation cars, with the rear platform extending deep into the body of the car and seating 32 persons, were rebuilt in SP's Sacramento shops for the 1923 season. "All-Day Lunch" cars, coaches with a counter at one end of the main compartment, were added in 1924 to serve sandwiches and drugstore fare at low prices.

Parlor cars were added to the *Daylight* in 1928, and special observation cars, designed by SP and built by Pullman, were delivered in 1930. They were painted with pearl-gray Pyroxilin lacquer to reflect the heat of the sun; window sashes were painted dark gray. For a brief season the entire *Daylight* wore this handsome livery.

During the 1920's the *Lark* attained premier status. The finest Pullman cars were assigned to the train, by now a favorite of film stars and businessmen. Two single-bedroom cars, the first in the West, were added to the *Lark* in 1929; they were followed in 1930 by two sunroom Pullmans named in the *Lark* series. Also in 1930 the *Lark* received elegant SP-owned lounge cars built by Pullman for the crack trains of the railroad. The exteriors of the cars were finished with special Mimex aluminum lacquer to reflect heat; the interiors contained complete club facilities: valet, barber shop, showers for men and women, soda fountain (in deference to the Volstead Act), and extra-large windows for sightseeing.

In 1931 the Oakland-San Jose-Los Angeles *Padre* was replaced by an Oakland section of the *Lark*, operating between San Jose and Oakland along the shore of San Francisco Bay.

REBUILT observation car 1724, once a twin of 1728 on the preceding page, displays its deep observation platform in San Francisco.

PASSENGERS on the platform enjoy the tang of the salty sea air as the Daylight Limited speeds south along the coast in the 1920's.

MOUNTAIN-TYPE 4357 is ready to lead a 1930's-era Lark south from San Francisco's Third Street Station to Los Angeles. The Lark was a favorite of movie stars: William Bendix, Ida Lupino, and Pat O'Brien arrive San Francisco (above) in May 1951 for a movie premiere.

Lark

Baldwin.

BALDWIN built P-10-class Pacific No. 2488 in 1924. Its 73½-inch drivers and trailing-truck booster produced 53,000 pounds of tractive force.

Pullman-Standard.

WELLS FARGO was still actively engaged in the express business in 1911 when Pullman built baggage-railway-post-office car No. 5033.

Pullman-Standard.

HEAD-END car design changed little in 17 years: Baggage-mail No. 5066 of 1928 differs in only a few details from car No. 5033 above.

Standard Steel Car Co.

COACH 2312 seated 90, was built in 1923 by Standard Steel Car Company. The initials on the side of the car attest to the continued corporate existence of the Central Pacific, which had become a part of SP in 1885.

Pullman-Standard.

COACH 2009 was completed in 1926 by Pullman and carried the initials of the Oregon & California. In 1928 the car was rebuilt to a parlor car.

326

All photos this page, Pullman-Standard.

DINER 10155 (above), built by Pullman in 1928, became one of the first air-conditioned cars in 1932 — note the duct along the roof. Diner 10000 (below) was an early steel diner, one of a group of nine built in 1914 for SP, CP, OSL, and C&A. Interior of 10000 (below left) had arched ceiling, art glass in the upper sash, and side lamps. In prosperous times SP's dining-car department employed 1900 persons.

THE Daylight observation cars of 1930 seated 74 in folding chairs, to which SP later added orange-and-black striped slipcovers.

OBSERVATION cars of 1930 had wide windows for sightseeing. They introduced a pearl-gray livery designed to reflect the sun's heat.

327

FORERUNNER of the streamlined Daylight locomotives were 14 GS–1's built by Baldwin in 1930. No. 700 was assigned to Texas & New Orleans.

BAGGAGE-BUFFET car 3229 (above) was built by Pullman in 1914 for SP limiteds. The interior (below) was masculine and club-like, with leather chairs, dark wood, and art-glass upper sash.

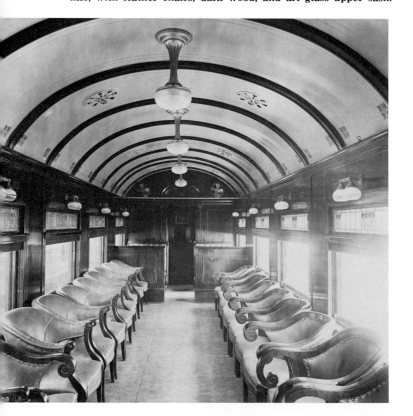

SHORE LARK (below) and Meadow Lark were built in 1930 for — what else? — the Lark. They each contained 3 single bedrooms, 2 compartments, a drawing room, a buffet, and a sunroom-lounge. Mission-style interior (above) was appropriate for the Lark's route.

NIGHT FERN (top), with 14 single bedrooms, was constructed by Pullman in 1929 and was one of the first all-room sleepers on the Lark. It was sold to the SP in 1948 when the Pullman Company was sold to the Buying Group of 57 railroads. At the time, SP was the third largest operator of Pullman Company sleeping cars in the country. Shares in the Pullman Company were allotted on the basis of the number of Pullman cars operated. Pennsylvania received the largest share — 16.18 per cent, followed by New York Central — 15.50 per cent, and Southern Pacific — 8.55 per cent. Poplar Junction (center), originally a standard 12-section, 1-drawing-room car, was rebuilt in 1939 with 6 sections and 6 double bedrooms. Windsor Forest (bottom) was a 10-section-restaurant-lounge car assigned to SP for service on the Coaster.

LOUNGE CAR 2912 (below) included almost everything a traveler wanted: barbershop, shower, observation room, card-playing and smoking areas, soda fountain. Aluminum lacquer reflected the sun's heat.

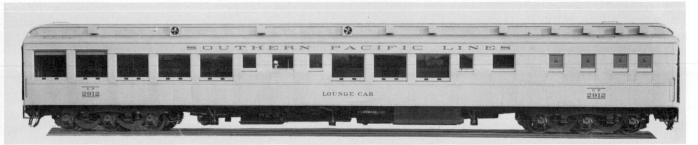

Daylight

All photos, SP.

The world's most beautiful trains

EARLY in 1937 two sets of luxurious cars and six streamlined steam locomotives headed west to California. The 12-car trains were built by Pullman in Chicago, while the 4-8-4's, classified as GS (for Golden State) and termed the largest and most powerful streamlined locomotives ever built, were the product of Lima Locomotive Works. Each of the complete trains, favorites of their historian, Richard K. Wright, was 960 feet long, weighed nearly 1000 tons, and cost 1 million depression dollars. They were painted in a stunning livery of red, orange, and black. Each car and locomotive bore on its flanks a new emblem: a circle symbolizing California's sun, a wing symbolizing speed, and, in flowing script, *Daylight*.

Southern Pacific termed the *Daylight* "the most beautiful train in the West," a claim which was soon expanded to "the world's most beautiful train." Few who saw the *Daylight* doubted the claim.

The new equipment entered service on March 21, 1937, on a 9¾-hour schedule. The new *Daylight* quickly became so popular that it often was unable to accommodate all the travelers who clamored to ride it. On January 5, 1940, therefore, new 14-car *Daylights* went into service. The 1937 equipment was reconditioned and became the *Noon Daylight* on March 30, 1940; at that time the existing *Daylight* became the *Morning Daylight*.

The *Noon Daylight* was annulled during World War II. On October 2, 1949, it was discontinued and its consist became the San Francisco-Los Angeles *Starlight*, which operated for 8 years before merging with the *Lark*. The *Morning Daylight* was renamed the *Coast Daylight* on August 8, 1952.

The *Daylight* concept was extended beyond El Camino Real on four occasions. On September 19, 1937, twin 8-car *Sunbeams*

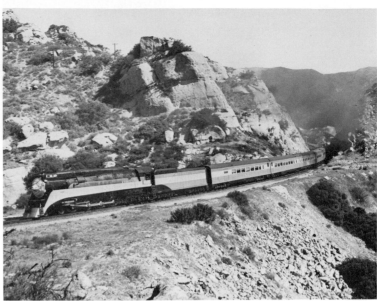

THE Shasta Daylight (far left) was the only Daylight dieselized at birth. The Coast Daylight's route follows the very edge of the Pacific for 113 miles (left) and winds through the Santa Susana Mountains (above). It is easy to see why construction of the Coast Line took so many years.

were placed in service between Houston and Dallas, making the 264-mile run nonstop in 4¾ hours. Soon each set of *Sunbeam* equipment was making a daily round trip, running in one direction as the *Hustler*. On July 4, 1941, the *San Joaquin*, operating between Oakland Pier and Los Angeles via Fresno and Bakersfield, received lightweight, streamlined cars and became the *San Joaquin Daylight*. June 2, 1946, saw through Los Angeles-Sacramento cars added to the *San Joaquin Daylight*, running the 57 miles between Lathrop and the state capital as the *Sacramento Daylight*. The *Shasta Daylight* was inaugurated July 10, 1949, covering the 714 miles between Oakland Pier and Portland in 15 hours.

Nor was the *Lark* forgotten in the modernization program. On May 1, 1941, it became the West's first all-private-room train. SP advertised it as "the newest and finest overnight train in America . . . completely streamlined — beautiful beyond description." Each *Lark* included refurbished head-end cars,

13 all-room Pullmans, and a triple-unit articulated "*Lark* Club," all painted a dignified two-tone gray, somewhat like the 1938 Twentieth Century Limited. The last few cars of the train, including the observation-lounge-sleeper, formed the *Oakland Lark*, running along the east side of San Francisco Bay between San Jose and Oakland Pier.

As rail passenger travel declined in the 1960's, Southern Pacific sought to discontinue both the *Shasta Daylight* and the *Lark*. The *Shasta Daylight* died slowly, after several years of triweekly and summer-only operation, but the discontinuance of the *Lark* became a *cause célèbre*, making newspaper headlines as humorist Stan Freberg matched wits with SP management. The *San Joaquin* and *Sacramento Daylights* operated until the advent of Amtrak, though barren of amenities. The *Coast Daylight* continued in operation under Amtrak, running through to Seattle triweekly as the *Coast Starlight* and making connections at Los Angeles to and from San Diego.

SLEEPERS with 6 sections, 6 roomettes, and 4 double bedrooms came to the Lark in 1942 and 1943. They appear just behind the mail car in the Lark leaving Burlingame for San Francisco, 18 miles away (far left), and ahead of the observation car — the former Muskingum River — in the train nearing its southern terminal (above). Heavyweight diners and lounges occasionally replaced the triple-unit Lark Club, as they did one overcast morning as the northbound Lark curved along the shore of the bay and into a tunnel near South San Francisco.

Lima Locomotive Works, author's collection.

MANY considered the 30 locomotives of the GS-4 class, built by Lima Locomotive Works in 1941, Southern Pacific's finest passenger power.

BAGGAGE-COACH No. 3303 was constructed in 1939 for the second set of Daylight equipment. Note such well-thought-out details as the flush-fitting baggage door, the baggage elevator, and the wind wing at the vestibule door to protect a train-man looking out to inspect the train.

Pullman-Standard.

COACH 2357 (right), with its smooth sides and high windows, was identical to Shasta Daylight cars. Built in 1954, it was one of the last long-haul passenger cars built for SP.

Pullman-Standard.

Pullman-Standard.

THE wing-type journal boxes of the trucks resembled a three-cornered hat, earned the nickname "Napoleon Bonaparte truck."

332

Pullman-Standard.

PARLOR CAR 3002 (above), built in 1939 for the Morning Daylight, had 27 revolving chairs and a drawing room seating 5. Parlor car of 1937 train (below) was decorated in shades of tan and green.

Pullman-Standard.

TAVERN-COFFEE SHOP car of the 1937 Daylight, with its semi-circular seats and multi-color indirect lighting, was so popular that full tavern cars such as 10313 (below) were built in 1938, along with coffee-shop cars. The 10313 became SP's first automatic buffet car.

Pullman-Standard.

BAGGAGE elevator (left) made a trial ascent while car was still on shop trucks. Coach 2493 (above) carried the San Joaquin emblem.

All photos, unless otherwise credited, Pullman-Standard.

THE 1939 and 1941 equipment included 203-foot 6-inch-long triple-unit coffee shop-kitchen-diner cars (top) that seated 152 for meals. London & North Eastern had used a similar concept in 1928.

DINER of the 1937 Daylight seated 40. The decor was green walls and carpet, rust upholstery. SP's salad bowl was a menu favorite.

THE ultimate in dining and lounge facilities for the Cascade of 1950 was provided by this triple-unit dormitory-kitchen-diner-lounge.

HEAVYWEIGHT lounge 2976 (right) was rebuilt in 1942 from a club-baggage car for standby Lark service.

PULLMAN built a pair of two-tone gray Lark Club triple units (above) in 1941. Advertised as "$247,000 worth of luxury for dining and lounging," they contained crew dormitory space and a kitchen in the first unit, a diner in the second, and a lounge in the third. The total length was over 200 feet. Interior view (right) looks across the articulation into the lounge.

Lark

THE high windows of triple-unit coffee shop-kitchen-diner 10262-10263-10264, built in 1949, mark it as built for the Shasta Daylight. During the mid-1960's it ran on the Coast Daylight.

DOME-LOUNGE 3601 was painted Union Pacific yellow and gray for Overland Route service. SP rebuilt seven Daylight cars into domes.

PASSENGERS on the Houston-Dallas Sunbeam of SP's Texas subsidiary, the Texas & New Orleans, were served meals on special **Sunbeam china in diner-observation-lounges 950 and twin 951. The frame of 950 was used as the basis for dome-lounge car 3606.**

EVEN baggage and mail rode in streamlined cars on the Shasta Daylight. No. 5001 later operated on the Cascade over the same route.

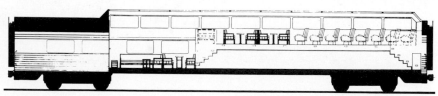

OBSERVATION-PARLOR car 2950 entered SP's Sacramento shops in 1954, was rebuilt to dome-lounge 3600 (far left). Most of the seating was on the upper level; dome glass continued over the lower-level lounge (left). A bar served the lounge, and there was a small crew dormitory. Drawing (above) shows a cross-section of SP's dome-lounge design.

Daylight *Sunbeam*

SP.

Pullman-Standard.

Pullman-Standard.

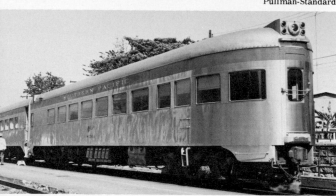

Douglas Wornom.

SIX parlor-observation cars (right) were built between 1937 and 1941 for the Daylights, differing only in minor details. They had a lounge area in the rounded rear end (upper photo) in addition to the usual complement of parlor chairs. Rear view shows the red neon tail sign. Parlor car 2954 (above) has the flat stainless-steel sides that SP began applying to Daylight equipment in 1958 for ease of maintenance.

Pullman-Standard.

All photos, unless otherwise credited, Pullman-Standard.

LARK Pullmans were numbered, not named. No. 106 is a 10-5, similar to the Cascade-series cars of the 1938 Broadway and Century.

THE luxury cars of the Lark were the 4-double-bedroom, 4-compartment, 2-drawing-room cars. The six cars later became SP 9100-9105.

EACH Lark carried four 13-double-bedroom cars like 300 (later SP 9350). The gray livery of the Lark was accented by an emblem similar to the Daylight's, with the train name in orange and a silver circle symbolizing the moon for the overnight run.

THE 1950 order of cars for the Cascade included new Pullmans for the Lark, such as No. 9039, with 10 roomettes and 6 double bedrooms.

Budd.

STAINLESS-STEEL 10-6's built by Budd in 1950 for the Sunset Limited sometimes were assigned to the Lark during seasons of heavy travel.

338

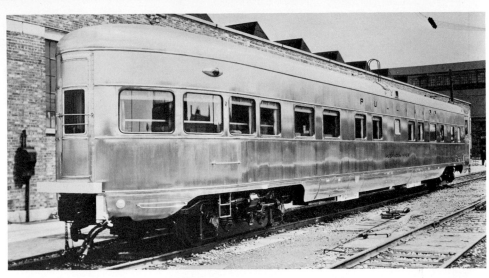

(ABOVE) American Milemaster was built for the 1939 New York World's Fair. Muskingum River (right) was an experimental stainless-steel car built in 1940. Both ran on the Arizona Limited before assignment to the Lark.

AS replacement cars, American Milemaster and Muskingum River were rebuilt with blunt observation ends (below), numbered 9500 and 9501. No. 9501 was wrecked in 1959; ex-American Milemaster became EMD's test car.

Pullman Company.

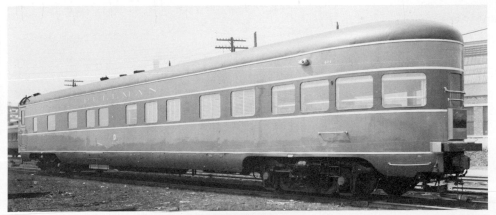

THE Lark's observation cars, 400 and 401, part of the Oakland section of the train, had a drawing room, a compartment, 2 double bedrooms, and a buffet. The lounge had deep-cushioned chairs and wood-paneled walls; on the rear was a neon tail sign. Both cars were wrecked in 1942.

1 ON September 30, 1965, an interesting era in American railroading ended quietly during the early morning rain in the Corn Belt. Passenger service on the Chicago Great Western Railway ceased as trains 13 and 14 slowly ground to their final halts in the Omaha and Minneapolis terminals respectively.

It was an era in which aggressive management of a modest grain belt railway strove hard to achieve passenger-train prominence. The record included one innovation after another: unique Mann Boudoir all-room cars of the 1880's; the elegant *Great Western Limited;* Electro-Motive Company's first gas-electric rail car; "The *Red Bird* — No-Stop Train"; pioneer rail-air services; and the renowned *Blue Bird,* forerunner of all diesel-electric streamliners. . . . The late Lucius Beebe would have termed them "fragrant memories."

Great trains

The small ro

CORN BELT ROUTE

Promoter of the Great Western and its predecessors — the Minnesota & Northwestern Railroad and the Chicago, St. Paul & Kansas City Railway — was Alpheus Beede Stickney, a Down East schoolteacher and lawyer from Maine who became a leading Middle West railroad entrepreneur. A. B. Stickney, also a builder of the Canadian Pacific and Great Northern, brought the Great Western into being and expanded it after overcoming early financial difficulties.

The Minnesota & Northwestern operated its first train on October 3, 1885, from Lyle, Minn., to St. Paul through a sparsely settled area which later became one of the most fertile agricultural regions of the United States.

At its peak, the Chicago Great Western operated 1500 miles connecting the states of Illinois, Iowa, Kansas, Minnesota, Missouri, and Nebraska, with terminals at Chicago, Kansas City, Omaha, St. Paul, and Minneapolis, in what has been titled "The Breadbasket of America."

of the Great Western

at did a big job for passengers until hard times intervened

GREAT WESTERN 1002

Author's collection.

FAMILY relaxed in privacy aboard all-room Mann Boudoir car on cover of this promotional brochure.

Great trains of the Great Western

In the beginning

IN November 1886, the Minnesota & Northwestern line from St. Paul reached Dubuque, Ia., where it connected with the Illinois Central Railroad to Chicago. A year later, on August 1, 1887, after completion of the half-mile-long Winston Tunnel in western Illinois, the Minnesota & Northwestern route to Chicago was opened, and the first through trains were placed in service between the Twin Cities and Chicago. Also in 1886, the Chicago, St. Paul & Kansas City Railway was incorporated in Iowa to construct a line from Waterloo via Des Moines to St. Joseph, Mo. On December 8, 1887, the Chicago, St. Paul & Kansas City Railway purchased all of the railway and property of the short-lived Minnesota & Northwestern Railroad.

For overnight passenger trains on the new system, A. B. Stickney negotiated a contract with Col. William D'Alton Mann for lease of his unique Mann Boudoir sleeping cars; and until February 1889, when George Pullman purchased the Mann enterprise, the Stickney trains carried the blue-and-gold all-room cars. In Europe several years previously Colonel Mann had helped organize a predecessor of the International Wagons-Lits Company. (See page 498.) During his later years Mann retired from railroading altogether and returned to New York City, where he published a gossip newspaper. After a stormy career he passed away in 1920 at the age of 81.

In 1889, the Chicago, St. Paul & Kansas City offered a $100 prize for a new herald. The winning design, submitted by a Wabash Railroad ticket agent, was a maple leaf on which the veins formed a map of the railroad. For the next two decades the Chicago Great Western was known as the "Maple Leaf System."

On January 16, 1892, in a complex financial maneuver, the Chicago Great Western Railway was incorporated to effect a reorganization of the Chicago, St. Paul & Kansas City Railway. A. B. Stickney became president of the new corporation.

Purchase of the Leavenworth & St. Joseph Railway in July 1893 ensured trackage rights into Kansas City, Mo. Completion of the line to Council Bluffs and rights over the Union Pacific afforded entry into Omaha. Through service into that Nebraska gateway city began on January 3, 1904.

Superintendent of Motive Power on the Maple Leaf road was a serious young man named Walter P. Chrysler. Chrysler was in charge of the main shops at Oelwein, Ia., at the time a trip to the 1908 Chicago Automobile Show changed the course of his life. While he was at the auto show his eyes fell upon a shiny white Locomobile trimmed with red. It was love at first

sight for Chrysler, who bought the $5000 car on the spot. Several years later Walter Chrysler left the CGW to work for the American Locomotive Company. In 1912 he finally entered the automobile industry with Buick.

Back in St. Paul, A. B. Stickney continued to pilot the Great Western under the most difficult conditions. Competition from the long-established neighboring railroads proved to be insurmountable, and the Maple Leaf Route entered a period of hard times.

Pullman-Standard.

FURNITURE CAR 50534 touted CGW's Maple Leaf Route slogan in 1903. Wabash ticket agent won a $100 contest for leaf herald design.

BLACK AND YELLOW folder of Minnesota & Northwestern in 1887 (right) announced Mann Boudoir car service to Chicago. Chicago, St. Paul & Kansas City's 1893 timetable (lower right) advertised "Fast Line" service through the "Garden Spot of America" to the Columbian Exposition in Chicago, lured readers inside with views of world's fair.

STEEL ENGRAVING depicts Chicago, St. Paul & Kansas City train with Mann car on the rear and fast-moving 4-4-0 leading the way.

Author's collection.

Author's collection.

Great trains of the Great Western

Collection of James Konas.

GREAT WESTERN LIMITED of 1908 gave riders view of University of Minnesota as train entered Minneapolis over NP bridge behind 2-6-2 911.

Author's collection.

"COMFORTS of Home and Club" were described in Corn Belt Route timetable of CGW.

The Felton era

SEPTEMBER 1, 1909, marked the beginning of the Felton era on the Chicago Great Western. On that date the property was sold at foreclosure and conveyed to a new ownership. Corporate headquarters were moved from St. Paul to Chicago.

Samuel Morse Felton was recognized as one of the most distinguished railway executives when he assumed the presidency of the newly organized "Corn Belt Route." His many worthy accomplishments included a reputation as "doctor of sick railroads." In that capacity he assisted his friend E. H. Harriman. Felton during the course of his career served as President of the Queen & Crescent Route, Alabama Great Southern, Chicago & Alton, Mexican Central, Pere Marquette, and finally the Chicago Great Western. During World War I he was appointed Director General of Military Railways and was awarded the first U. S. Distinguished Service Medal bestowed on a civilian.

Sam Felton promptly set about reviving the ailing Corn Belt Route. Fifteen million dollars was authorized for betterments: new motive power and rolling stock, and improved right of way with automatic electric block signals. A new crack train, the *Great Western Limited*, was placed in service between Chicago and the Twin Cities.

The *Limited* was proclaimed "the highest type of passenger train operated anywhere." "No other train so good as this," stated another advertisement during an era when the Chicago-Twin Cities trade was coveted by seven competing routes: CGW, Chicago & North Western, Burlington, Milwaukee Road, Rock Island, Illinois Central-Minneapolis & St. Louis, and Soo.

The *Limited* was refurbished with luxurious Pullman equipment, including compartment-observation cars newly withdrawn from the New York Central's *Twentieth Century Limited*. Standard sleepers contained electric fans and white enameled washrooms. Easy-riding coaches had dark red plush upholstery. Elegant buffet cars completed the consist.

Departure at both terminals was at dinnertime, with arrival scheduled for the following morning after breakfast.

BUFFET CAR 142, Pullman-built in 1903, was termed a "house car" and was planned to look like a residence. Smoking room had Empire finish with oak woodwork and ormolu decoration.

Pullman-Standard.

Chicago Great Western Railroad

the Legionnaire

CHICAGO·ROCHESTER·ST. PAUL·MINNEAPOLIS

Chicago Great Western
TO
ROCHESTER
NEW
No-Stop Train
Commencing July 15th

NOW
COMBINED RAIL
AND AIR SERVICE
via
Chicago Great Western
and Universal Air Lines System to
ST. LOUIS-
CLEVELAND
Safety - Speed - Comfort - Reliability

The glorious Twenties

DURING the decade of the 1920's the Great Western inaugurated three unique de luxe trains: "The No-Stop Rochester Train — *Red Bird*"; the *Legionnaire*; and the *Blue Bird*. In addition, the Corn Belt Route purchased the first gas-electric rail car built by the newly incorporated Electro-Motive Company.

On July 15, 1923, the road introduced the "No-Stop Train," predecessor of the *Red Bird*, between the Twin Cities and Rochester, Minn. Scheduled time was 3 hours 25 minutes. Equipment included an all-steel buffet-parlor-observation car serving "famously good meals." Reduced fares were an extra feature of the train. Increased demand for service to Rochester resulted from the growing fame of the Mayo Clinic established by Dr. William Mayo in 1889. Continued expansion of the medical center caused steadily increasing patronage of the Great Western service.

The Great Western had the distinction of being the first customer of the Electro-Motive Engineering Corporation of Cleveland, predecessor of the great General Motors Diesel locomotive division. In 1923 Electro-Motive's struggling engineers, working in conjunction with St. Louis Car Company and the nearly bankrupt Winton Automobile Company of Cleveland, developed "Car Number One," M-300, which was consigned to the Chicago Great Western. The CGW agreed to purchase the rail car if it would pull a 35-ton trail car at 50 mph and "run for 30 days in regular service with no more than two 15-minute delays at final terminals due to mechanical trouble."

For one month, August 1924, Electro-Motive M-300 operated between Fort Dodge and Mason City. Fast troubleshooting, brilliant innovations, after-hour toil, and numerous prayers kept the record unblemished. The railroad bought M-300, and the new company survived its first major crisis.

Also in 1924, a trip by Samuel Felton to England had an interesting reaction on the railroad. The simplified styling and colorful liveries of English locomotives impressed the Great Western's Chairman, who ordered the *Rochester Special* "No-Stop Train" refurbished promptly upon his return from

EMD.

FIRST Electro-Motive gas-electric, CGW M-300, was built by St. Louis Car in 1924; developed 175 h.p.

FREE of external piping and fitted with a flanged stack, Baldwin-built 4-6-2 No. 925 exhibited CGW's English style leanings.

Great trains of the Great Western

DINING CAR 197 and mate 196 were built by Pullman in 1916 for CGW Limited operating between Chicago and the Twin Cities.

CLUB CAR 143 and mate 144 measured 72½ feet coupler to coupler; were built by Pullman in 1911 for Great Western Limited. Advertising by CGW stated that steel car 143 "has no peer."

OBSERVATION 167 and mate 168 were steel cafe-parlors built by Pullman in 1915. The 80-foot 5-inch cars contained smoking room, parlor, cafe, and kitchen; were painted red and gold in 1924 for CGW's famous train, the Red Bird.

Great trains of the Great Western

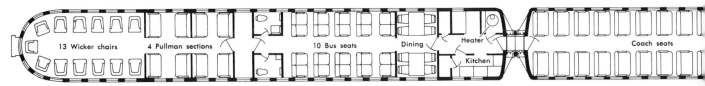

OFFICIAL portrait of Blue Bird of 1929 reveals that wholesale reconstruction of equipment could not quite hide its McKeen car ancestry. Motor train was painted blue with gold leaf trim.

PRAIRIE-TO-PACIFIC conversion, No. 916, displays red-and gold livery introduced in 1924 for Twin Cities-Rochester Red Bird

abroad. Brooks 4-6-2 No. 916 and four cars were painted red with gold leaf striping and lettering. The new train soon became known as the *Red Bird*.

In connection with the continuing improvement of passenger operation, the *Legionnaire* was chosen as the prize-winning name for the Chicago-Rochester-Twin Cities overnight inaugurated on January 16, 1925. Selection of the title was the result of a contest in which 60,000 names were submitted. *Legionnaire* paid tribute during the post-World War I era to ex-soldiers of the nation, many of whom were in the employ of the road. The all-steel train carried the latest types of equipment, including Pullmans from Chicago for Minneapolis, Rochester, Des Moines, and St. Joseph. At Oelwein, Ia., hub of the system, the Kansas City-Minneapolis car was switched. Rearranging the cars at Oelwein for transfer to other terminals was a long-standing Great Western practice.

The most extraordinary Great Western passenger train of

all was placed in service between the Twin Cities and Rochester on January 13, 1929. The unique equipment consisted of three lightweight McKeen rail cars, rebuilt and luxuriously outfitted at the road's Oelwein shop. The new train, christened *Blue Bird*, was painted entirely in blue except for the running gear and the cooling system on the motor-car roof. All striping and lettering was in gold leaf.

The head-end motor car contained an Electro-Motive 300-h.p. six-cylinder gasoline engine and mail and baggage compartments. The second car was a comfortable day coach. The third and last car was an unusual parlor-club-cafe-lounge car with bucket-type bus seats and 4 Pullman-style sections for invalids en route to the Mayo Clinic — the first Pullman accommodations to be built in a gas-electric train. *Railway Age* noted the provision of practically every modern convenience, refinement, and innovation to please the most fastidious traveler. Because of its internal combustion motive power, lightweight construction, and unusual advanced styling, the *Blue Bird* has been justifiably termed the forerunner of the streamlined train in America.

Great Western General Passenger Agent Roy A. Bishop was one of the early advocates of combined rail-air service. In 1929 he developed a train-plane arrangement with Universal

PLANS show interior configurations of (right to left) Blue Bird's motor-mail-baggage car 1000; coach trailer 1001; and cafe-parlor-Pullman-lounge trailer 1002. The photo depicts the red-and-gold Rochester Special of 1924, which was later renamed the Red Bird.

13 Wicker chairs   4 Pullman sections   10 Bus seats   Dining   Heater   Kitchen   Coach seats

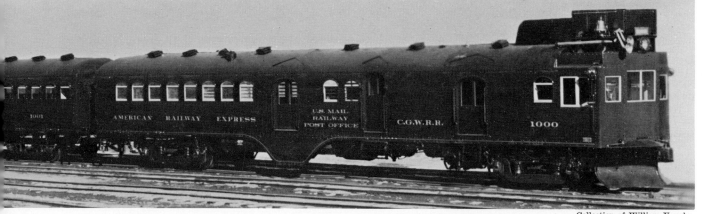

Collection of William Vaughn.

Author's collection.

Air Lines System. Passengers from the Twin Cities, Des Moines, and Waterloo traveled overnight by train to and from Chicago. Special connecting motor coaches shuttled between Chicago's Grand Central Station and the Municipal Airport, where trimotored airplanes connected with Cleveland or St. Louis.

Great Western passengers from the West en route to New York used the Cleveland flight to overtake the eastbound NYC *Twentieth Century Limited* in the Forest City, thereby gaining an extra half day in Chicago for business or shopping.

The decade of the 1920's ended with great optimism for the future of the passenger service.

Plans and photo, collection of William Vaughn.

MINNESOTAN crosses Fox River at St. Charles, Ill., in August 1934 with 4-6-0 509 and five cars, including Pullman restaurant-sleeper.

Great trains of the Great Western

The final years

THE 1929 stock market crash, followed by the death in 1930 of Sam Felton, hastened the end of the extraordinary passenger services on the Great Western.

First to go was the rail-air service which had barely "got off the ground." In March 1930, the *Legionnaire* was renamed the *Minnesotan*, and most of the amenities were eliminated. In 1931 the *Blue Bird* was withdrawn; one year later the *Red Bird* was abolished. During 1933 the famed Great Western dining cars were replaced by Pullman-operated combined restaurant-sleepers with grill-type meals. Gone forever were the renowned $1.50 table d'hote dinners "with a hint of 'old Virginny' in the cooking," served "not for profit, but for that intangible asset good will." Clearly, hard times had come to the Great Western.

Passenger operations never recovered their former glory. Unlike most American railroads, the Great Western profited little from World War II traffic. The great postwar streamlined passenger train era never quite arrived either — except for three lightweight baggage cars built by Pullman-Standard in 1946 and two aging ex-*Hiawatha* coaches purchased second-hand from the Milwaukee Road in 1961.

In 1948 a group of shareholders became deeply concerned about the condition of the railroad and its future. New management was brought in to rebuild the road and exploit the freight traffic potential of its main lines, particularly the St. Paul-Kansas City route. The new executives quickly set about to make the Great Western a freight-carrying railroad. Track improvement, complete dieselization, and industrial development were the order of the day. Within several years the Chicago Great Western was one of the most efficient railroads in the country, with one of the highest ratios of gross ton-miles per train-mile.

By 1953 more than one half of passenger train-miles were eliminated, along with all parlor, buffet, and Pullman sleeping cars. The remaining mainline passenger services consisted of one local train per day offering baggage and mail accommodations. Passenger operation into Chicago ended in 1956; Minneapolis-Kansas City service was discontinued in 1962.

The once great passenger operation dwindled to trains 13 and 14, successors to the Twin Cities-Omaha *Nebraska Limited*. When the U. S. Mail contract was not renewed, the end came quickly. On September 30, 1965, "varnish" trains on the Chicago Great Western passed into history.

On April 27, 1967, the Interstate Commerce Commission unanimously approved merger of the Chicago Great Western Railway into the Chicago & North Western Railway after specifying measures to protect the competing Soo Line Railroad and also the employees of the merging lines.

COMING AND GOING: The Minnesotan departs Forest Park, Ill., in the summer of 1934 with Pacific No. 930 on the point and Pullman restaurant-sleeper Old Elm Club carrying the markers. A fascinated youth occupies the "railfan's seat" at the rear.

353

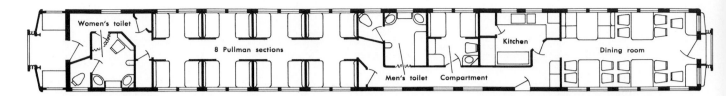

OLD ELM CLUB and twin Rochester Club were 1917-model 16-section sleepers rebuilt in the depression to 8-section, 1-compart-ment, kitchen, 18-seat dining room cars when hard times bumped full dining cars out of the Chicago Great Western's timetable.

Great trains of the Great Western

TRAIN 12, the Mill Cities Limited, weaves through the throat of Kansas City Union Station as it departs for Minneapolis at 12:45 p.m. on March 24, 1949. Behind Pacific No. 928 are three head-end revenue cars, a coach, and a Pullman restaurant-sleeper.

James G. LaVake.

THREE-CAR train 6 on the GN's bridge at Minneapolis in 1952 includes midtrain Railway Express car that was the only light-weight equipment purchased new by the CGW. Diesel and consist are painted in post-World War II maroon with stripes.

Collection of V. Allan Vaughn.

EX-HIAWATHA lightweight coach was purchased from Milwau-kee Road in 1961 and painted maroon, sans striping. No. 200 oper-ated in passenger service until CGW terminated all varnish in 1965 — a far cry in time and speed from its Hi service behind 4-4-2's.

OLYMPIAN

1 TWO THOUSAND years before the birth of Christ, the ancient Greeks believed that Vulcan, the blacksmith son of Juno, had wrought upon his forge on Mount Olympus the sun chariot which Apollo daily drove across the heavens. This marvelous vehicle was believed to have wheels of gold, spokes of silver, and a seat of chrysolites (topaz) and diamonds.

Forty centuries later, a great new American transcontinental train was built for the Chicago, Milwaukee & St. Paul and the Chicago, Milwaukee & Puget Sound railways to operate between Chicago and the Pacific Northwest. It was completed in 1911 and ready for inspection, but the new flagship lacked a name. Of hundreds

submitted, _The Olympian_ — "Fit for the Gods," was chosen as the most appropriate title for the new transcontinental "chariot." _The Olympian_ and a companion train, _The Columbian_, began operation on May 29, 1911.

The new through passenger line from Chicago and the Twin Cities to Seattle and Tacoma had been conceived by the "St. Paul Road" (CM&StP) and its Puget Sound subsidiary (CM&PS). The route was the shortest between Chicago and the Pacific Northwest, and its main line had been engineered to the highest standards, constructed with minimum grades and curves, and protected with block signals. The immense undertaking cost 200 million dollars. No expense had been spared to ensure

Both photos, Kaufmann & Fabry, courtesy of CM&StP.

The OLYMPIAN

Fit for the gods

the greatest degree of safety and comfort to passengers.

Twenty complete train consists — the first ones of steel construction to operate between Chicago and the Northwest — were required to equip _The Olympian_ and _The Columbian_. _The Olympian_'s equipment was finished on the interior with expensive carved hardwoods. All of its cars were electric-lighted throughout with Mazda lamps.

"The West has never had a train approaching [_The Olympian_] in excellence. The East has none of equal desirability for all classes of travel." — _CM&PS brochure._

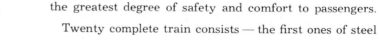

BARNEY & SMITH steel observation car Alaska on the Olympian in 1926 sported a ruby-glass drumhead and striped awnings.

357

The OLYMPIAN

Orange-and-maroon transcontinentals

HISTORICALLY, there were three generations of *Olympians*. May 28, 1911, marked the birth of the original train, all-steel and steam powered. The first Nos. 15 and 16 were composed exclusively of railroad-owned and -operated equipment beautifully painted yellow-orange with maroon trim and gold lining. The sleeping cars were touted as having "longer-higher-wider berths." In 1916 the railroad completed the first section of electrified line over the Continental Divide and proclaimed "The dawn of the electrical era in railroading."*

The new *Olympian*, "Queen of the Transcontinental Trains," began service on August 1, 1927. Under the terms of a new contract with the Pullman Company, the St. Paul Road sleeping cars were replaced with new orange-and-maroon Pullmans. Electrification of the railroad continued until, ultimately, 656 miles of electrified line had been built. At a memorable auction on November 22, 1926, the bankrupt Chicago, Milwaukee & St. Paul was sold for 140 million dollars. Corporate transfer to the new owner, Chicago, Milwaukee, St. Paul & Pacific (The Milwaukee Road), became effective midnight, January 13, 1928.

The third and final *Olympian* — the diesel-powered *Olympian Hiawatha* — was launched on June 29, 1947. In order to meet new competition (i.e., the *Empire Builder* and *North Coast Limited*), the *Olympian Hi* had to be pressed into service with both streamlined and heavyweight equipment. Complete streamlining was achieved in 1949 when new Pullmans and bedroom-Skytop Lounges arrived from Pullman-Standard. Super Domes were added in 1952. The P-S Skytops externally were similar to previous *Hiawatha* solarium cars, but contained more glass area forward.

Despite quality service and intensive promotion, the *Olympian Hiawatha* lost money and was discontinued on May 22, 1961. Contributing to its demise were first-generation jet airliners and competing trains, including UP's *City of Portland* which, ironically, had been operated jointly by the Milwaukee Road since 1955. Through Pullmans for Seattle on the *City* were handled beyond Portland by the former *Train of Tomorrow*.

*In February 1973, the Milwaukee Road announced plans to phase out the electrified operation owing to cost of upgrading and equipment replacement.

DONE! Last-spike ceremony for CM&PS was held on May 19, 1909, 4 miles west of Garrison, Mont., in the Bitter Root Mountains.

CM&StP.

CMStP&P.

EVEN train gates at Chicago Union Station carried out the Hiawatha theme (above). Meanwhile, passengers begin check-in for Olympian Hiawatha.

PROMOTION of electric locomotion: CM&StP 2-6-6-2 battles a bipolar in a tug-of-war staged at Kent, Wash., on March 6, 1920.

DIESELS for the 1947 Olympian Hi: Fairbanks-Morse "Erie-builts" emblazoned with chrome trim and gray, orange, and maroon colors.

359

EARLY EXPLORERS never had it this good! Passengers in an open-air observation car on the westbound Olympian circa 1939 (above) "explore" the wilds of the Big Belt Mountains near Lombard, Mont.

LARGEST electrics on the CMStP&P were the Baldwin-Westinghouse EP3's. (Below) EP3 pauses on Clear Creek trestle near Falcon, Idaho (in the Bitter Root Mountains) in 1929 with the Chicago-bound Olympian.

ALCO-GE bipolar No. E4 (ex-10253) escorts the Olympian Hiawatha through the Cascade Mountains in 1951. The 265-ton electrics were sometimes referred to by crews as "caterpillars."

The OLYMPIAN

SLEEKNESS of Class F5 4-6-2 No. 3123 (right) was somewhat emphasized by its pronounced headlight. Alco built 50 of these 69-inch-drivered Pacifics in 1910 to supplement 20 F5's built in the CM&StP shops. Note that 3123 is lettered for the CM&PS.

Alco.

AC&F.

FRESH from the shops, CM&StP baggage-RPO 650 (above) weighs in at 118,300 pounds. American Car & Foundry built the car in 1913. Olympian's electric lights were powered by a dynamo in the baggage car (below); the dynamo itself was powered by steam from the locomotive. An electrician accompanied the Olympian at all times.

The OLYMPIAN

Kaufmann, Weimar & Fabry, courtesy of CM&StP.

CM&StP.

EIGHTY-ONE-FOOT CM&PS tourist sleeper B-9 (below) was built by Pullman in 1911 for the original Olympian. Interior contained a large smoking room, a small kitchen with a cooking range, and — for the economy minded — 14 sections upholstered in rattan (above).

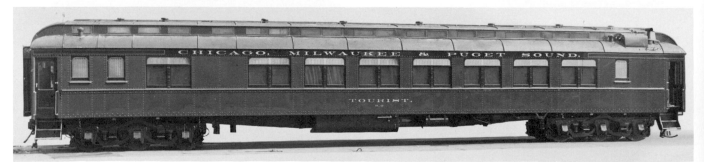

Pullman-Standard.

362

CM&StP diner (left) was one of 20 dining cars built by Pullman in 1911 for Olympian and Columbian service. The eight cars lettered for CM&StP were identified by letters only: G, J, Q, V, Y, Z, AB, and AC. The 12 CM&PS dining cars were numbered 4505-4516.

ONEIDA (above) was one of the railroad-owned sleepers that operated on the first version of the Olympian. It had 10 sections, 2 compartments, and 1 drawing room. Compartment interior of CM&StP Barney & Smith sleeping car (below right) featured fine wood paneling for which the Dayton (O.) carbuilder was famous.

ALBERTON (below) contained a ladies' tea room, men's club room, smoking and writing rooms, library, bath, barbershop, and tailor facilities. Its observation-lounge (above) was furnished with in-laid Cuban mahogany walls and a beamed ceiling. Alberton was one of 10 such Barney & Smith cars built between 1910-1912.

THE BARNEY & SMITH CAR CO.
BUILDERS.
DAYTON, OHIO. 1910

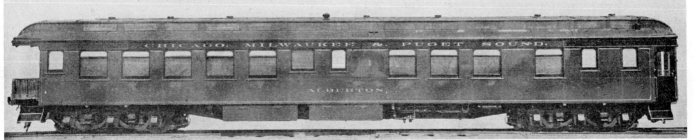

NORTHERNS often could be found wheeling the Olympian over the Idaho Division. Baldwin built Class S-1 No. 9700 (above) in 1930.

BIPOLARS such as 10250 (above) could transform 3000 volts into 3480 h.p. to conquer the 2.2 per cent ruling grade of the Cascades.

Alco-GE built five of these CM&StP Class EP-2's (1-B+D+D+B-1) in 1918. No. 10251 was donated to the St. Louis Museum of Transport.

READY for the 1927 Olympian, tourist car 5706 stands outside Milwaukee shops after being rebuilt and fitted with wide letterboards and roller-bearing trucks. Originally numbered B-7, the car was built by Pullman for the Olympian of 1911.

The OLYMPIAN

COMPLETED in 1931, wide-windowed diner 5143 (below) and twin Dan Healy were among the last heavyweight cars built by Pullman. The two rolling restaurants served on the Pioneer and Olympian, and were supervised by George Rector. Wood-paneled interior (left) contained spacious 2-4 seating for 36 persons.

Pullman-Standard.

SLUMBER came easy in 8-section, 2-compartment, 1-drawing-room Okoboji (above), one of 62 Pullmans built in 1927 for the Olympian.

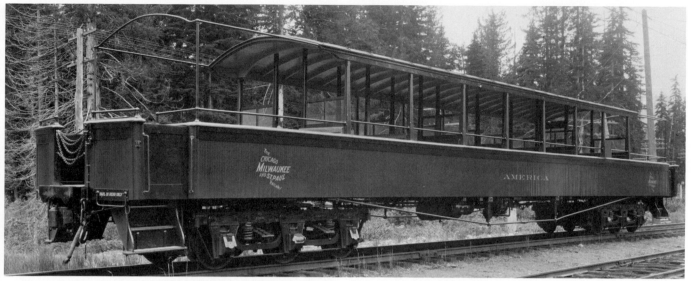

CMStP&P.

TRAIN travelers proclaim, "See America best — by rail!" But in the 1920's and 1930's patrons could see rails best from America (above) and other wooden-seat open-air cars — built from old sleepers, parlors — attached to the Olympian in electrified zones.

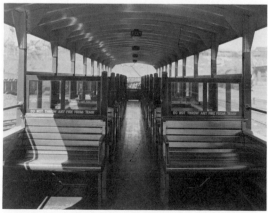

CMStP&P.

HIGH WINDOWS of Pullman observation-lounge City of Everett (left and below) allowed passengers a fine view of the Rockies and Cascades. Floodlight above platform was for sightseeing at night. Car also had two baths, barbershop, and a soda fountain.

Both photos, Pullman-Standard.

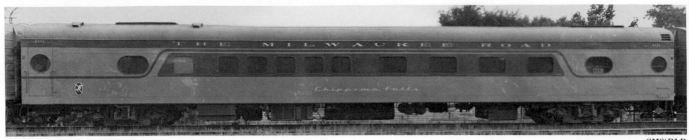

WIDER, longer berths were a feature of the Touralux cars built at Milwaukee shops in 1947. Chippewa Falls (above), intended for the exclusive use of women and children, was fitted with 24 coach seats and 8 sections. Tulare (below) had 14 sections and later was renamed Mt. Stuart. Touralux interior (facing page) had Milwaukee Road's traditional wood-veneer decor.

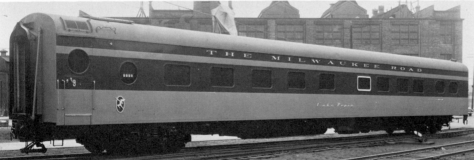

RAILROAD-BUILT diners on the Olympian Hiawatha (above left) seated 40 in seats for two, angled toward windows (for scenic side orders). Lake Pepin (left) was one of ten Lake-series 10-roomette, 6-double-bedroom sleepers built by Pullman in 1948 for the Olympian Hi. Cars had the cast Hiawatha emblem.

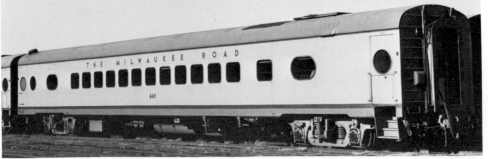

GRAY and armour-yellow livery à la Union Pacific, shown on coach No. 660 (left), was applied to Hiawatha cars after the mid-1950's. Originally No. 660, nee 550, was a 48-seat car built by the railroad in 1948 for general Hiawatha service. It was rebuilt in 1957 to contain 40 leg-rest seats for Overland service.

Pullman-Standard.

SIGHTSEEING (above) was pleasant under glass — 325 square feet on each of 10 Milwaukee Road Super Domes (below) that Pullman-Standard delivered in late 1952. The cars were painted harvest orange and royal maroon.

Kaufmann & Fabry, courtesy of CMStP&P.

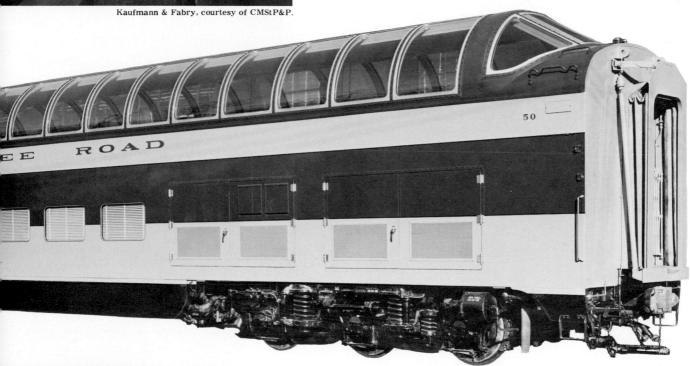

Pullman-Standard.

The OLYMPIAN

Both photos, Pullman-Standard.

COFFEE CREEK (above) had 8 bedrooms and a Skytop Lounge. Pullman-Standard built six of these cars in 1947. The lounge area (left) was styled by designer Brooks Stevens.

The Golden State Limited

THE Golden State Limited departs from Los Angeles for Chicago's La Salle Street Station on May 22, 1924. Patrons bid their farewells from seven of the train's nine sections in a record-breaking movement on the first day of lowered summer fares.

The golden way to the Golden State

IN 1902, the Chicago, Rock Island & Pacific Railway and the El Paso & Rock Island Railway were linked at Santa Rosa, N. Mex., near Tucumcari. Driving of the spike which joined the railroads near the Pecos River produced the Golden State Route, a Chicago-California transcontinental line operated by the Chicago, Rock Island & Pacific; El Paso-Northeastern System (later El Paso & Southwestern System); and Southern Pacific.

To celebrate the completion of the "Low-altitude Route" (and the 50th anniversary of the first Rock Island train),* a de luxe hotel on wheels was created. The *Golden State Limited* — introduced on Sunday November 2, 1902, for the winter season in the Golden State — was advertised as "the most luxuriously equipped train in the world." The route of the new *Limited* was Chicago-Kan-

*The first RI passenger train ran from Chicago to Joliet, Ill. on October 10, 1852.

sas City-El Paso-Los Angeles. A through San Francisco Pullman was operated in connection with the SP *Owl.* Running time was 68 hours, Chicago to Los Angeles; 87 hours, Chicago to San Francisco. The first consist included a Rock Island Atlantic-type locomotive and olive-green wooden Pullmans trimmed with gold and heavily varnished.

For more than 60 years, the *Limited* provided "The Golden Way to the Golden State." (Between May 1903 and December 1904 operation was suspended.) From 1905 to 1906 the train was routed via the Chicago & Alton Railway between Joliet, Ill., and Kansas City. Daily, year-round service was established on January 2, 1910, from Chicago, and on January 6, 1910, from Los Angeles. On December 1, 1919, a San Diego Pullman was added, by connection at Yuma, Ariz., with the San Diego & Arizona

BROCHURE introduced a seasonal Limited in 1902.

and Tijuana & Tecate railways — via Tijuana, Mexico.

Not until the depression and the dawn of the streamlined era did the *Golden State Limited* falter; World War II interfered with the construction of lightweight cars ordered to complete the streamlining of the consist and permit reduction in scheduled time to match the competing limiteds of the Santa Fe and C&NW-UP.

Following World War II, Rock Island officials planned what was to be the ultimate version of the *Limited* — the *Golden Rocket* of 1947. Regrettably, that ill-fated train never traveled a mile.† Instead, the streamlined *Golden State* (no longer termed *Limited*) was inaugurated in 1947. This train survived until February 21, 1968, when Rock Island No. 4 completed its final run from California to La Salle Street Station — on time.

†See *Some Classic Trains*, pages 220-225.

A WORLD WAR I vintage Golden State Limited crosses the bridge over the Canadian River near Logan, N. Mex., with a Santa Fe baggage car and Santa Fe dining car behind CRI&P Vanderbilt-tendered Pacific No. 969.

CRI&P, author's collection.

TWO Golden State cars served in the short-lived Arizona Limited (above) which ran for only two seasons. Red, silver, and maroon 2000-h.p. No. 623, one of four such CRI&P locomotives, was styled by Otto Kuhler and built by Alco-GE in December 1940.

CRI&P.

WESTBOUND travelers depart Chicago's La Salle Street Station in 1924. Colorful drum sign portrays oranges with green leaves.

Serving the famed and fortuned

THE most opulent era of the *Limited* was during the prosperous 1920's when Rock Island and Southern Pacific steam power pulled luxurious all-steel cars built by the Pullman Company. The *Golden State Limited* was recognized as superior and de luxe. During its first three decades of operation, it competed favorably with the renowned Chicago-California luxury limiteds of the Santa Fe and the Chicago & North Western-Union Pacific. The "exclusively first-class" train regularly carried 10 Pullman sleepers from Chicago, Des Moines, Kansas City, Minneapolis, Memphis, and St. Louis through to Santa Barbara and San Diego as well as to Los Angeles. Each day six complete *Limiteds* (some in several sections) paraded across the continent — three westbound and three eastbound.

The *Golden State Limited* was a favorite of personages of the day. Chewing-gum magnate William Wrigley Jr. wrote:

> "I had the pleasure of returning from Los Angeles yesterday on the new *Golden State Limited*. Without exception it was the most comfortable and pleasing ride I have ever had from the Pacific Coast to Chicago."

Notre Dame's "Fighting Irish" football players, along with legions of fans, traveled aboard the *Limited* when their annual game with the University of Southern California "Trojans" was played on the Coast. When film idol Rudolph Valentino died, his body was carried to its final rest aboard the great screen lover's favorite train — the *Golden State Limited*.

IDENTICAL TWINS, Rock Island No. 1671 and El Paso & Southwestern No. 40, wooden observation-smoking cars, were completed by Pullman for the Golden State Limited in 1906, when both the CRI&P and EP&SW were part of the Frisco-Rock Island system.

Pullman-Standard.

TWENTY-NINE redcaps link arms in front of new Alco-built 4-8-2 No. 4033, class M50, considered gigantic when built in August of 1924.

LETTERED for the Golden State Limited, 1925 Pullman club car No. 6505 (above) was a combination baggage-club car complete with men's shower. It had a Harriman-style roof. (Left) Attendant pours White Rock Water (minus the whiskey) during Prohibition as patrons study the routing of the Limited. Note the Havana cigar box.

ROCK ISLAND diner No. 8030 (below) served RI's "Golden State Meals — The Best on Wheels" in a Spanish decor with 4-2 seating (above). The car was constructed by the Pullman Company in 1929. Film actor Adolphe Menjou kindly wrote that "the cuisine [on No. 3] is especially worthy of praise. Every meal was a pleasure."

EL PASO & SOUTHWESTERN dining car 877 was built by American Car & Foundry in November 1924, the year SP acquired the EP&SW.

CARS Rock Land and Island Chalet, built in 1929, contained "oversize dressing rooms." Twenty Rock-series sleepers had 8 sections, 1 drawing room, and 2 compartments. Fifteen Island-series cars had 10 sections, 1 drawing room, and 1 compartment.

PULLMAN Golden State was one of 10 Golden-series observation cars built in March 1924 for service on de luxe trains. The car contained 3 compartments (above left), 2 drawing rooms, a lounge (above right), and a women's lounge with a shower bath.

The finest tra

I "THE Finest Trains on Earth" — that was the name given by George M. Pullman to the superb trains constructed in his own Pullman Palace Car Company shops for service on the Chicago, Burlington & Quincy between Chicago and St. Paul-Minneapolis. The year was 1897. Mr. Pullman, who was then only months away from his death, was generous in his praise. Indeed, in this case he had reason to be. The Chicago-Twin Cities run was among the most competitive in the United States.

AN early poster advertised Burlington Route's selection as the line to carry the fast mail.

ns on earth

Varnish without equal, here or abroad

Although the traffic was divided among seven railways,* three roads fought for the lion's share: Burlington; Chicago & North-Western; and Chicago, Milwaukee & St. Paul. In addition, the premier trains on the Burlington's two major competitors had been built by the arch rivals of George Pullman. The new *North Western Limited* of the North-Western Line was fresh from the Buffalo Shops of the Wagner Palace Car Company; and the *Pioneer Limited* of the St. Paul Road, "bound in covers of yellow and gold," was produced in the Dayton (O.) works of Barney & Smith.

Mr. Pullman, when viewing the new Burlington trains

---

*Chicago & North-Western; Chicago, Milwaukee & St. Paul; Chicago Great Western; Chicago, Rock Island & Pacific; Illinois Central-Minneapolis & St. Louis; and Wisconsin Central.

at Chicago's Union Station, said: "These are the finest cars that ever stood on wheels, and I make the assertion without fear of contradiction, that nothing to equal them has ever been built."

The two *Limiteds* cost over $100,000, and were described by the *Railroad Car Journal* as "the two handsomest trains of cars ever built in any country, with the possible exception of the World's Fair (1893) Trains built by Pullman and Wagner." The St. Paul *Pioneer Press* announced, "It is the finest regular train on earth." The Minneapolis *Tribune* commented, "Nothing finer has been constructed in the World's history." From the East, the Philadelphia *Press* stated, "This limited express train has no equal in America or abroad."

TWO separate five-car trains comprised the Burlington Limited in 1897. Here cars St. Paul, Parthenon, Apollo, Alma, and Winona rest behind No. 357, a Class A-1 4-4-0 built in the railroad's West Burlington (Ia.) shops in 1886.

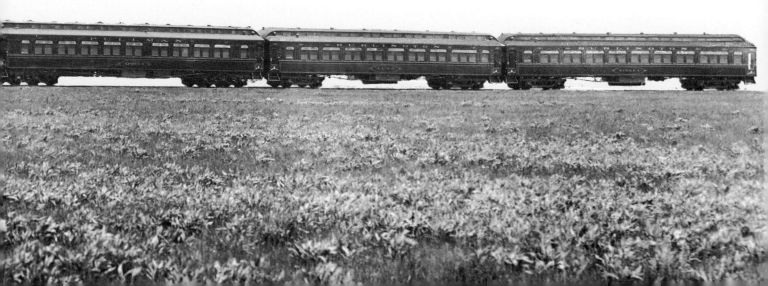

FOUR of the Limited's new cars — resplendent in Pullman green with gold leaf — posed for an official portrait at Pullman in 1897.

Electric lights and whist boards

BURLINGTON Nos. 47 and 48, the *Limited*, between Chicago and St. Paul-Minneapolis, consisted of two trains, identical in construction, equipment, and finish. Each train comprised five cars: combination buffet-library-baggage car; compartment sleeping car; ordinary open-section sleeping car; reclining-chair car; passenger coach. Outside, all cars were of the standard Pullman dark green, ornamented with gold leaf. On the buffet-library car was painted the black-and-white trademark of the Burlington Route.

After an inspection trip to Galesburg, Ill., on May 25, 1897, and an unusual off-line run over the Big Four to Cincinnati

ROOMS of the Angelo featured luxurious fringed upholstery and polished woodwork with inlaid medallions.

on May 26 with a delegation from the Chicago Commercial Club, the *Limited* was exhibited along the line of the Burlington. It was placed in revenue service on June 2, 1897, on the overnight run between Chicago and the Twin Cities, 442 miles via Savanna, Ill., and the Mississippi River Scenic Line.

The new cars embodied all the best and newest ideas of the Pullman establishment. Passengers were pleased with the new method of vestibuling the ends of cars. The vestibules were the full width of the car platform, and in fact formed a little observation room, with glass doors reaching from roof to floor, from which the traveler could safely and comfortably enjoy the scenery along the line.

The whole train was lighted by electricity and also by an auxiliary Pintsch gas system. A new storage-battery system provided the electricity in order to avoid the noise incident to the use of a dynamo. A publicity brochure described the unique method of furnishing electric light:

> The Burlington cars have a new arrangement. Close to the traveler's shoulder on the side of the car are sockets to receive an electric light bulb. All the traveler has to do when he wants such a light is to call the attendant, who will place the bulb, which will be conveniently at hand, in the socket. Presto! He has a light that eclipses the brilliancy that is shed from the roof of the car. The act of thrusting the bulb into place establishes the electric lighting connection.

The combined buffet-library-smoking-baggage cars *Minneapolis* and *St. Paul* contained a grand sideboard, well stocked with all the liquors, beverages, and cigars likely to be sought by the traveling public. The Minneapolis *Journal* of June 2, 1897, stated:

> The buffet smoking car is one of the most convenient cars of its kind ever put on wheels. All the chairs are of wicker work and are luxurious. Besides all the periodicals and literature usually provided, there are duplicate whist boards, which shows how every wish of the traveler has been anticipated. At one end, in large gold letters, are the words, CHICAGO — ST. PAUL — MINNEAPOLIS, in the center a large trademark of the Burlington under which is the word LIMITED (but goodness only knows what is limited in the way of beauty, comfort, and luxury).

The compartment cars *Angelo* and *Apollo* were splendid in their appointments. They contained nine separate rooms — seven compartments and two drawing rooms. The Burlington brochure stated, "It is hardly possible to imagine that a king or a queen of one of Europe's big empires could wish of anything more magnificent to travel in." Each room was a complete apartment with toilet and sanitary facilities artistically concealed. Hand-rubbed wood trim included vermilion wood, St. Jago (Santiago) and Tabasco mahogany, Circassian walnut. The woodwork was richly filled with marquetry of colorful species of trees: green holly, amaranth, primavera, black ebony, rosewood, tulip, satinwood, thuya, English oak (throughout the car were 70 varieties of wood).

The ceilings had curved arches and were decorated in silver and gold leaf on a Nile green background. Flowered upholstery, draperies, and carpet were different in each room.

The standard sleepers contained 16 sections of highly polished vermilion wood upholstered in blue plush. Light blue ceilings were decorated with gold and silver. Each of the upper-berth panels contained a medallion panel of marquetry reported to have cost an additional $500 per car.

The twin chair cars *Alma* and *Maiden Rock* were finished in mahogany with marquetry and catered to passengers who preferred the economy of reclining chairs to a Pullman berth. "Nothing in the way of chair cars hitherto placed on railroad tracks can vie with the new ones of the Burlington Route," declared a company brochure.

Two day coaches, *Winona* and *Savanna*, were provided for local passengers. They too were decorated with choice specimens of marquetry and ornamentation. Each car was equipped with the most modern toilet accessories and a commodious smoking room.

Later, a dining car was operated between Chicago and Rochelle, Ill. It served dinner in the evening on the way to Rochelle and breakfast in the morning on the return to Chicago. The dining car seated 24 and was cooled by electric fans. Each table was equipped with an electric "call" to summon the conductor or steward. Decorations were all in gold. The table settings were of heavy gold and silver plate made especially for the train. Each evening the crystal vases were filled with freshly cut flowers. Of the service, S. S. McClure, publisher of the well-known *McClure's Magazine*, wrote:

> I have traveled on most of the important railroads in America and Europe, and have dined on such of them as have restaurant cars. I would rather dine on a Burlington Route Dining Car than on any railroad dining car that I know of in the world.

Charles Austin Bates, prominent American financier, declared in *Criticisms*:

> The Dining Car Service of the Burlington Route is about the best there is. On every table in the Dining Car appears a fresh bunch of American Beauty roses, one of which the waiter affixes to your coat when you have finished with your meal. The cloth is changed with each guest, no matter how little it is soiled. The menu, though not long, is wonderfully well selected and admirably served.

Finally, the Burlington's brochure publicizing the *Limited* pondered the following question:

> The journey on one of these superb trains sets the passenger to wondering what will be the next great improvement in railway travel — how it will be possible to make any great improvement on the comfort and conveniences of the Burlington Road. Unless an entire hotel can be set on wheels, it is hard to imagine what more can be done to make flying across the country in railway trains an easy and attractive experience.

Dining-Car Service

DINING CAR CRESTON

DINNER

Split Pea Soup, 20c.
Queen Olives, Individual Bottles, 15c.   Assorted Pickles, 10c.
Celery, 15c.
Raw Oysters, half dozen, 25c.
Boiled Salmon, Egg Sauce, 35c.
Boiled Ham and Cabbage, 50c.   Roast Wild Duck, 50c.
Roast Turkey, Cranberry Sauce, 45c.
Prime Roast Beef, 45c.
Rib Ends of Beef, with Brown Potatoes, 35c.
Baked Chicken Pie, 35c.   Baked Pork and Beans, 25c.
Boiled or Mashed Potatoes, 10c.
Braised Sweet Potatoes, 10c.
Sweet Corn, 10c.   Cauliflower, 10c.   Stewed Tomatoes, 10c.
Lobster Salad, 25c.
Apple Pie, 10c.   Pumpkin Pie, 10c.
Cabinet Pudding, 15c.   Plum Pudding, Brandy Sauce, 15c.
Assorted Cake, 15c.   Ice Cream, 15c.
Assorted Fruit in Season, 15c.
Preserved Fruit, Individual Package, 20c.
Roquefort or Club House Cheese, 15c.
Bent's Water Crackers, 10c.
Coffee or Tea, per pot, 25c.   Coffee or Tea, per cup, 10c.

NO SERVICE LESS THAN 25 CENTS TO EACH PERSON.

Any inattention to duty on this car please report to L. N. Hopkins, Commissary, C. B. & Q. R. R., Chicago.

DENVER ARTESIAN WATER USED ON THESE TABLES.

CONTEMPORARY Burlington menu offered roast wild duck for 50 cents, lobster salad for 25 cents, and plum pudding with brandy sauce for 15 cents. Denver artesian water also was served.

AMERICAN STANDARD sisters of Burlington & Missouri River No. 210 pulled the Limited. In 1897 this particular engine was used on the Chicago-to-Denver Mayham Special that made a fast but futile run to race a father to his dying son's bedside.

STEAM SHOVELS used in construction of the line overcame the forces of nature and cut through the rugged countryside.

Building a transcontinental

THE Confederation of Ontario, Quebec, and the Maritime Provinces was effected on July 1, 1867. During the decade that followed Canada came to be regarded as a homeland for immigrating colonists from Europe. Then, with the attainment of political stability in the Dominion, a need arose for a railway to open up the West and link the Pacific Ocean with eastern Canada.

The safeguarding of Canadian interest in the western prairies also became an urgent matter. There was a growing feeling in Ottawa that the United States government was resolved to do anything short of war to secure possession of the western territory. The expanding populations of Manitoba and British Columbia had joined into confederation with the understanding that they would be connected by rail with eastern Canada.

Pressure for construction of the Pacific Railway steadily increased. Government efforts to induce the Grand Trunk Railway to undertake the task were to no avail. Early efforts on the part of the Government itself to build the line in Manitoba progressed slowly; and there was no plan for the formidable crossing of the Rocky Mountains.

As railroad building in the western United States increased, Canadians became more apprehensive about invasion by the Americans. When British Columbia threatened to secede, the Ottawa government in 1880 finally started construction of the railway eastward from the Pacific Coast across the mountains. This effort generally proved fruitless.

Finally, during 1880 a syndicate of Canadian and British railway men and bankers was formed by George Stephen

(later Lord Mount-Stephen), president of the Bank of Montreal. Associated in the venture were Duncan McIntyre, Richard B. Angus, John S. Kennedy, and James J. Hill. In a contract with the Canadian government dated October 20, 1880, the group agreed to have a 2900-mile railway in operation between Montreal and Vancouver within 10 years. In return, the developers were to receive 25 million dollars in cash; 25 million acres of land; and the two segments of railroad (then under construction by the Government) consisting of 712 miles and estimated to be worth 27.7 million dollars.

In 1881 the new Canadian Pacific Railway commenced construction, completing only 130 miles of line west from Winnipeg by year's end. January 1, 1882, saw the arrival of American-born William C. Van Horne, former general superintendent of the Chicago, Milwaukee & St. Paul Railway. Van Horne (later Sir William) was placed in charge of construction; he was soon joined by Thomas G. Shaughnessy, also from the St. Paul

382

STEAM-OPERATED hand car came with a vertical boiler.

TOOL CAR No. 1 cleared the track of rocks and obstructions.

LOCOMOTIVE thirst was quenched by this water tower at Emory.

PRIVATE CAR Eva later was used on the Esquimalt & Nanaimo.

Road. Van Horne promptly announced that he would build 500 miles of track during 1882. By shipping English and German rail to New Orleans, then up the Mississippi River Valley to Winnipeg, Van Horne began laying the iron road immediately after the spring thaw. Working furiously, he completed over 500 miles of track before the next winter freeze.

The following year CPR rails reached Calgary in the west, and considerable work was accomplished east of Winnipeg and north of Lake Superior. It was at this time that Canadian-born James J. Hill, who favored a line south of Lake Superior (across the state of Minnesota), left the CPR to concentrate on development of the St. Paul, Minneapolis & Manitoba Railway, which became the Great Northern Railway in the U. S.

While armies of workers laid the iron across the western prairies and the muskeg of Ontario, 7000 Chinese laborers blasted their way through the Coast Range in British Columbia. By 1884, after constant battle with the forces of nature, includ-

ing landslides and snow avalanches, the summit of the Rockies was reached.

The Government section of line from the Pacific Coast had progressed eastward to Kamloops Lake. At that point CPR forces took up the work and carried the line toward a connection with the workers advancing westward across the Rockies.

Finally, on a rainy November 7, 1885, in the forest at Craigellachie, B. C., high in the Eagle Pass of the Columbian Range, 2553 miles from Montreal and 351 miles from Vancouver, Donald Smith hammered the last spike during a modest ceremony which sealed the ribbon of steel from the St. Lawrence to the Pacific.

Unlike the excitement that accompanied the meeting of the Union Pacific and the Central Pacific at Promontory, Utah, in 1869, the ceremony at Craigellachie was only the first step in the completion of the Canadian Pacific. Traffic had not been developed, equipment was not yet provided, the telegraph line

FRASER RIVER BRIDGE was supported by stone masonry piers.

TUNNEL No. 17 was black-powder-blasted through solid rock.

CONSTRUCTION LOCOMOTIVE No. 7, Kamloops, was built by Baldwin in 1884 and sold to the Intercolonial Railway in 1887.

was not even constructed. It wasn't until June 28, 1886, that the line opened for regular passenger service; freight service did not begin until July 6, 1886.

In 1887 the Lachine Bridge over the St. Lawrence was finished, and in 1889 the road across the state of Maine to Saint John, N. B., was placed in operation. Additional trackage connected the main line with Sault Ste. Marie, Ont., and also extended the CPR to Toronto and Detroit.

By the turn of the century interest in Empire trade stimulated the development of a fleet of magnificent company-owned steamships which extended the CPR across the Pacific and Atlantic oceans.

Barney & Smith of Dayton, O., delivered the first sleeping

IN August 1883 the first train to arrive at Calgary, Alta., was greeted by an honor guard of Royal Canadian Mounted Police.

THE last spike was driven by Sir Donald Smith at Craigellachie, B. C., on November 7, 1885, completing 4325 miles of railway.

cars owned by the CPR in May 1882. The three cars, named *Montreal, Ottawa,* and *Toronto,* were 58 feet 10 inches long and were built with 6-wheel trucks and open platforms.

In June 1886, the first de luxe passenger equipment for the new transcontinental line was received in Montreal. *Railroad Gazette*'s June 4, 1886, issue described eight new sleeping cars and six dining cars patterned after designs furnished by Vice-President W. C. Van Horne. Barney & Smith, previously favored by Van Horne during his tenure at the CM&StP, again was selected to be the builder. The cars were assigned to the *Pacific Express* (westbound) and the *Atlantic Express* (eastbound).

The new cars were built with exteriors of varnished solid mahogany; interiors were satinwood, inlaid with brass and mother-of-pearl in Japanese designs. Parisian marble lavatories contained fittings of beaten bronze. Clerestory window ventilators were of colored Venetian glass; upholstery was sea-green plush; floors were covered with Turkey carpets.

Passengers from the United States traveled via the Manitoba-Pacific Route between St. Paul-Winnipeg-Vancouver on Jim Hill's St. Paul, Minneapolis & Manitoba Railway to Winnipeg, and Canadian Pacific to the West Coast. This route remained in operation until Hill completed his Great Northern Railway to Seattle in September 1893, at which time the CPR purchased a controlling interest in the Soo Line and inaugurated its own Soo-Pacific Route from St. Paul.

385

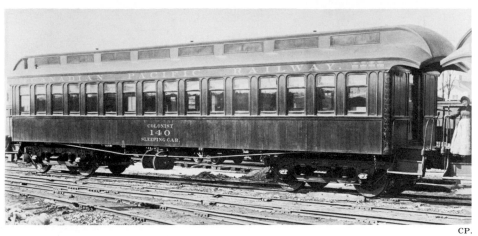

COLONIST sleeping cars were unique to Canadian railroading, and were similar to earlier equipment in the United States known as Immigrant cars. At the turn of the century thousands of immigrants spent their first nights in Canada aboard the cars.

FIRST-CLASS coach No. 426 had narrow vestibules and brass grillwork. One could relax in copper-red plush seats, enjoy a cigar in the smoking room, or read a book by the light of the oil lamps. The 1890 car was rebuilt to cafe car No. 42 in 1907.

TOURIST CAR No. 1064, built in June 1898 by the James Crossen plant of Cobourg, Ont., was one of the first wide-vestibule cars on the Canadian Pacific. It was 58 feet long and had 4-wheel trucks with equalizers. Oil lamps provided illumination.

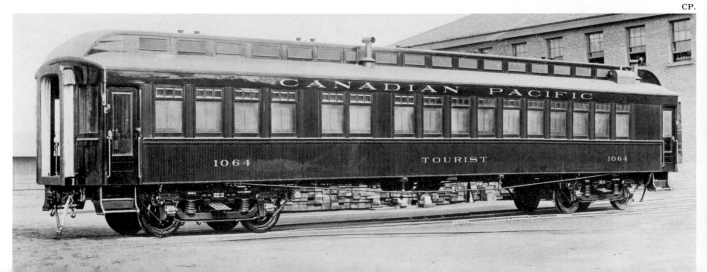

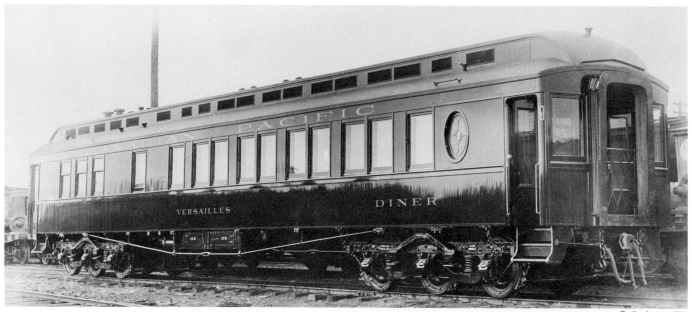

VERSAILLES, an elegant example of a 12-wheel dining car, contained luxurious tasseled drapes (below).

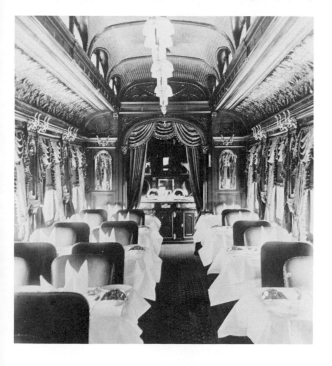

MOOSEHEAD, a sleeping car built by Barney & Smith of Dayton, O., in 1890, had rich velvet upholstery and a mahogany interior (above).

THE Imperial Limited was advertised as "near perfection in railway equipment." Pacific No. 1104, railroad-built in 1906, trailed seven Honduras-red mahogany cars.

The Imperial Limited

ON June 23, 1899, the Canadian Pacific inaugurated the *Imperial Limited*. Advertised as "the only transcontinental train run under one management," it operated daily between Montreal and Vancouver in 100 hours, offering what was described as "the fastest service from the Atlantic to the Pacific aboard superb equipment." Toronto passengers were served by a Grand Trunk sleeper connection at North Bay, Ont.

Beginning June 11, 1900, the *Imperial Limited* also became a Soo Line train from St. Paul to Vancouver, crossing the border at Portal, N. D. The Soo cars joined the Montreal section at Regina in Assiniboia (now Saskatchewan). The Soo Line-CPR *Imperial Limited* was the forerunner of the *Soo-Pacific Train De Luxe* of 1907 between St. Paul, Minn., and the Pacific Coast via the Crow's Nest Pass through the Kootenay.

Early CPR advertising folders described the new *Imperial Limited* trains as approaching "near perfection in railway equipment." Each consisted of two or more Palace sleepers, a tourist sleeper, a dining car, and a baggage car. The exteriors were uniformly finished in varnished Honduras-red mahogany of the "well-known Canadian Pacific standard."

In describing the Palace sleeping cars and the dining cars the reporter was enthusiastic:

> The sleeping cars intended for the service — the *Monrepos, Lorraine, Lausanne, Chantilly, Narbonne, Soissons, Trianon, Vincennes, Fontenoy,* and *Rochelle* — are designed after the charming style of Louis Quinze, and are magnificent creations of their kind. The elaborate decorations are exquisitely beautiful, being chiefly in ivory and gold, which give a general effect of superb, yet tasteful luxury. Each car has eight sections, two large staterooms furnished with lavatory, etc., and a spacious smoking compartment. The main saloon is finished in prima verra [sic], the upholstering throughout being in velour frappé, and the draperies

Author's collection.

BROCHURE described train's luxuries, services.

SOO-PACIFIC, seen here near Field, B.C., in 1907, had an open observation car that enabled sightseers to view the scenery. Passengers sat on plain wooden slat seats.

Railway & Locomotive Historical Society.

harmonizing in color and richness with the other furnishings.

The dining cars rival the sleepers in the chasteness of their embellishments. The dining room is finished in red-figured mahogany, with ceilings of embossed Lincrusta-Walton, old gold in color, and the floor is carpeted with green Brussels. The kitchen and pantry are fitted with every modern convenience that will insure the choicest viands and service.

The first observation cars on CPR appeared in 1890. They were unique passenger cars produced in the company shops to enable sightseeing passengers to view the magnificent scenery of the Canadian Rockies. These early cars, later known as "mountain observation cars," were built with raised cupolas at each end that were early versions of dome cars. Several variations of the mountain observation emerged. One series that appeared about 1907 was similar to a gondola car with rows of wooden slat seats (and no roof). These were old passenger cars with bodies cut down to the belt rail. Later models built during the 1920's contained partially glazed sides and a roof.

The first conventional brass-railing observation-lounge-

sleeping cars on CPR appeared in 1909. They were the famous *Glen* and *Mount* series, with 3 compartments, 1 drawing room, buffet, and lounge.

An unusual type of sleeping car unique to Canadian railroading was the Colonist car, which was similar to earlier equipment in the United States known as the Immigrant car. Colonist cars provided settlers with minimal sleeping accommodations, but no bedding or linen, as were furnished on tourist, or second class, sleeping cars. Thousands of immigrants from Europe who arrived in Canada at the turn of the century spent their first nights in Canada aboard Colonist cars.

On May 3, 1914, shortly after the outbreak of World War I, a new international route between Montreal-Toronto-Detroit-Chicago was established. Double-daily service in connection with the Michigan Central commenced with the *Canadian* and the *Michigan Central Limited*, later designated the *Dominion Overseas*. The latter train advertised "assured connections with Atlantic steamships at Montreal," and became a favorite of European travelers on the new line between Canada and the United States.

Freeman Hubbard, collection of Railroad Magazine.

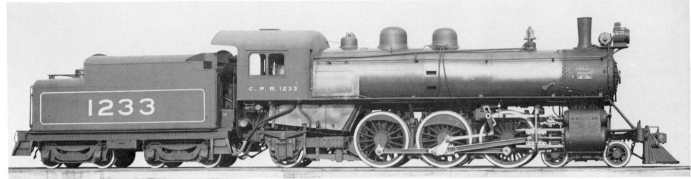

PACIFIC No. 1233, outshopped by American Locomotive Company in 1906, had 69-inch drivers and 21 x 28-inch cylinders.

DOMINION EXPRESS baggage car No. 1987 is shown in natural varnished mahogany.

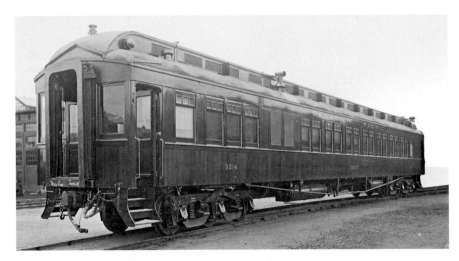

TOURIST CAR No. 3014 was built in 1913 by Canadian Car & Foundry. The simple interior (above) consisted of plain, varnished wood paneling and smooth leather upholstery.

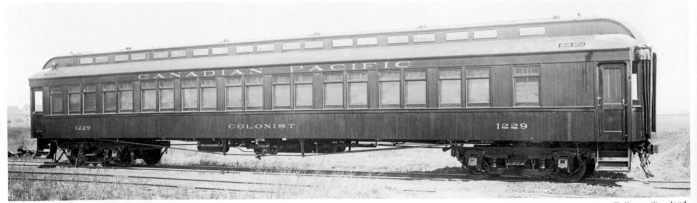

COLONIST CAR No. 1229, an eight-wheeler, was built by Pullman-Standard in 1905; car possessed vestibules at both ends.

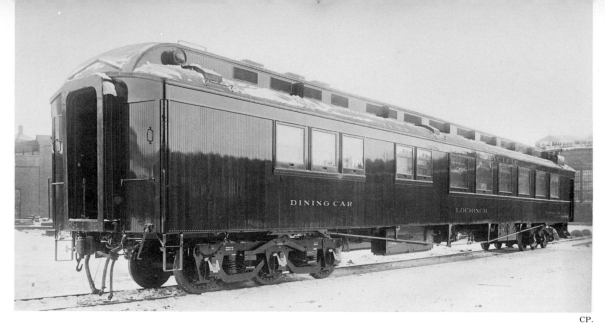

DINING CAR Lochinch, constructed by Canadian Pacific in 1913, was fitted with Krupp steel-tired wheels.

RARE Barney & Smith photo shows Soo Line dining car 1108 lettered "Soo-Spokane Line" for 1907 Soo-Pacific Express.

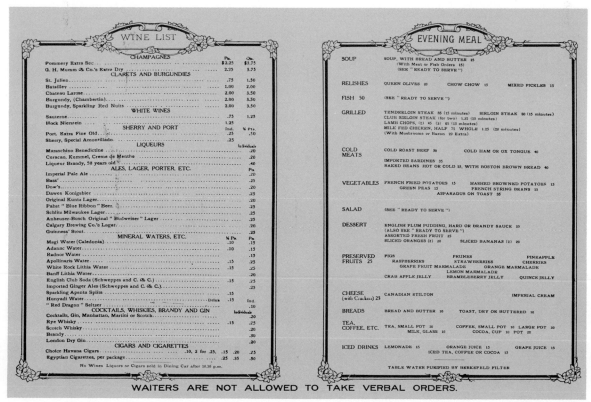

WINE LIST

CHAMPAGNES

	Pts.	Qts.
Pommery Extra Sec	$2.25	$3.75
G. H. Mumm & Co.'s Extra Dry	2.25	3.75

CLARETS AND BURGUNDIES

St. Julien	.75	1.50
Batailley	1.00	2.00
Chateau Larose	2.00	3.50
Burgundy, (Chambertin)	2.00	3.50
Burgundy, Sparkling Red Nuits	2.00	3.50

WHITE WINES

Sauterne	.75	1.25
Hock Nierstein	1.25	

SHERRY AND PORT

	Ind.	¼ Pts.
Port, Extra Fine Old	.25	.50
Sherry, Special Amontillado	.25	

LIQUEURS

	Individuals
Maraschino Benedictine	.20
Curacao, Kummel, Creme de Menthe	.20
Liqueur Brandy, 50 years old	.40

ALES, LAGER, PORTER, ETC.

	Pts.
Imperial Pale Ale	.20
Bass'	.25
Dow's	.20
Dawes Konigsbier	.25
Original Kuntz Lager	.20
Pabst " Blue Ribbon " Beer	.25
Schlitz Milwaukee Lager	.25
Anheuser-Busch Original " Budweiser " Lager	.25
Calgary Brewing Co.'s Lager	.20
Guinness' Stout	.25

MINERAL WATERS, ETC.

	¼ Pts.	Pts.
Magi Water (Caledonia)	.10	.15
Adanac Water	.10	.15
Radnor Water		.15
Apollinaris Water		.25
White Rock Lithia Water	.15	.25
Banff Lithia Water		.20
English Club Soda (Schweppes and C. & C.)	.15	.25
Imported Ginger Ales (Schweppes and C. & C.)		.25
Sparkling Apenta Splits	.15	
Hunyadi Water	Drink	.15
" Red Dragon " Seltzer		.10

COCKTAILS, WHISKIES, BRANDY AND GIN

	Individuals
Cocktails, Gin, Manhattan, Martini or Scotch	.20
Rye Whisky	.15 .25
Scotch Whisky	.20
Brandy	.30
London Dry Gin	.20

CIGARS AND CIGARETTES

Choice Havana Cigars	.10, 2 for .25, .15	.20	.25
Egyptian Cigarettes, per package	.25	.35	.50

No Wines Liquors or Cigars sold in Dining Car after 10.30 p.m.

EVENING MEAL

SOUP — SOUP, WITH BREAD AND BUTTER 25 (With Meat or Fish Orders 15) (SEE " READY TO SERVE ")

RELISHES — QUEEN OLIVES 20   CHOW CHOW 15   MIXED PICKLES 15

FISH 50 — (SEE " READY TO SERVE ")

GRILLED — TENDERLOIN STEAK 85 (15 minutes)   SIRLOIN STEAK 80 (15 minutes)
CLUB SIRLOIN STEAK (for two) 1.25 (15 minutes)
LAMB CHOPS, (2) 45 (3) 65 (15 minutes)
MILK FED CHICKEN, HALF 75 WHOLE 1.25 (20 minutes)
(With Mushrooms or Bacon 20 Extra)

COLD MEATS — COLD ROAST BEEF 50   COLD HAM OR OX TONGUE 40
IMPORTED SARDINES 35
BAKED BEANS HOT OR COLD 25, WITH BOSTON BROWN BREAD 40

VEGETABLES — FRENCH FRIED POTATOES 15   HASHED BROWNED POTATOES 15
GREEN PEAS 15   FRENCH STRING BEANS 15
ASPARAGUS ON TOAST 35

SALAD — (SEE " READY TO SERVE ")

DESSERT — ENGLISH PLUM PUDDING, HARD OR BRANDY SAUCE 25
(ALSO SEE " READY TO SERVE ")
ASSORTED FRESH FRUIT 25
SLICED ORANGES (2) 20   SLICED BANANAS (2) 20

PRESERVED FRUITS 25 — FIGS   PRUNES   PINEAPPLE
RASPBERRIES   STRAWBERRIES   CHERRIES
GRAPE FRUIT MARMALADE   ORANGE MARMALADE
LEMON MARMALADE
CRAB APPLE JELLY   BRAMBLEBERRY JELLY   QUINCE JELLY

CHEESE (with Crackers) 25 — CANADIAN STILTON   IMPERIAL CREAM

BREADS — BREAD AND BUTTER 10   TOAST, DRY OR BUTTERED 10

TEA, COFFEE, ETC. — TEA, SMALL POT 10   COFFEE, SMALL POT 10 LARGE POT 20
MILK, GLASS 10   COCOA, CUP 10 POT 20

ICED DRINKS — LEMONADE 15   ORANGE JUICE 15   GRAPE JUICE 15
ICED TEA, COFFEE OR COCOA 15

TABLE WATER PURIFIED BY BERKEFELD FILTER

WAITERS ARE NOT ALLOWED TO TAKE VERBAL ORDERS.

IN 1912 the menu for the evening meal featured club sirloin steak for two people at a cost of $1.25.

Both photos, CP.

ORNATE sleeping car Rochelle (above) posed at Canadian Pacific's Hochelaga carshops in Montreal, where the car was built in 1898. The elaborate interior was designed "after the charming style of Louis Quinze" in a white-and-gold pattern (below left). It was one of the few sleeping cars with a bathtub, an innovation that preceded showers aboard cars.

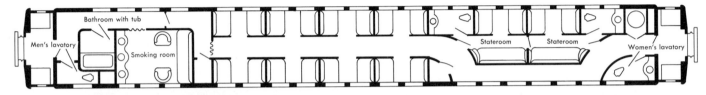

Both photos, Pullman-Standard.

SLEEPING CAR Kanaka, Pullman-built in 1913, conformed to rigid CPR specifications. Honduras mahogany exterior was finished with boiled linseed oil and four coats of varnish. Colorful leaded art-glass clerestory sash graced the interior (above).

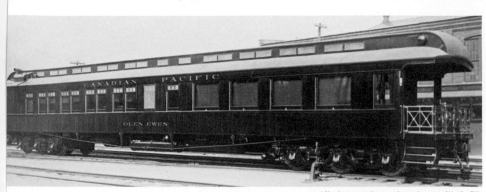

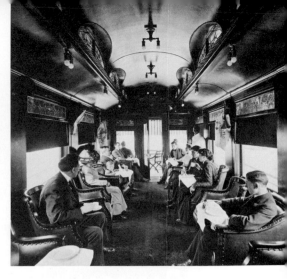

GLEN EWEN was one of the first cars on CPR with the conventional open-end observation platform, lounge, and compartment. The lounge section (right) provided large, comfortable chairs. Later version Mount MacDonald (below) was resplendent when new in 1909.

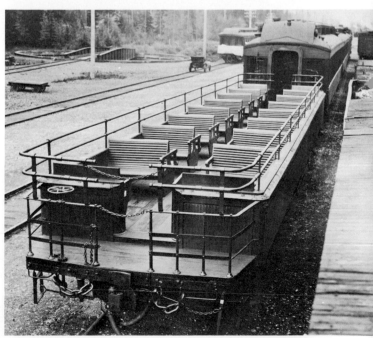

MOUNTAIN observation car 86 was an 1890 precursor of dome cars. Open-air version (above) was constructed in 1907.

THE Trans-Canada Limited crosses Stoney Creek Bridge in the Selkirk Range.

The era of steam and steel

FIRST-CLASS coach No. 999, built in June 1912 at Angus Shops, ushered in the era of steel equipment on CPR. The last wooden sleeping and dining cars were outshopped in 1913, although Canada's entry into World War I during 1914 precluded extensive construction of new steel rolling stock.

With the postwar mass production of steel cars and the application of steel sheathing to many wooden Canadian Pacific cars after World War I, color-matching of the natural mahogany equipment presented a problem. The first steel passenger cars on CPR were painted a special orange-yellow developed to imitate the color of mahogany. This practice prevailed until officials in Montreal finally decided to change the color of all CPR passenger equipment, both wooden and steel, to the rich tuscan-red enamel used by CPR's subsidiary Soo Line (and the Soo-owned Wisconsin Central).*

Soon after the 1918 armistice, a new train was inaugurated. June 1, 1919, marked the beginning of the great *Trans-Canada*

*Information about the change of colors was provided by Andrew Merrilees of Toronto and James Shields of Montreal, both of whom have done extensive research on the subject.

Limited, all-sleeping-car trains 7 and 8, between Montreal and Vancouver. Trains 9 and 10 were the *Trans-Canada* connection over the new CPR line between Toronto and Sudbury, Ont. Only first-class passengers were carried. The "Quickest Train Across Canada" advertised " 'Class' Right Through," with no extra fare. The *Imperial Limited* continued as a year-around transcontinental service between Montreal-Toronto and Vancouver.

Each year the summer season heralded the *Trans-Canada Limited*, proclaimed as "Canada's Premier Train" and "the fastest transcontinental and longest distance all-sleeping-car train in the world." Companion summer train on the Chicago-Vancouver run via St. Paul-Minneapolis was the Soo Line-CPR *Mountaineer*, inaugurated on June 10, 1923.

The summer of 1926 brought two new name trains on the "Montreal and Boston Line": the daytime run was named the *Alouette*; the overnight train was called the *Red Wing* and carried ex-*Soo-Pacific* Barney & Smith observation-compartment cars on the rear end.

The expansive prosperity of 1928 also ushered in a unique joint service between Boston and Halifax via the Boston & Maine-Maine Central-Canadian Pacific-Canadian National. Within the year, on September 30, 1928, double-daily service

DOUBLEHEADING in the Rockies is train No. 8. "The Quickest Train Across Canada" carried only sleeping-car passengers.

was established by both the *Pine Tree Acadian* and the *Gull*.

In an editorial headed "The Best Train in the World," the Vancouver *Star* of May 11, 1929, said:

> Readers of Kipling will recall that, after locomotive No. 007 had made his famous emergency run with the working equipment, he was promoted to regular duty at the front end of the nickel-plated *Millionaires' Special*. That was more than 20 years ago; and while the *Millionaires' Special* was the last word in luxury on roads then, 007, proud as he was of the first passenger train he drew, would have found it far outclassed had he desired to hook on to any of the 12 *Trans-Canadas* that open their season tomorrow. Nor anywhere in his own land, the United States, would he have found equipment to equal that provided for its de luxe service by the Canadian Pacific Railway.
>
> Twelve new trains have been provided for the operation of the *Trans-Canada*, 10 of which will be in motion at one time, while the other 2 will be in the yards awaiting their turns of the rota. One of them is now in Vancouver ready to begin service from this terminal. It was on exhibition today. It is well worth visiting, whether one expects to travel by it or not, for it shows the enormous advances that have been made in recent years in providing the comforts and conveniences of railway journeying, advances that are ultimately reflected in varying degree in the equipment of other and less costly trains, so that gradually the whole standard is raised.
>
> The 12 trains, as already remarked, are new. They are entirely of Canadian construction, having been built to Canadian designs, by Canadian artificiers and of Canadian materials, at the Angus Shops, Montreal. They have cost, approximately, 1 million dollars each as they stand on the tracks. Recent improvements embodied in trains elsewhere and a number of new ones only to be enjoyed aboard these trains have been included.
>
> There are bathrooms, ladies' smoking rooms, and card rooms. There is a solarium-lounge, which is really an observation-coach equipped with vita-glass windows that keep out the sun glare but let in the health-giving ultra-violet rays. The compartments in the compartment car are arranged *en suite* for the convenience of family parties. The diner is richly upholstered in blue and gold in keeping with the other appointments of the train, the whole of which are at once highly artistic and most comfortable. The train, in short, is a superb hotel on wheels. It may be added that, as the baggage car carries only the personal effects of the passengers, a large part of it has been converted into a sleeper where the dining-car crew can rest in comfort and enjoy their scanty hours of leisure.
>
> Since 24 men are required for each train, the *Trans-*

TRAIN No. 7, the Dominion, with 2-10-4 No. 5924 on the point, stops at the station of the famous resort area of Banff, Alta., in 1950.

THE Mountaineer, an all-sleeping-car train, traveled the 2172 miles between Chicago and Vancouver in 73 hours via Soo and CPR.

Canada service will cost at least $3000 a day in wages alone. Adding the other expenses, it will hardly be directly profitable to the company. Indirectly, however, it will have great value. It will not only be an excellent advertisement for all the company's services, but it will attract to Canada the wealthy tourists from the United States, who insist on having the best obtainable no matter what the price.

Finally, it will place the company in the proud position of running the finest passenger trains on this continent, and therefore the finest, from the standpoint of equipment, in the world.

During the winter of 1929 trains 3 and 4 (Toronto-Vancouver) became the *Dominion*. In the twilight of prosperity during the summer season of 1931, CPR transcontinental service reached its peak with a parade of five daily trains: the all-sleeping-car *Trans-Canada* (Montreal and Toronto-Vancouver); the *Imperial* (Montreal-Vancouver); the *Dominion* (Toronto-Vancouver); the all-sleeping-car *Mountaineer* and the *Soo-Pacific* (Chicago-Vancouver).

The fat yellow timetable dated April 26, 1931, which chronicled this record fleet, listed 618 passenger trains and 17,723 scheduled station stops each weekday over the rail line of the CPR "All Red Route."

This prosperity lasted for only one season: the depression of the 1930's took its toll in 1932 with a general cutback in service that continued until the outbreak of World War II in September 1939.

Notwithstanding the difficult economic period, CPR had the distinction of operating the "Fastest Train in the World." Between April and September 1931, train No. 38, the *Royal York* (Toronto-Montreal), was scheduled to operate between Smiths Falls, Ont., and Montreal West, Que., a distance of 124 miles in 108 minutes at an average speed of 68.9 mph. A report of this exploit by Canadian railway historian Omer Lavallée can be found in the April 1966 issue of *Canadian Rail*.

Locomotive Nos. 2850 to 2859.
Class—H-1-d.
Cylinders—22 inches diameter by 30-inch stroke.
Drivers—75 inches diameter. (Six)
Boiler Pressure—275 pounds per square inch.
Tractive Power—45,250 pounds.
Tractive Power with Booster—57,250 pounds.

	With Booster	Without Booster
Weight on Engine Truck	61,400	61,000
Drivers	186,700	186,700
Trailer Truck	115,900	105,800
Total Engine	364,000	353,500
Tender	293,500	293,500
Total Engine and Tender	657,500	647,000

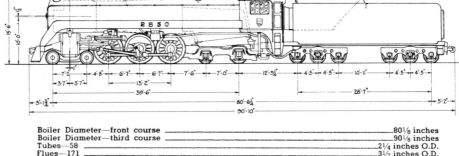

Boiler Diameter—front course	80⅛ inches
Boiler Diameter—third course	90⅛ inches
Tubes—58	2¼ inches O.D.
Flues—171	3½ inches O.D.
Length of boiler tubes and flues	18 feet 3 inches
Firebox Length	131 inches
Firebox Width	88⅞ inches
Grate Area	80.8 square feet

HEATING SURFACES—

Tubes and Flues	3,465 square feet
Firebox and Arch Tubes	326 square feet
Total	3,791 square feet
Superheater	1,542 square feet
Combined	5,333 square feet

TENDER

Water Capacity	12,000 imperial gallons
Coal Capacity	21 tons

Montreal Locomotive Works.

HUDSONS 2800-2809 of subclass H-1-a were built by Montreal Locomotive Works in 1929. No. 2803 was retired in April 1959.

CP.

ROYAL HUDSONS such as 2862 were delivered to Canadian Pacific in 1940 with cast-brass crowns decorating each running board.

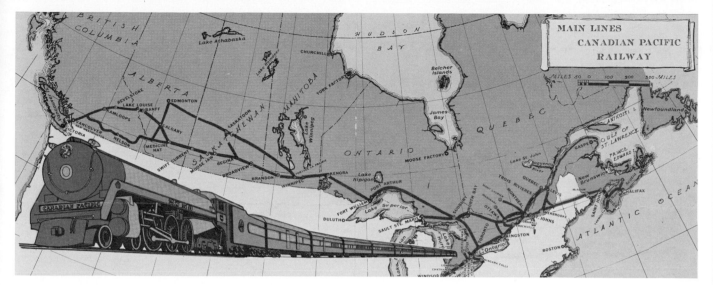

MAIN LINES
CANADIAN PACIFIC
RAILWAY

QUEEN OF THE RAILS in Canada is locomotive 2850, beautifully lined Canadian Pacific Railway engine, powerful and capable of high speeds, which successfully completed the record-breaking task of hauling the royal 12-car train of His Majesty King George VI and Her Majesty Queen Elizabeth 3100 miles across Canada.

The trip passed without incident to mar the giant locomotive's record, although never heretofore has such a train accomplished such a lengthy run on the North American Continent without change of engine. . . .

When the locomotives of the 2800 series were built to specifications and designs from the office of H. B. Bowen, Chief of Motive Power and Rolling Stock, Canadian Pacific Railway, Montreal, the object was to produce a locomotive which could travel great distances without relief. How well they succeeded was demonstrated by the record royal run — a performance which could just as well have been accomplished by any of the 60 Canadian Pacific 2800-series locomotives.

The locomotive is a mass of shining stainless steel, royal blue, silver, and gold. The semi-streamlined front bears the royal arms over the headlight which is sunk flush with the boiler-casing; Imperial Crowns decorate each running board; the crest of the Canadian Pacific appears beneath the window of the cab, and on the tender, the King's arms 4 feet high are blazoned in relief.

The general decorative scheme comprises a background of deep blue on the underframe, smokebox, trucks, wheels, front of engine, and all marginal work on engine and tender. The sides of tender, cab, and running boards are painted royal blue, with lining of gold leaf. A panel of aluminum leaf laid in diagonal squares, matching the panel on the cars of the royal train, extends half way on the tender. The panel is outlined in gold. The jacket on the locomotive, handrails on it, the tender, and other trim are in brush finish stainless steel. Gold leaf has been employed on the engine numbers, which are cast in relief.

Power, speed, and an attractive appearance are the outstanding features of this locomotive, one of 40 of the same type built in the past two years for the Canadian Pacific Railway. Twenty others of the same series were constructed in 1929-1930. In regular service these locomotives have been used on runs approximating a thousand miles between Toronto and Fort William and in western Canada.

The locomotives are attractive in appearance, following the popular streamlined construction first developed in the lightweight high-speed Jubilee engines. The exterior is smooth and modern in appearance with no projecting headlight, smokestack, or domes. Sloping lines of the front plates merge into the horizontal lines of run-boards and boiler in such a manner as to convey an appreciation . . . for sustained high speed inherent in the design.

Author's collection.

CPR'S only 4-8-4's, the 1928 home-built 3100 and 3101, were a fixture on Toronto-Montreal night trains. They had 75-inch drivers.

CP.

THROUGH baggage car 4909 was built with passenger-car trucks.

401

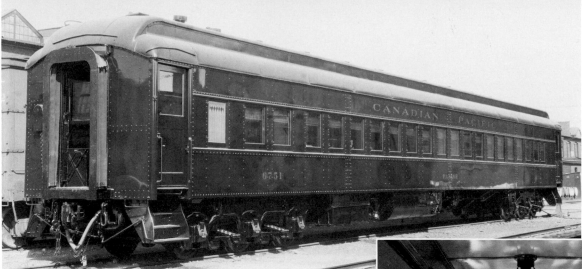

ONE assignment of parlor car 6751 and 13 sisters was the Trans-Canada Limited between Montreal and Ottawa. Cars were 84 feet long over buffers and offered 23 gaily upholstered easy chairs (right).

STOCKTON, one of 50 "S" series sleeping cars built in 1931, had a configuration of 12 sections, 1 drawing room. It measured 75 feet 6 inches over its frame and weighed 181,100 pounds. The mahogany interior (above) had floral-patterned upholstery.

CANADIAN PACIFIC RAILWAY.

COMPARTMENT-OBSERVATION CAR Mount McKay, last of Canadian Pacific's brass-railed Mount series, had 3 compartments, 1 drawing room.

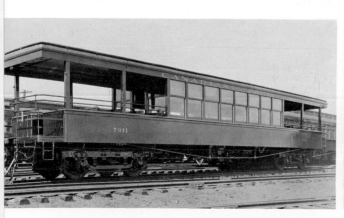

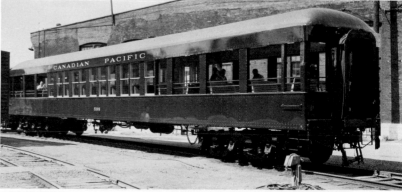

TWO variations of mountain observation cars are these wood (7911) and steel (598) versions that served in the Age of Steam.

CLUB, baggage, and sleeping car No. 4485, built in 1929, contained 6 sections which were used as a club for male passengers in the daytime, and as sleeping quarters for the dining-car crew at night.

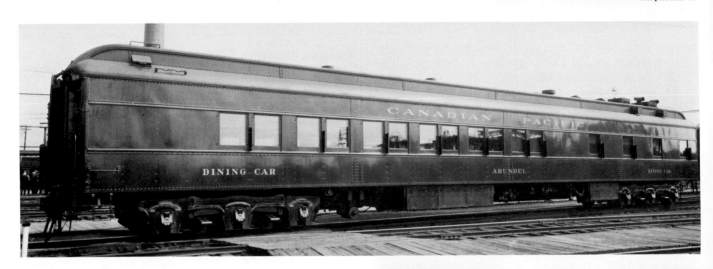

DINING CAR Arundel was one of 15 cars built in 1929 that were named for British castles. The blue-and-gold interior (above) consisted of inlaid wood paneling and seating for 33 patrons.

CANADIAN PACIFIC DINING CAR SERVICE

THE DOMINION

Dinner Suggestions

$1.00

| Consomme Clear | Clam Chowder |

Choice of........Pacific Coast Fish   Ham Steak   Chicken Omelet
Boiled New Potatoes   New Beets or Cabbage
Salad Bowl

Choice of........Diplomat Pudding   Apple Pie
Canadian Cheddar Cheese with Crackers   Ice Cream with Cake

Bread   Rolls

Tea   Coffee   Milk   Buttermilk

$1.25

Green Onions and Radishes or Fruit Cocktail

Consomme Clear   Clam Chowder

Choice of........Lamb Chops with Bacon
Calf's Liver with Onions
Assorted Cold Cuts with Potato Salad

New Potatoes in Cream   New Beets or Cabbage
Salad Bowl

Choice of........Diplomat Pudding   Apple Pie
Canadian Cheddar Cheese with Crackers   Ice Cream with Cake

Bread   Rolls

Tea   Coffee   Milk   Buttermilk

$1.50
"RED BRAND" SIRLOIN STEAK DINNER
BROILED CHICKEN
(Including selections from the $1.25 Dinner)

It will be a great aid to the service and avoid any possibility of mistakes if passengers will kindly ask for meal order blanks, and upon them write their orders, because stewards and waiters are not allowed to serve any food without a meal check.

T. M. McKeown, Manager, Sleeping, Dining and Parlor Cars, Restaurants and News Service.

7-8—Wpg—12-37
1 E

DINNERS were a special treat on the Dominion in 1937.

CP.

REVELSTOKE — an 8-section, 2-compartment, 1-drawing-room sleeping car — was one of 29 cars of the "R" series turned out in the year 1929.

CP.

LAKE WINDERMERE, one of five Lake-series sleepers built in 1928, operated on overnight runs in eastern Canada and had 4 compartments, 1 drawing room, buffet, and parlor.

Pullman-Standard.

ALTHOUGH Pullmans were a rarity on CPR, Clover Knoll, a 1936 rebuild, operated for several summers on the Mountaineer.

ACF.

BELGRADE, a 12-section, 1-drawing-room sleeping car, was built by ACF in 1921 for Soo Line-CPR service.

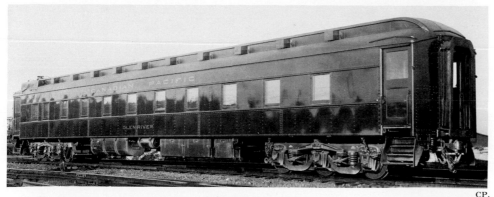

CP.

SLEEPING CAR Glen River had 10 compartments. Traditionally, CPR built many of its own cars at Montreal.

407

SUNLIGHT glints off the stainless-steel exterior of the Scenic Dome observation car as the Canadian approaches Mt. Eisenhower.

The Canadian

DURING 1954 and 1955 Canadian Pacific received 173 stainless-steel cars. The new equipment, ordered for two transcontinental trains in each direction, was built in Philadelphia by the Budd Company. Seven types of cars were furnished: 18 baggage-dormitory; 30 coaches; 18 dome coach-buffets; 18 dining cars; 71 sleeping cars of two types; and 18 dome observation-sleepers. In all, 18 consists were delivered, the first dome-equipped trains in Canada.

The *Canadian* was selected as the name of the premier train, the *Dominion* was continued as the name of the companion service. Before Confederation and the building of CPR, no generic term described British North Americans. Confederation created "Canadians." In honor of the Canadian Pacific Railway as the instrument of Confederation, the name *Canadian* was chosen for the new all-stainless-steel streamliner.

The first two cars, a sleeper and a Scenic Dome observation, were delivered in Montreal in July 1954. A 10,000-mile transcontinental exhibition trip followed, during which over 200,000 persons visited the two cars. Indians, cowboys, miners, seamen, hunters, rangers, plainsmen, city people, farmers, and country folk — some of whom had traveled hundreds of miles — came to examine the exciting new railway cars. It was the first time in decades that a train had created such a stir in Canada.

The new streamlined *Canadian* continued the high standards established by CPR; operating in connection with the company-owned steamships, airlines, and elegant hotels, the new trains were widely advertised and enthusiastically received. During 1967, the Canadian World Fair year of Expo 67, the silver streamliners carried record loads to and from Montreal.

By 1970, when the operation of passenger trains was considered uneconomic by CP Rail (the designation for the railroad since 1968), the Canadian Transport Commission ordered CP to continue operation of the *Canadian* under Government subsidy. Permission to discontinue the train was denied on the basis of its importance to the nation, and a subsidy of more than 1 million dollars per month was granted the railway to ensure the continuation of service. ⌶

Both photos, CP.

ALGONQUIN PARK, with 3 double bedrooms, 1 drawing room, and lounge, was one of 18 cars named for Canada's national and provincial parks. The lounge (above) had paintings and murals furnished by members of the Royal Canadian Academy of Arts.

Budd Company.

SILVER-AND-MAROON Canadian rides through the majestic snow-covered Canadian Rockies.

INTERIOR of dining car Louise (right) had glass partitions etched with Canadian birds. Bulkheads carried colored crests of noted dining rooms in Canadian Pacific hotels for which cars were named.

UNITY was one of 22 tourist cars with 14 sections that were rebuilt from standard sleeping cars by Canadian Pacific in 1956.

410

Budd Company.

FORTY-TWO Manor-series cars, named for Canadians of British origin, had 4 roomettes, 5 double bedrooms, 1 compartment, and 4 sections.

Budd Company.

CHATEAU LA SALLE had 8 duplex roomettes, 1 drawing room, 3 double bedrooms, and 4 sections. The series honored French Canadians.

CP.

SKYLINE DOME coffee shop-coach included 26 reclining coach seats, coffee-shop seating for 23, and a small kitchen under the dome.

Author's collection.

DOMELINER cruise train Canadian awaits departure time from Montreal's Windsor Station.

ACROSS CANADA

"The National Way"

¹ THE Latin motto *A Mare Usque Ad Mare* (From Sea to Sea) under the Canadian coat of arms aptly describes the Canadian National Railways which binds the country together as a national entity. The Canadian National, one of the world's largest railways, was neither conceived nor built as a system. It is the result of an amalgamation of many government and privately sponsored railways which, because of economic conditions, were brought under one management to serve the people of Canada, the second largest nation in the world.

The Canadian National Railways Act passed in Parliament in 1919 created the CN and became the original source of the company's strength. In due course there were brought under unified management and operation six railway enterprises, private and public, listed in the order they began operation: Grand Trunk, Intercolonial, Canadian Northern, Newfoundland, National Transcontinental, Grand Trunk Pacific.

PASSENGERS aboard the transcontinental Super Continental view Windy Point near Jasper, Alta. The scenic miles unfolding in this vista are only a few of 22,375 that CN claimed — out of a total of 38,896 rail miles in Canada — in an early brochure and map.

412

ACROSS CANADA

The National Way

CANADIAN NATIONAL-GRAND TRUNK

The Greatest Transportation System in the World.

22,375 miles of railway.

102,000 miles of telegraph lines.

For fares, reservation of berths, and further information apply to any agent of the Canadian National-Grand Trunk Railways

GREAT WESTERN DIVISION bill of fare of the 1880's offered beefsteak pie with sweet corn fritter for 25 cents.

Grand Trunk Railway and Great Western Railway of Canada

THE Grand Trunk Railway of Canada was incorporated by an act of Parliament in 1852 to develop a railway system in Canada and the United States. The term "Grand Trunk" signified a line running from east to west in Canada through Quebec and Ontario, connecting the ports of Montreal, Que., and Portland, Me., with railways in the Midwestern United States and with lake steamer lines at Port Huron, Mich.

Two predecessors of the Grand Trunk, the St. Lawrence & Atlantic in Canada and the Atlantic & St. Lawrence in the United States, were incorporated in 1845 to connect Montreal with Portland and to provide a port for the Canadian city during its landlocked winter season. Both were amalgamated with the Grand Trunk in 1853. All originally were built to the wide track gauge of 5 feet 6 inches, which for 20 years was the "standard" gauge in the settled parts of Canada. In 1856 the Montreal-Toronto line was completed; in 1859 Grand Trunk reached Sarnia, Ont., and a Port Huron ferryboat connection.

Canada's first common-carrier railway, the 4-foot 8½-inch Champlain & Lawrence of 1836, was absorbed by the Grand Trunk in 1864, extending the GTR to the United States border at Rouses Point, N. Y.

A major Grand Trunk undertaking was construction of the Victoria Bridge over the St. Lawrence between 1854 and 1859. The original structure was a single-track iron tubular bridge with a total length from bank to bank of 9155 feet. During 1898 the tube was replaced by a double-track truss structure.

In 1882 the Grand Trunk absorbed the Great Western Railway of Canada, which connected the Niagara frontier with Sarnia and Windsor, Ont. For 20 years the Great Western had acted as a bridge road between the New York Central at Niagara Falls and the Vanderbilt-controlled Michigan Central at Detroit — serving as part of a through New York-Chicago route for Vanderbilt traffic in the days when ownership of the "Lake Shore" route from Buffalo to Chicago via Cleveland was in doubt. Its value in this regard was suddenly and completely negated in 1876, when Vanderbilt secured his own line in Canada by leasing the recently completed and generally parallel Canada Southern.

However, the Grand Trunk completed its own line into Chicago in 1880, setting the stage for the 1882 amalgamation with the Great Western. (A Great Western subsidiary in Michigan gave it access to Grand Haven, and from there to Milwaukee by car ferry across Lake Michigan.) The Great Western, like the Grand Trunk, had been built to the 5-foot 6-inch gauge. Both had been converted to 4 feet 8½ inches in 1873 and 1874.

In 1905 the Grand Trunk purchased the Canada Atlantic Railway, a 466-mile line known as the Algonquin Park Route. Built by lumberman J. R. Booth to connect Georgian Bay with Ottawa, the line also reached the U. S. border at Alburgh, Vt., providing service between Ottawa and Boston and New York.

The Grand Trunk and Great Western relationships with the Pullman Company were both of long standing. The first hotel car, *Western World*, was built for George Pullman in 1867 by the Great Western Railway in its shops at Hamilton, Ont. The first Pullman Palace cars for Grand Trunk service were built in 1870 at the Point St. Charles shops of the GTR in Montreal. For many years all sleeping cars on the Grand Trunk were operated by the Pullman Company on an association basis: Pullman and Grand Trunk jointly owned the cars and shared the profits from operations. Pullman cars on the Grand Trunk and Great Western were built in both railways' Montreal shops until 1881, when the Pullman works in Chicago was completed; some Pullmans for use on the Grand Trunk were built at the Pullman Detroit shops in 1883.

The Pullman-Grand Trunk partnership continued for many decades. After Pullman became a major car builder, many of the passenger coaches and dining cars owned by the Grand Trunk were constructed in Pullman shops. All of the sleeping cars operated on Grand Trunk lines were owned by the Pullman Company. Even after the Grand Trunk Railway was absorbed into the Canadian National System in 1923 the long-term Pullman sleeping-car contracts remained extant over these former Grand Trunk routes: Montreal to Ottawa, Toronto, Detroit, and Chicago; Montreal to Portland, Boston, and New York; Toronto to Philadelphia and New York; and Chicago to Philadelphia and New York via Sarnia and Buffalo.

WINE LIST.

CHAMPAGNES

	PINTS.	QTS.
Perrier Jouet Pale Dry Creaming	$1.75	$3.00
Pommery, "Sec."	2.00	3.50
G. H. Mumm's Dry Verzenay	1.75	3.00
Louis Roederer	2.00	3.50
Dry Monopole	2.00	3.50

CLARETS

Barton & Guestier, Floriac		60
Johnston's St. Estephe	75	1.25
Johnston's Medoc	75	1.00
St. Emilion		1.00
Ludon		75

WHITE WINES

Haut Sauterne, Barton & Guestier	1.00	1.75

ALES, STOUT, SPIRITS, ETC.

St. Louis "Budweiser" Lager Beer		25
Bass' Pale Ale		25
Carling's Amber Ale		15
Carling's London Lager		15
Guinness' Dublin Stout		25
GIN — Old Tom, Booth's	glass, 10	1.00
" "Hollands"	10	1.00
BRANDY — Hennessy's Cognac	15	1.50
" C. V. P. Old "	"	1.25
WHISKY — Old Rye	"	10
SHERRY — Misa	15	1.50

MINERAL WATERS, ETC.

	BOTTLE
Imperial Soda Water	15
" Ginger Ale	15
" Seltzer Water	15
Apollinaris Water	20
Lemonade	per glass 15

CIGARS

Imported Cigars	each 12½ and 15
Cigarettes	per package 10

Author's collection.

WINE LIST was on page opposite menu.

GRAND TRUNK timetable of June 1879 (above left) pictured Montreal's Victoria Bridge on cover page and presented a system map in color on the inside pages. Great Western and Michigan Central folder of 1878 (above right) advertised Wagner cars on all trains.

Railway & Locomotive Historical Society.

PACIFIC No. 200, built at Point St. Charles in 1911, was typical of GTR passenger power. As CN's No. 5578, she was scrapped in 1961.

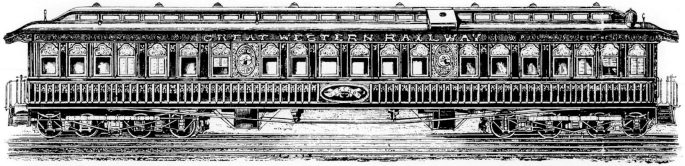

Author's collection.

VICEROY, an early Pullman hotel car, was built in 1867 at the Hamilton (Ont.) shops of the Great Western by William A. Robinson, the road's locomotive superintendent. The 66-foot-long car rode on 16 chilled cast wheels and cost $20,000, exclusive of curtains, velvet upholstery, electroplated fittings, china, and bedding — interior items which were supplied by George M. Pullman.

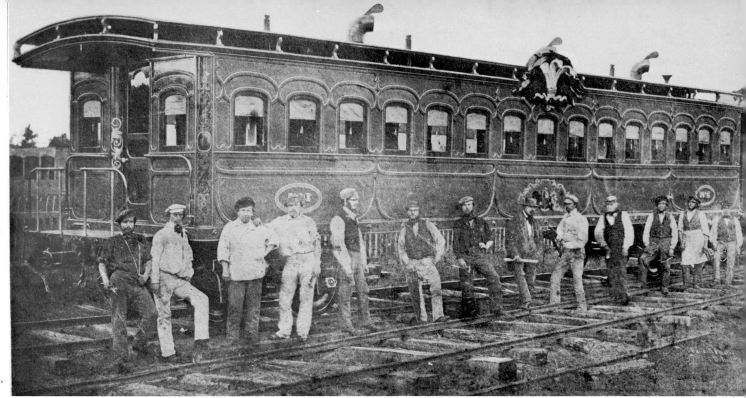

ROYAL VISITS have long commanded regal rail accommodations. For the 1860 visit to Canada and the U. S. of the 19-year-old Prince of Wales (who became King Edward VII in 1901), the Brantford (Ont.) shops of the Buffalo & Lake Huron Railway built a special car featuring a royal blue exterior with a carved wood gold-and-white royal coat of arms coronet and feathers. Shopmen posed with the car, which had an anteroom, retiring room, and three compartments furnished with silks, marble, and polished wood.

GREAT WESTERN RAILWAY passenger car No. 88 was built in 1872 by Harlan & Hollingsworth (later AC&F) in Wilmington, Del. The interior (right) reveals a stove, lavatory, and a silver-plated drinking tap at the front end of the ornately decorated coach.

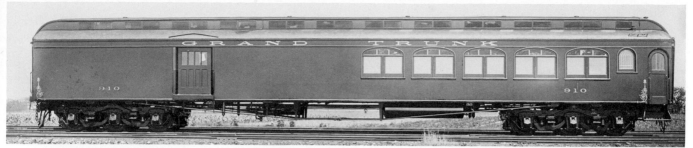

COMBINATION baggage-and-coach cars numbered 908-910 were built by Pullman in 1904. "Stone system" of electric lighting was used.

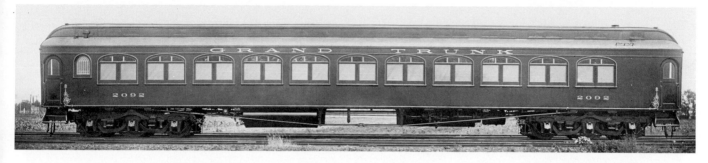

SIX wide-vestibuled coaches delivered in 1904 were billed as "models of modern science," rode on Krupp steel-tired wheels.

IN 1904 Pullman built two diners for the International Limited, the Montreal to Chicago train inaugurated in 1900. Interior view (left) illustrates mahogany trim, black leather upholstery, and art glass windows.

FOUR cafe-parlor cars, Nos. 2607-2610, also entered service in 1904. Two-tone green plush, Wilton carpets, and mahogany trim with marquetry design helped comprise interiors (right) of 73-foot-long cars.

417

GRAND TRUNK parlor car No. 2527 seated 27 people. The 1914 Pullman had statuary bronze hardware; later was named *La Croix* by CN.

CENTRAL VERMONT dining car (above and left) ran in New England States Limited with cars from New York and Boston to Montreal.

THE 12-section, 1-drawing-room Pullman *Sabara* entered GTR Chicago-Montreal-Boston service in 1891; interior view shows a similar car.

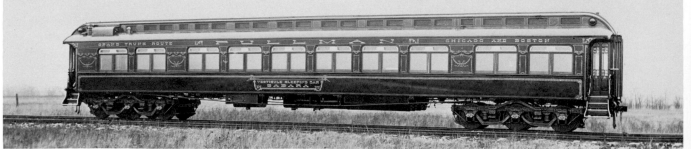

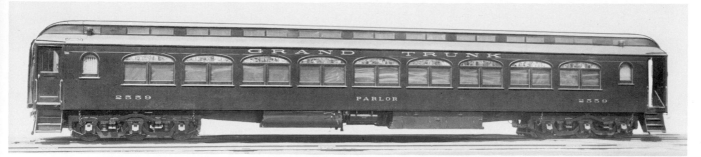

AMENITIES of 73-foot-long, 35-passenger parlor car No. 2559 included a library. The 1914 car later became CN's Calabogie.

OTTAWA and Georgian Bay were linked by the Canada Atlantic, which used this Baldwin 4-4-2. Grand Trunk bought the line in 1905.

NATURAL wood exterior of an 1899 Canada Atlantic parlor car was similar to early CPR finish. Chairs of Edwardian velvet plush, decorated with fringe then in vogue, offered stylish comfort.

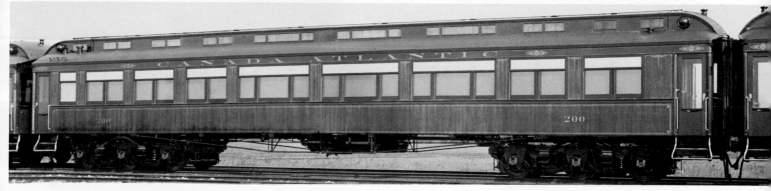

ACCORDING to the 1913 timefolder, the Ocean Limited required 25 hours westbound, 25½ hours eastbound.

IN 1913 Ocean Limited patrons left Montreal at 7:30 p.m. aboard such cars as the eight-year-old Tantramar; train left Halifax westbound at 8:20 a.m.

Intercolonial Railway

THE Intercolonial Railway and the Prince Edward Island Railway of Canada were known as "The People's Railway." They comprised 1600 miles in the eastern provinces of Quebec, New Brunswick, Nova Scotia, and Prince Edward Island, from Montreal and Rivière du Loup, Que., to Quebec, Saint John, N. B., and Halifax and Sydney, N. S.

One of the conditions of Confederation in 1867 was that a railway be built by the newly constituted Dominion government to connect Halifax with the St. Lawrence River at or near Quebec City. Considerable controversy developed over the selection of the route to be followed through New Brunswick. Because of military and economic considerations, and also because of the disputed boundary line with the state of Maine, the northern — and longest — route along Chaleur Bay was chosen. On Dominion Day, July 1, 1876, the line was opened for traffic from Halifax to Levis, Que., opposite Quebec City. In 1890 the Intercolonial was extended east to Sydney. By 1898 ICR had purchased trackage and secured running rights from the Grand Trunk Railway to permit through operation from Halifax and Saint John to Montreal via Rivière du Loup.

The Intercolonial was not built primarily as a commercial enterprise; it was built to serve the economic and political needs of Canada. Its very construction was one of the resolutions adopted in 1864 that formed the basis of the articles of Confederation that united eastern Canada, western Canada, and the Maritime Provinces. The road was built at high cost through a sparsely populated country. Soon after its completion it was subjected to competition from the shorter Canadian Pacific route from Montreal across the state of Maine to Saint John. For these reasons the Intercolonial was never a financial success, but it served a most useful purpose in developing the Eastern seaboard of Canada.

De luxe service on the Intercolonial dates from the 19th century. The *Maritime Express* connecting Montreal and Halifax was inaugurated on March 1, 1898. It was advertised as "Canada's Famous Train, One of the Finest on the American Continent." A second train, the *Ocean Limited*, was added on July 3, 1904. The *Maritime Express* and the *Ocean Limited* operated from the old North Street Station in Halifax, which was demolished in the Halifax explosion of December 6, 1917, and later was replaced by CN's combined Hotel Nova Scotian and station. In the early days the trains consisted of ICR Ten-Wheelers and wooden cars finished in the Empire style of the Victorian era. Many of the Intercolonial sleeping and dining cars were constructed by Pullman Company at Chicago or by Canadian Car & Foundry.

WOOD CARS and a 1901 Alco (Manchester) 4-6-0 identify the Maritime Express of the early 1900's. No. 69 became CGR 615, CN 1522.

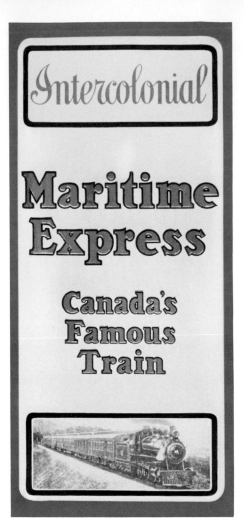

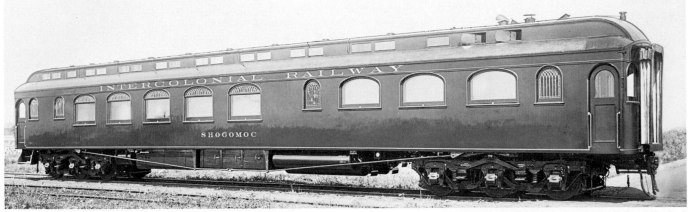

SOME 130 scenic illustrations were used in a brochure to publicize "Canada's Famous Train, the Maritime Express, Connecting Montreal, Quebec, St. John, Halifax, and the Sydneys."

TWIN dining cars Shogomoc (below) and Escuminac were built by Pullman in 1905. Shogomoc became CN 1208; Escuminac CN 1209.

Pullman-Standard.

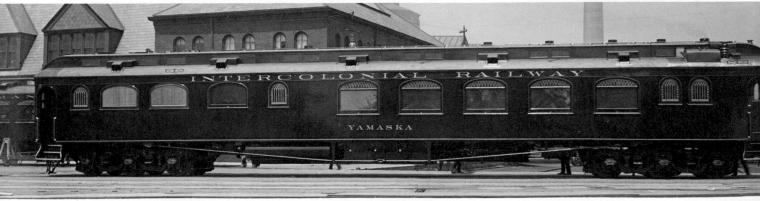

Pullman-Standard.

YAMASKA and other dining cars made day runs from Montreal and Halifax to Ste. Flavie, Que.; waited overnight for next trains.

All photos, Pullman-Standard.

FRONTENAC, a 1912 Pullman product, became CN diner 1229. **ICR** also used diners between Halifax and Antigonish on Sydney trains.

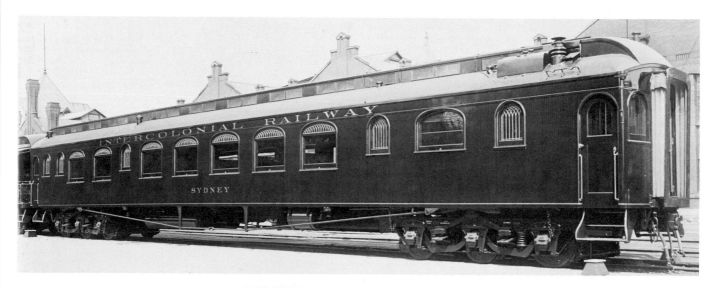

SYDNEY, a 1904 Pullman named after the Nova Scotia city, had 10 sections, 2 drawing rooms — and berths (left) with a mirrorlike finish.

STEEL UNDERFRAMES and interiors of Pullman green plush identified Rossignol and two other 10-2 sleepers acquired in 1913.

RARE builder photo from Barney & Smith (above) shows Canadian Northern's Duluth, built in Dayton, O., in 1908. Interior views of Barney & Smith cars (right and below) depict a porter making up a berth and passengers en route across Canada's prairies. Note CN hatbags next to window, leaded-glass dome at end of car.

TRANSCONTINENTAL service was the mission of Cobourg, a 12-section, 1-drawing-room sleeper built by CC&F at Turcot in 1915.

FORT GARRY was one of seven 1916 steel-underframe Fort cars from CC&F that became prototypes for Canadian National series.

CANADIAN NORTHERN boasted of "snow-white linen, burnished silver, hot-house blooms, choice dainties and edibles . . . that make dining a delight . . . " The subject of such inspired copy-writing were dining cars such as those shown in the interior views (above) and No. 56, a 1907 Barney & Smith graduate on the CN roster as No. 9005 when the photo (below) was taken.

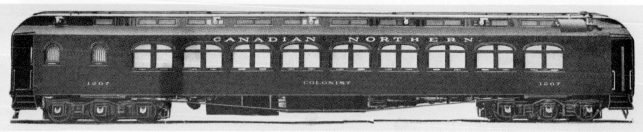

HOW MANY grandparents of residents of Canada's rich Prairie Provinces came west as poor immigrants on cars such as this one?

427

FIRST GTP passenger train from Prince Rupert, B. C., photographed at Milepost 45 on June 14, 1911, had box cars in the consist.

Grand Trunk Pacific and National Transcontinental railways

AFTER 1900 Canada witnessed a period of expansion and increased immigration. As the Prairie Provinces prospered and the Canadian Pacific Railway proved successful, interest in railroad construction continued. Moreover, CPR's single-track line between Winnipeg and the lakehead at Fort William was unable to accommodate the shipment of the abundant wheat crops to the East.

Both the newly organized Canadian Northern in the West and the venerable Grand Trunk in the East wished to share in the growing long-haul traffic that originated in the western provinces. Proposals to unite the two lines were made, but all negotiations failed. An earlier Grand Trunk offer to build from North Bay, Ont., to the Pacific Coast had not been acceptable to the Government for fear that traffic from western Canada would be diverted from the Canadian ports of Halifax and Saint John by the Grand Trunk to its American terminus at Portland, Me.

After lengthy and complex — and frequently bitter — negotiations between Parliament and the Grand Trunk, the National Transcontinental Railway measure became law on July 18, 1903. Under its terms the Grand Trunk was granted a charter and financial assistance to build a railway, the Grand Trunk Pacific, from Winnipeg to the Pacific Coast. At the same time, the Canadian government was to build the National Transcontinental Railway from Moncton, N. B., on the Atlantic seaboard, to Winnipeg via Quebec City. The NTR was to be financed by Government funds and built to Grand Trunk specification. Upon completion it was to be leased to the new Grand Trunk Pacific. A proposed GTP branch line from Prince George, B. C., to Vancouver later was built by the province of British Columbia as the Pacific Great Eastern Railway.

Surveys for the gigantic 3600-mile undertaking were made during 1903 and 1904. Construction of the two-part, 200-million-dollar line began in 1905. The GTP was completed from Winnipeg through the Yellowhead Pass to Prince Rupert, B. C., in 1914; the NTR was completed in 1915, except for the great Quebec cantilever bridge over the St. Lawrence which collapsed twice during construction and was not operational until 1917. Financial difficulties forced actual operation of the NTR

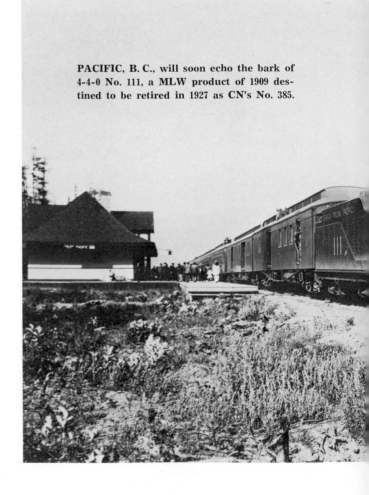

PACIFIC, B. C., will soon echo the bark of 4-4-0 No. 111, a MLW product of 1909 destined to be retired in 1927 as CN's No. 385.

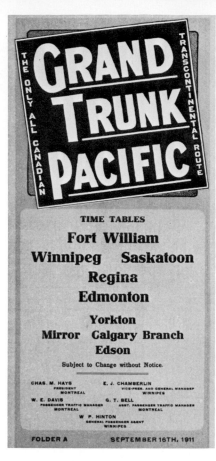

TIME TABLES

Fort William

Winnipeg   Saskatoon

Regina

Edmonton

Yorkton

Mirror   Calgary Branch

Edson

Subject to Change without Notice.

CHAS. M. HAYS
PRESIDENT
MONTREAL

E. J. CHAMBERLIN
VICE-PRES. AND GENERAL MANAGER
WINNIPEG

W. E. DAVIS
PASSENGER TRAFFIC MANAGER
MONTREAL

G. T. BELL
ASST. PASSENGER TRAFFIC MANAGER
MONTREAL

W. P. HINTON
GENERAL PASSENGER AGENT
WINNIPEG

FOLDER A   SEPTEMBER 16TH, 1911

THE ONLY ALL CANADIAN
TRANSCONTINENTAL ROUTE

CANADIAN GOVERNMENT RAILWAYS
GRAND TRUNK RAILWAY SYSTEM
TEMISKAMING & NORTHERN ONTARIO RY.

Toronto
North Bay
Timagami
Cobalt
Englehart
Cochrane
Hearst
Graham
Minaki
Winnipeg

FOLDER T-C No. 1   JULY 13, 1915

Author's collection.

Author's collection.

GRAND TRUNK PACIFIC was open only to Edson, Alta., when the folder (above left) was issued in 1911; the Transcontinental Line folder of 1915 (above right) announced the beginning of Toronto-Winnipeg service over three railroads aboard the National.

CN.

to quickly pass on to the Canadian Government Railways.

Both lines offered de luxe passenger service as soon as they were opened, and in 1915 it was possible to travel from coast to coast over the new route, with one transfer at Winnipeg. West of Winnipeg, GTP service was maintained by trains 1 and 2, which contained new electric-lighted sleeping, tourist, dining, and parlor cars. The equipment was built by Pullman at Chicago in line with the long-standing Grand Trunk-Pullman relationship.

East of Winnipeg, NTR's *National* carried electric-lighted sleeping cars, dining cars, and first-class coaches built by Pullman and National Steel Car of Canada. Inaugurated on July 13, 1915, westbound and on July 18 eastbound, the *National* traversed the joint lines of the Grand Trunk, Temiskaming & Northern Ontario (Ontario Government Railway), and National Transcontinental — which by that time was operated by the Canadian Government Railways. The route between Toronto and Winnipeg took the train via North Bay and Cochrane, Ont.

The NTR-GTP was advertised as "The All-Canadian Transcontinental Route," a pointed reminder that the Canadian Pacific route crossed northern Maine and the Canadian Northern line passed through Minnesota. Two elegant GTP hotels, the Fort Garry in Winnipeg and the Macdonald in Edmonton, Alta., offered a welcome break in the 5-day journey between Toronto-Winnipeg-Vancouver. The GTP also operated the twin-screw sisterships, *Prince Rupert* and *Prince George*, which provided service from Prince Rupert north to Alaska and south to Vancouver, Victoria, and Seattle, Wash., through "The Norway of America."

The climate that had generated optimism for railroad construction turned stormy as it encountered a business recession in 1912, followed by a period of inflation brought on by the outbreak of World War I in 1914. Construction costs for completing the NTR and GTP skyrocketed, and development of western provinces slowed beyond the point of spawning sufficient traffic and revenues. When further financial assistance by the Government was refused to the Grand Trunk Pacific, the Government took over GTP operation as receiver in 1919.

429

COLONIST sleeping car with 4-wheel trucks left the Pullman shops in 1913 for immigrant service on the Grand Trunk Pacific.

TOURIST CARS provided spartan sleeping accommodations at low fares. No. 3414 was one of five tourist cars with 6-wheel trucks out-shopped by Pullman in 1913. The interior view shows the plain berth fronts and leather upholstery; lights were not yet installed.

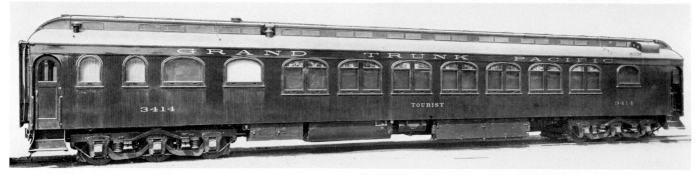

THIRTY-SEAT dining car arrived on the Grand Trunk Pacific in 1913. It became Canadian National's 1212 after amalgamation in 1919.

430

LUXURY indeed rode Canadian rails in 1909 when parlor-cafe 3900 (later CN's Echelle) came from Canadian Car & Foundry. There were 29 richly appointed chairs plus the buffet. A window at the end of the car off the vestibule aided operation at the rear of the train.

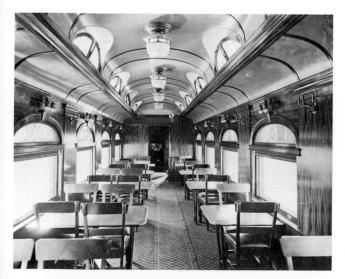

HANDSOME paneled interior (above) competed with scenery and meals for diner's attention in 30-seat No. 4000 (CC&F 1911).

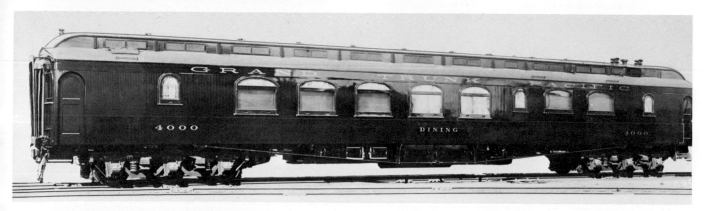

THE TRANS-CONTINENTAL LINE

CN.

PARLOR-CAFE 3907 joined the GTP fleet from Pullman in 1913; it received a new number (720) plus a name (Roseway) on CN.

THE National was approximately nine years old when 4-6-2 5576 and eight cars appeared in a Canadian National photo circa 1924.

Pullman-Standard.

Pullman-Standard.

TASMANIA and nine other sleeping cars that came from Pullman in 1911 were named after countries in the British Empire.

432

Pullman-Standard.

COACH No. 241 of the Ontario Government Railway (Temiskaming & Northern Ontario) was one of the early steel passenger cars in Canada, built in June 1914. The 12-wheeler saw service along the 253.6-mile North Bay-Cochrane (Ont.) route.

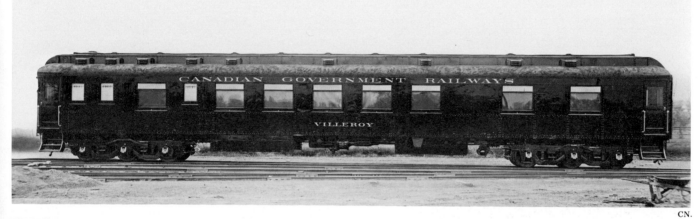

CN.

VILLEROY was one of eight "V" series sleeping cars (10 sections, 2 drawing rooms) for Canadian Government Railways that were the first all-steel sleeping cars built by a Canadian firm. National Steel Car Corp., Hamilton, Ont., had the honor in 1916.

Pullman-Standard.

LOCHBROOM was delivered to Canadian Government Railways by Pullman in 1918 as one of 14 "L" series steel sleeping cars.

Pullman-Standard.

DUGALD, one of seven "D" series steel-exterior dining cars, rolled off the Pullman production line for CGR in October 1918.

433

CANADIAN NATIONAL

Amalgamation

RAILROAD BUILDING in Canada during the early part of the 20th century was slowed by a business recession and eventually was brought to a halt after the outbreak of World War I. The two new transcontinental railway systems, the Canadian Northern and Grand Trunk Pacific, were in financial trouble before they were completed. Construction costs and operating expenses had been inflated by the war; money had become difficult to borrow. The situation was aggravated because the credit of both the Canadian government and key Canadian banks had been heavily committed to financing the new railways as well as the 1914-1918 war. The situation became desperate when further loans were requested by the Canadian Northern and Grand Trunk Pacific in 1916. In order that rail service in Canada would not be disrupted, and Canadian credit, both public and private, would not be threatened, emergency Government assistance was furnished. In addition, a Royal Commission was established to recommend a solution to the grave problem.

In 1917 the two-man majority of the Commission, Sir Henry Drayton, chairman of the Canadian Board of Railway Commissioners, and Sir William M. Acworth, an English railway authority, submitted their report; a minority view was proposed by A. H. Smith, president of the New York Central System. The Drayton-Acworth findings reluctantly recommended that the Canadian government take over the privately owned Grand Trunk, Grand Trunk Pacific, and Canadian Northern railroads and operate them with the Government-owned Intercolonial and National Transcontinental as one publicly owned system, the Canadian Government Railways (a name already used in conjunction with Government control of the Intercolonial and National Transcontinental).

During 1918 Parliament implemented some of the recommendations by taking over the Canadian Northern. The Government authorized use of the new title "Canadian National Railways" to denote the publicly owned enterprise. Two years later, in February 1920, the Grand Trunk Pacific, including its steamships, hotels, and telegraph system, also was entrusted to the Canadian National Railways.

The Grand Trunk, because of its obligations to the Government in connection with the GTP, remained to be dealt with. In 1921 a Board of Arbitration deemed that Grand Trunk common and preference stock had no value. This finding was upheld by courts of appeal, and the Government assumed operation of the Grand Trunk until 1923, when formal amalgamation into the Canadian National System occurred.

A new board of directors faced the problem of uniting all the personnel and fixed plant into one system. Sir Henry Thornton, former general superintendent of the Pennsylvania "Lines West," and later the Long Island Railroad, was recruited from his post as general manager of the Great Eastern Railway of England to become chairman and president. He took the varied pieces of the competing railroads and transformed them into a manageable and unified railroad.

BROCHURES from 1927 (above left) and 1929 (above right) promote new train operations.

THE Continental Limited races across eastern Canada in the 1930's behind 4-8-4 No. 6153.

CN.

Train No. 1 of the Canadian National was the *Continental Limited* from Montreal to Vancouver (No. 2 eastbound). It began service on December 3, 1920, via a 2938-mile route over trackage of the Grand Trunk from Montreal to Ottawa, the former Canadian Northern to North Bay, the T&NO to Cochrane, Ont., the former Grand Trunk Pacific to Edmonton, and an amalgam of the former Canadian National and GTP to Jasper and Vancouver. Through cars from Winnipeg to Prince Rupert operated over the former GTP from Jasper. The Montreal-Vancouver running time was 108 hours 10 minutes. Beginning in 1925 the summer consist also included a Chicago-Jasper Park sleeping car via the C&NW to Duluth and the former Canadian Northern to Winnipeg. Also in the 1920's, the first mountain observation cars were operated during the summer months between Jasper and Kamloops on the Vancouver line.

Because of its magnitude, the Canadian National Railways operated a large number of distinguished trains over many routes: the *National*, Toronto-Winnipeg; the *Ocean Limited* and the *Maritime Express*, Montreal-Halifax; the *International Limited*, Montreal-Chicago; the *New Yorker-Chicagoan*, New York-Chicago via the Lehigh Valley; the *New Englander*, Montreal-Boston via the Grand Trunk subsidiary, Central Vermont; the *Washingtonian* and the *Montrealer*, Quebec-Ottawa-Montreal-Washington, D. C., via CV, B&M, NYNH&H, and PRR, using the Hell Gate Bridge route through New York City.

Between 1920 and 1931, Canadian Car & Foundry built new steel coaches, diners, compartment-observation cars, and tourist and standard sleepers. The railroad operated the sleeping cars, except on lines specified under former Grand Trunk-Pullman Company contracts. On many Canadian National trains provisions were made that contributed to the comfort of long-distance passengers: large smoking rooms, garment hangers, special luminous night buttons, thermos bottles for iced water, boot boxes, and 4 p.m. tea service in the observation-buffet cars. In 1924 CN experimented with radio entertainment: a network of 11 radio stations across Canada was established by the radio department of the company, with receiving sets in parlor cars of important trains. This network became the nucleus of the Canadian Broadcasting Corp. in 1932.

In 1927 substantial improvements were made in Canadian National service. Trains 3 and 4, formerly the *National* between Toronto and Winnipeg, became the *Confederation*, a through transcontinental via Port Arthur and Regina to Vancouver, commemorating the 60th anniversary and Diamond Jubilee of Canadian Confederation (1867-1927). A second new train, the *Maple Leaf*, supplemented the *International Limited* between Montreal and Chicago. The third addition to the timetable was the all-sleeping-car *Acadian* between Montreal and Halifax on the route of the *Ocean Limited* and the *Maritime Express*.

The prosperous year of 1928 brought two more de luxe trains in an unusual co-operative venture between Canadian National and Canadian Pacific: the *Down Easter* between New York and Halifax via the New Haven-Boston & Maine Central-CP-CN; and the *Pine Tree Acadian* from Boston to Halifax over the B&M-MEC-CP-CN. Also in 1928, the *Gull* was added to the Boston-Halifax joint service.

New Pullman cars for the Grand Trunk-Pullman lines, and new CN equipment for the other important trains on the system, were added from 1929 to 1931. The depression and World War II soon halted the construction of new heavyweight equipment on "The Largest Railway System in America."

CN.

IN 1927 the Confederation rumbled across Cisco Bridge in British Columbia to span both the Canadian Pacific and the Fraser River.

CN.

CANADIAN NATIONAL

FORT-SERIES observation car on the Continental Limited in Montreal's old Bonaventure Station in 1924 displayed a radio antenna.

Author's collection.

CAPE TRAVERSE, a 2-compartment, 6-section open-end observation, brings up the rear of the Ocean Limited in Truro, N. S., in 1940.

A BIG USER of 4-8-2's in passenger service, CN took delivery of 73-inch-drivered 6055 from Montreal Locomotive Works in 1930.

A DESIRE to eliminate poor vision resulting from smoke blowing past locomotive cabs led to 1936 construction by MLW of five stream- lined 4-8-4's. No. 6400 had 77-inch drivers and was resplendent in green and black with gold striping and a red CN herald.

IN 1928 Westinghouse and Baldwin furnished the plans for build- ing No. 9000, North America's first diesel large enough to match the specs of a 4-8-2. The V-12 Beardmore engines from Scotland developed 2660 h.p. in carbodies assembled by Canadian Locomo- tive at Kingston, Ont. During World War II one unit was armor- plated to pull an artillery train on the Prince Rupert (B. C.) line.

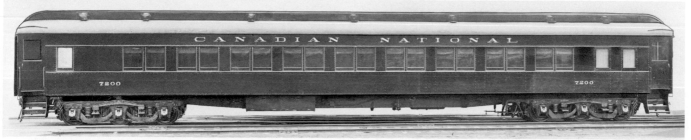

LONG AFTER U.S. roads required Immigrant cars, Canadian Northern was obliged — in 1919 — to buy 50 Colonist cars from Pullman.

437

PORT ELGIN, a 75-foot 6-inch composite sleeper outshopped by CC&F at Montreal in October 1931, was configured (below) for 6 sections, 1 drawing room, and 4 chambrettes (single bedrooms).

TORONTO (left), an all-steel 12-section, 1-drawing-room sleeper built by Canadian Car & Foundry in 1919, was 73 feet 6 inches long; displayed an interior (above) of green plush and mahogany berths.

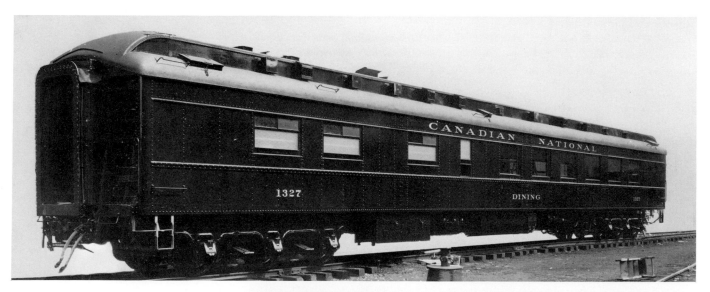

WALNUT VENEER from a 400-year-old tree at Oxford, England, and candelabras highlighted interior (left and right) of diner 1327 (above), built by CC&F in June 1930.

CANADIAN
NATIONAL

CANADIAN NATIONAL dining cars rarely were named. One exception was St. James, outshopped by Canadian Car & Foundry in 1921.

TWIN Pullman cars Mount Mansfield (above) and Mount Royal contained 10 sections plus an enclosed observation-lounge (right). In 1928 both cars were assigned to the Central Vermont-Boston & Maine New Englander, Nos. 302 and 325, for Montreal-Boston service.

CANADIAN NATIONAL

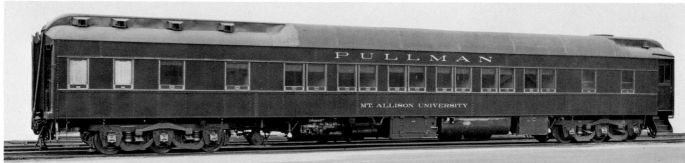

MT. ALLISON UNIVERSITY was a 12-section, 2-double-bedroom Pullman sleeping car named for a Sackville (N. B.) school.

PULLMANS in Canada generally were allotted to international runs. McNamee was one of 225 "Mc" series cars with the 12-section, 1-drawing-room plan. Railroad name on the letterboards of 27 cars leased to CN was unique on a Pullman-owned car.

442

CC&F, courtesy of Canadian Railroad Historical Association.

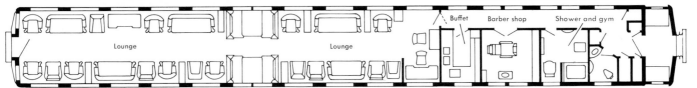

Lounge   Lounge   Buffet   Barber shop   Shower and gym

LUXURY rode the Confederation in 1930 when six Bay-series lounge cars came from CC&F. Georgian Bay (above) had a radio-equipped lounge (left) paneled in English silver harewood plus a tiled shower and a barbershop (below). Bay cars were CN's answer to CPR's River series (see page 404), but the little-used cars were converted into parlors during the depression.

CN.   CN.   CN.

Pullman-Standard.

GEORGIAN BAY (different than CN car at top of page) and sisters Alexandria Bay and Murray Bay were built in 1929 for the International Limited. Cars had unusual plan: drawing room, 2 compartments, 3 single bedrooms, buffet-lounge, and sunroom.

BROCHURE had schedule, blurbs. Author's collection.

THE Overland was a fine sight, whether arriving beneath the Mansard roof of St. John's station during World War II (above), or loping cross-country (below) on a weekly schedule that variously read from 24 to 27 hours from Port-aux-Basques.

The Newfie Bullet

ON March 31, 1949, Newfoundland became the tenth province of Canada. On that date the Government-owned Newfoundland Railway, a 700-mile 3-foot 6-inch narrow-gauge system connecting Port-aux-Basques with the capital city of St. John's, became part of the Canadian National.

Work on the railroad was started by an American company in 1881; but it remained for Robert (later Sir Robert) G. Reid of Montreal to complete the line across the island to Port-aux-Basques in 1898. Thereafter, the line entered into a period of financial difficulty until it was taken over by the Newfoundland government in 1922. Steamships operated by the Newfoundland Railway connected North Sydney on the Nova Scotia mainland with Port-aux-Basques across Cabot Strait.

Crack passenger train on the 547-mile run between Port-aux-Basques and St. John's during the Age of Steam was the *Overland Limited*, operating one day a week in each direction. The companion train was Nos. 1 and 2, the triweekly *Foreign (Canada) Express*. Comfort was the keynote: standard sleeping cars, unsurpassed dining-car service, and courteous attendants were an intimate part of the Newfoundland service. A railroad brochure stated:

> Trains are not operated so much for revenue as for the delectation of patrons. And, so far as cuisine and general service are concerned, are run in accordance with the standard of much larger and more pretentious railway systems.

When the CN assumed operation of the rail and steamship routes in Newfoundland, the *Overland Limited* soon acquired Nos. 1 and 2 and became the *Caribou*, affectionately known as the "Newfie Bullet."

In 1965 the Newfoundland portion of the Trans-Canada Highway was completed. Driving time between Port-aux-Basques and St. John's was about half as long as train time, and Newfoundlanders began deserting the train in favor of the automobile. CN first announced its intention to abandon the *Caribou* in May 1967. Formal approval of the discontinuance by the Canadian Transport Commission's Railway Transport Committee was granted on July 3, 1968. The new Road Cruiser buses that substituted for the trains proved successful, and the *Caribou* made its last run on July 3, 1969 (except for an emergency run in early 1971, when blizzards blocked the Trans-Canada Highway).

Collection of TRAINS Magazine.

CN.

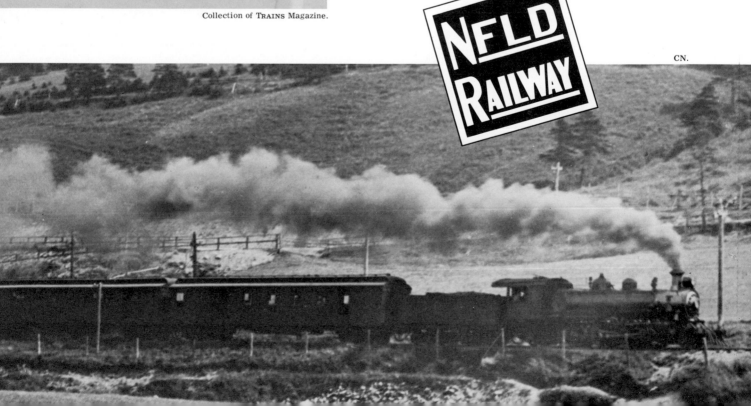

MIKADO No. 1007 (MLW 1941) was one of 12 Class S 152 engines that came from various builders between 1941 and 1944 and bolstered six North British Locomotive Company 2-8-2's delivered from 1935 to 1941. The dual-service Mikes had 48-inch drivers. Tender had "tilted wafer" herald.

THE 4-6-2's, including Belpaire-boilered 196 (Baldwin 1926), were bumped to light passenger and freight runs by the 2-8-2's.

SIX Pacifics, Nos. 190-195, were built by Baldwin in 1920. Their 52-inch drivers produced 20,000 pounds of tractive effort.

TREPASSEY was typical of the old wooden sleeping-car stock: It was fabricated in 1898 by Crossen Car at Cobourg, Ont.

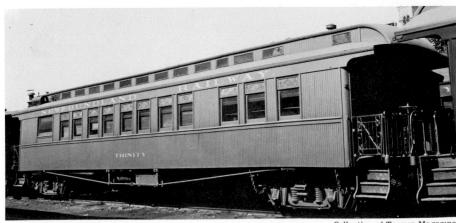

WOOD SLEEPERS such as Trinity still were in service when a snowstorm marooned a passenger train for 17 days in 1941.

TO ASSIST its military operations in New-foundland in the 1940's, the U. S. provided funds for new equipment. Sleeper Flower's Cove (plus coaches) came in 1943, was shopped by CC&F in 1952 (above and below).

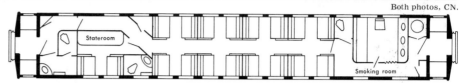

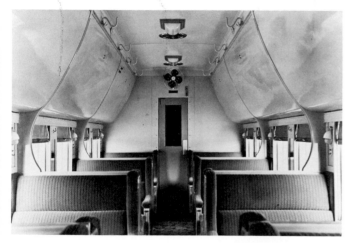

ROAD promoted "Unsurpassed Dining Car Service."

FERRYLAND first saw the light of day in 1926 at American Car & Foundry at Ber-wick, Pa. Car had 8 sections, 1 drawing room.

FOGO was an observation-sleeping car with 8 sections, 1 drawing room, and a brake-man's observation platform. It came to the Newfoundland Railway from CC&F in November 1943 as part of the railroad's wartime equipment upgrading program.

A new image

DURING the all-out effort expended on World War II (1939-1945), passenger mileage on the Canadian National tripled and the revenue from freight doubled. For the first time in its history the road earned an annual surplus, although in the process it depleted its resources of plant and equipment.

After the war, priority was given to replacing locomotives and freight cars, but in 1953 Canadian National contracted for 59 million dollars' worth of new passenger equipment with one of the largest orders ever placed by a North American railroad. Canadian Car & Foundry supplied 218 coaches and Pullman-Standard constructed 141 sleeping, dining, and parlor cars. During 1954 all mainline trains were re-equipped with lightweight streamlined cars. Every effort was made to distribute the rolling stock in such a manner that all Canadians benefited from the new trains.

To conclude a decade of modernization — and with the years

of amalgamation far behind — Canadian National in 1960 adopted a new corporate image (keynoted by the famous "toothpaste" CN logo) to project its character as a unified, efficiently operated, up-to-date railroad serving Canada and the United States.

During the early 1960's, when most American railroads were abandoning passenger service as fast as they could, Canadian National embarked on an aggressive program to encourage rail travel. With lightweight and modernized conventional rolling stock and facilities, the road instituted the concept of "traveliving," complete with many on-train innovations. A new "Red, White, and Blue" fare structure featured lower prices during off-peak travel periods. Schedules were speeded up. In 1963, for example, the running time of the Montreal-Vancouver *Super Continental* (introduced in 1955) was reduced to 68 hours 40 minutes westbound. From 1967 to 1971, a companion

Both photos, CN.

WHETHER the vista depicted booming Montreal's skyline or the Canadian Rockies, striking trains such as the Ocean (above) and Super Continental (right) contributed to CN's new image.

train named the *Panorama* offered twice-daily service with the *Super Continental*. By 1970 Canadian National was carrying nearly twice the number of passengers it had in 1960.

In an attempt to break away from the limitations of conventional rolling stock, CN undertook the study of a totally new concept in railroad passenger equipment and service. The result was an arrangement with United Aircraft of Canada to lease five TurboTrain trainsets of seven cars each for service in the Montreal-Toronto corridor. The TurboTrain was designed by Sikorsky Aircraft, a division of United Aircraft. Each bidirectional trainset had power dome cars at both ends with five low-level cars sandwiched in the middle. Four Pratt & Whitney modified aircraft-type gas-turbines in each dome car gave TurboTrain a maximum speed of 120 mph and furnished power for the auxiliaries. A single-axle air-cushion suspension system enabled the articulated cars to take sharp curves at 90 mph. The sleek aluminum-skin exterior was capped by an orange-red fiber-glass nose.

The interior resembled that of an airplane, with full carpeting and tinted, draped windows. Seating was provided for 302 passengers — 70 in Turboclub (first class) and 232 in Turboluxe (coach). Conventional dining was replaced by at-the-seat food service rendered by hostesses for first-class passengers and buffeteria pick up for coach patrons.

TurboTrains compared favorably with air travel both in fare structure and downtown-to-downtown travel time between Montreal and Toronto (335 miles in 3 hours 59 minutes for an average speed of 84 mph). The trains were well received by the public when they were placed in operation on December 12, 1968, but the service was interrupted once and later suspended because of technical problems. In 1973 the trainsets faced an uncertain future.

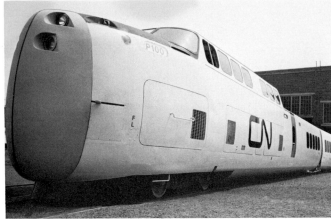

TURBOTRAIN was an imaginative but trouble-plagued response to the quest for a dynamic passenger train concept in the air age.

RAPIDO, crack Montreal-Toronto high-speed daylight train utilizing conventional equipment, is ready for boarding in Toronto.

IN 1950 Canadian Car & Foundry built 20 "I" series cars according to plans and specifications supplied by Pullman-Standard. Lightweight Indigo had 24 duplex roomettes riding over conventional 6-wheel drop equalizer trucks. Upon delivery Canadian National presented the green cars (the roof and trucks were painted black) to the public as "The Latest Thing in Sleeping Cars."

ALMOST at opposite ends of the vast CN transcontinental system, the Ocean (left), sporting a distinctive Skyview observation car purchased from the Milwaukee Road, crosses Beloeil Bridge in Quebec, and (right) the Super Continental enters Edmonton, Alta.

ALL-ROOM SLEEPER Mount Robson was one of six Mount cars with 5 compartments and 3 drawing rooms ordered for transcontinental service. Interior (above) shows drawing room; exterior (above right) highlights black, green, and gold paint scheme.

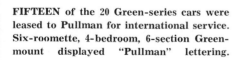

FIFTEEN of the 20 Green-series cars were leased to Pullman for international service. Six-roomette, 4-bedroom, 6-section Greenmount displayed "Pullman" lettering.

ALL 52 "E" series cars were assigned to Canadian routes. Eastport had 8 duplex roomettes, 4 bedrooms, and 4 sections. "Maple leaf" livery preceded "new image."

BUCKLEY BAY had 10 roomettes and 5 bedrooms. Of six Bay-series cars, four were leased to Pullman for Canadian domestic service.

COACH 5515 had plenty of roster mates: 218 streamlined, 80-seat cars were delivered by CC&F in 1954. Photo was taken later when car wore CN's new-image blue-and-off-white livery.

TRAVELERS could eat and sleep aboard the 8-section, 1-bedroom, and dining room-kitchen-pantry White Rapids, one of four White cars built in 1954. They became dining-lounge cars in 1964.

FOURTEEN dining cars, represented here by No. 1338, served as many as 40 passengers at a time in a modern, dignified setting.

SIX dinette cars were termed "drugstore counters on wheels." Each car seated 26 at a counter where hot meals were served.

VALLEYFIELD and five other 10-section, 1-bedroom, and buffet Valley-series cars were rebuilt into dining-lounge cars in 1964.

TWENTY revolving seats in the parlor section of parlor-buffet Beaverhill Lake were added in Canada after the interior (left) was photographed at the Pullman shops. Buffet section seated 16. In 1965 the car was remodeled by CN to 48-seat meal-service car No. 1362.

Both photos, Pullman-Standard.

CN SUBSIDIARY Grand Trunk Western operated buffet-club-dining cars Diamond Lake and Silver Lake (below), first on the Maple Leaf, later on the Chicago-Detroit Mohawk. Interior view (above) shows 15 revolving chairs and part of the dining area.

introducing the **"EXECUTIVE CLUB"** a new concept in business travel

CN

CN OFFERED "Executive Club" travel.

LAKE CHAPLEAU (above) was one of six 34-seat Lake-series parlor cars remodeled to club cars in 1965 for Rapidos. Lake O'Brien (below) had novel (for railroads) 2-1 seating for 43 persons. Liquor pantry at end of car furnished beverage service.

CN.

BUILT as 7-compartment-observation-lounge cars with buffet for charter to special groups, Burrard (above) and Bedford later were assigned to the afternoon Rapidos' short-lived "Executive Club" service, a de luxe ride-and-dine offering aimed at businessmen.

CAPE CHIGNECTO and seven other Cape cars had 2 compartments, 2 bedrooms, and buffet-lounge. CN and Pullman each operated four.

BEST SEAT in the house: CN's passenger "offensive" reached full pitch with 1964 purchase of glass-enclosed Skytop observation cars (above left) and six Super Domes (above right) from CMStP&P.

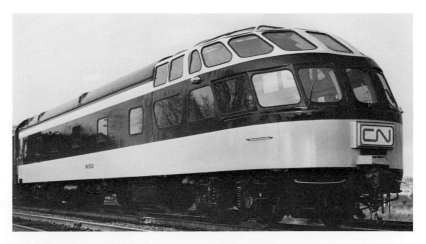

SKYVIEW LOUNGE Malpeque (right) was one of six 8-bedroom lounge-observation cars of Creek series built in 1949 for the Olympian Hiawatha and modernized by CN for Montreal-Halifax service. CN assigned the domes, such as Jasper (below), to Winnipeg-Jasper-Vancouver service, called them Sceneramic Cars.

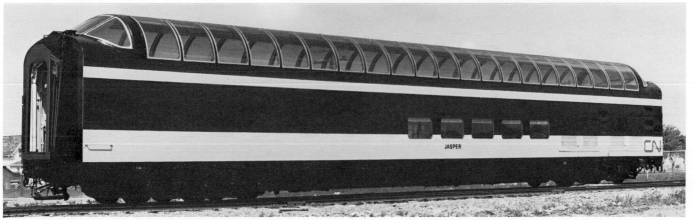

¡MEXICANO

Mexican luxury trains . . . and their Mopac connections

1 SOUTH of the Rio Grande, or *Rio Bravo del Norte* (Fierce River of the North), lies the Latin American republic of Mexico. Much of this beautiful country is covered by the rugged Sierra Madre and vast deserts; the remainder consists of warm fertile valleys and lush green jungles.

The original inhabitants of Mexico were the ancient Indians. They comprised about 50 tribes, including the Aztecs, Mayas, and Toltecs whose great pre-Columbian temples, palaces, and pyramids rank among the wonders of the world.

In 1876, after decades of unrest in the country, Porfirio Diaz seized the government and ruled as dictator until 1911. During this era of stability Diaz encouraged investors from other countries to develop the mines and oil fields of Mexico. Railroads were built and the country prospered.

Tourists from *Los Estados Unidos* seeking warmer climates in the wintertime were attracted also by the pre-Columbian ruins. In Mexico they found a nearby land of sunny skies and amazing antiquities, easily accessible without the rigors of an ocean voyage.

Jim Shaughnessy.

BRIGHT colors are a hallmark of National of Mexico's diesels, as attested by these orange-yellow-and-olive EMD cab units sitting at the Mexico City engine terminal. Alco hood units (right) lift train No. 1, the northbound Aztec Eagle, into the mountains south of Huichapan.

Jim C. Seacrest.

DE LUJO!

Author's collection.

SEÑORITA with a rose over her ear
decorated the cover of the July 1906
National Lines of Mexico timetable

TOUR OF ALL MEXICO

UNDER ESCORT OF REAU CAMPBELL, GEN. MGR.

THE AMERICAN TOURIST ASSOCIATION

A Private Train of Pullman Wide Vestibule Cars, Drawing Rooms, Compartments, Parlor, Library, Music Room, with the

LARGEST DINING CAR IN THE WORLD

Built by Pullman for The American Tourist Association, and the famous

OPEN TOP CAR CHILILITLI.

The only observation car that really and truly observes, going via IRON MOUNTAIN ROUTE. Leisurely itinerary, with long stops, including 3 CIRCLE TOURS in the TROPICS and to the RUINED CITIES in the SOUTH of MEXICO. All distasteful personally conducted features eliminated. Exclusive and independent movement assured.

TICKETS INCLUDE ALL EXPENSES EVERYWHERE

Address

THE AMERICAN TOURIST ASS'N

1418 MARQUETTE BLDG.
CHICAGO, AND

Agents Iron Mountain Route

H. C. TOWNSEND, G. P. & T. AGT., ST. LOUIS, MO.

Author's collection.

A BEVY of American beauties wave from the rear platform of the open-top observation car Chililitli, joyous no doubt because "all distasteful personally conducted features" have been eliminated from their trip to Mexico.

Pennsylvania Tour to MEXICO

MEXICANO DE LUJO!

FOUR-WEEK tour of Mexico which was operated by the Pennsylvania Railroad in 1892 cost $450 from New York and Philadelphia. The train was advertised as "an exact counterpart of the world-renowned Pennsylvania Limited."

Pullman-Standard.

SUPERB (Pullman 1889) of Montezuma Special contained 6 drawing rooms, each furnished with a different wood and décor treatment.

ESPANOLA, a 10-section-buffet Pullman built in 1880 for narrow-gauge service in Colorado, went south of the border in 1900. Photo depicts car immediately after shopping by Pullman for operation over Mexico City-Veracruz Interoceanic Railway of Mexico, whose attractions included the "Grandest Scenery on Earth."

URUAPAN — a narrow-gauge 10-section Pullman rebuilt with 8 sections, 1 drawing room for Mexican National.

CHILILITLI — the open-top, open-side observation car that "really and truly observes" — is shown in a rare builder's plate of 1897.

QUANTZINTECOMATZIN ("the noble eater of the Royal dish") of American Tourist Association was built by Pullman in 1902.

The Sunshine Route in steam and diesel

> The *Sunshine Special* — universally recognized as a train with few equals and no superiors — is famed the country over. Its giant oil-burning locomotives are the standard for speed and safety and cleanliness. Its crews are models for friendly, hospitable courtesy. — *Luxurious Comfort on the Sunshine Special*, Missouri Pacific Lines brochure, 1927.

FROM the day of its inauguration on December 5, 1915, the *Sunshine Special* was recognized as one of the outstanding trains on the continent. It brought about closer and more effective communication between the St. Louis gateway, the Southwest, and Mexico. The *Sunshine* was the premier train of the MP-NdeM route until the post-World War II era, when it was superseded by the streamlined *Texas Eagle* and *Aztec Eagle*.

During the great age of steam and steel, the *Sunshine* (MP Nos. 1-21-201 and 2-22-202 and NdeM Nos. 1 and 2) operated from St. Louis, Mo., and Memphis, Tenn., south and west to Texas-Louisiana-Mexico City-Los Angeles. Employing complex arrangements of connecting trains, through cars were switched at Little Rock, Ark., and Longview, Tex. Co-operating in these unusual movements were the Missouri Pacific Lines, Texas & Pacific, Southern Pacific, National Railways of Mexico, and the Pullman Company. The Los Angeles-St. Louis *Sunshine* traveled the route pioneered by the Southern Pacific *Sunset Limited* of 1897-1898 when it operated from California to Chicago on the Missouri Pacific Lines and the Alton. All sections of the *Sunshine* carried through sleepers and handsome de luxe Spanish lounge cars complete with shower baths and soda fountains. Missouri Pacific dining cars operated through to Mexico City with American and Mexican crews.

In 1926 Raymond & Whitcomb, the venerable Boston travel merchants actively associated with tour travel to Mexico since 1885, created the most luxurious mode of land travel in America. Duplicating the splendid features of an ocean cruise in variety and luxury of accommodations, Raymond & Whitcomb offered the Land Cruise Liners, advertised as "among the world's finest and most unique trains."

Each train consisted of seven or eight cars, some of which were specially designed for the Land Cruise Liners: entertainment cars equipped with gymnasium, recreation room, library-lounge, and barbershop; and special sleeping cars created by the Pullman Company with real beds, dressing

Raymond & Whitcomb.

LECTURER Burton Holmes snapped this Land Cruise train crowd.

Harold K. Vollrath.

SUNSHINE SPECIAL enters Marshall, Tex., in April 1937 behind the 12-wheel tender of burly-looking Texas & Pacific 4-8-2 902.

MEXICANO DE LUJO!

The SUNSHINE SPECIAL

tables, and connecting bathrooms. An observation car, a dining car, and a baggage car completed each consist.

Attentive and competent cruise staffs included cruise director, hostess, and a full complement of porters, maid, valet, gymnasium attendant, barber, and hairdresser.

Itineraries of the Land Cruises varied in length from 28 to 65 days and included summer and winter visits to "ports" throughout the resort areas of North America.

The first Land Cruise train to Mexico operated during the 1929-1930 winter season from San Antonio to Mexico City and return, with a week stopover in Mexico City. In 1930-1931 a side trip to Guadalajara was added; but in September 1931, when the last Liner "docked" in Chicago after the Labor Day weekend, the end was at hand. The economic depression which started in 1929 had made continued operation unprofitable. The Liner's Pullmans were scattered throughout the land. The entertainment cars were assigned to the *Florida Special*, and from 1937 to 1941 the Overland Route's *Forty-Niner* carried the Liner's special private-room sleeping cars and dining-kitchen set.

During the winter seasons from 1936 to 1939, in the brief period of prosperity between the depression and World War II, Raymond & Whitcomb again operated Land Cruise trains to Mexico via El Paso. During these seasons conventional Pullman equipment was operated in place of the glamorous custom cars.

Author's collection.

BROCHURE cover featured train, Indians.

In the same period, from June 1937 until December 1940, the Missouri Pacific and National Railways of Mexico operated the fabled *City of Mexico* via Laredo. This de luxe weekly tourist special, advertised as "The Finest International Train in the World," departed from St. Louis every Sunday evening at 5:30 and arrived in Mexico City on Tuesday evening, $47\frac{1}{2}$ hours later. Departure from Mexico City was on Thursday afternoons and arrival in St. Louis on Saturday mornings.

The luxurious through equipment included two 12-1 sleepers; two 8-2-1 sleepers; one 6-3 all-room car; a Missouri Pacific dining car which featured American and Mexican cuisine; and a Missouri Pacific Spanish lounge car with showers, radio, and soda fountain. All train attendants spoke English as well as Spanish.

Inauguration of the streamlined *Eagles* between St. Louis-Kansas City-Omaha on March 10, 1940, marked a progressive step in the history of the Missouri Pacific, but expansion of the blue-and-gray lightweight fleet was halted by World War II.

Six years later the colorful timetables issued by the Missouri Pacific announced an innovation for travelers on the Sunshine Route. Effective in July 1946, through New York-to-Mexico

Author's collection.

CITY OF MEXICO of 1937 departed St. Louis every Sunday.

MP.

LIGHT USRA 4-8-2 No. 5324 as rebuilt with higher drivers and boiler pressure, disc driving wheels, roller bearings, and a solid pilot.

AC&F.

UNIQUE Sullivan-Renshaw-designed RPO 2129 (built 1911) featured exposed structural framing, much like modern-day box cars.

City Pullman cars were inaugurated via the New York Central and Pennsylvania to St. Louis. Also of interest was the announcement of a 12-million-dollar order for new streamlined equipment for the *Sunshine*:

> With the inauguration of new equipment, the *Sunshine Special* will become the *Sunshine Eagle*. Eastern lines that now operate through sleeping cars via the *Sunshine* have also ordered new streamlined cars to match those being built for the *Sunshine Eagle*.
>
> Two of the four new *Eagle* trains will operate between St. Louis and Dallas-Fort Worth-El Paso, and two between St. Louis and Houston-Galveston-San Antonio and Mexico City, the latter service in connection with the National Lines of Mexico.

A LONG blue-and-gray Sunshine Special leaves St. Louis behind 4-8-2 No. 5340 in 1945.

WITH her vertical-lift coupler tucked away, Mopac 4-6-2 6621 leads Sunshine Special through North Little Rock, Ark.

MEXICANO DE LUJO!

The SUNSHINE SPECIAL

MOUNTAIN 5309 unwinds with a train which could be either a Sunshine Special or the famous City of Mexico limited.

SOUTH of San Antonio the consist and power of Sunshine Special were reduced, as shown in 1938 shot of it behind 4-6-0 384.

MOPAC express car 4194 was built in 1923 by American Car & Foundry. Clerestory roof and riveted-steel construction were typical of the era.

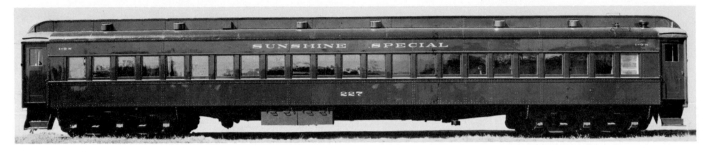

COACH 227 built by AC&F in 1924 for MP's International-Great Northern featured roomy smoking compartment, train name on letterboard.

DINING CAR No. 1015 was constructed for Texas & Pacific in 1920 by Pullman. Cantaloupe pie was a T&P dining-car specialty.

Unfortunately, the grandiose plan never materialized because the National Railways of Mexico did not acquire streamlined Pullmans for the through-service pool. As a result, the *Sunshine Eagles* were hastily renamed *Texas Eagles* and were placed in service on August 15, 1948, from St. Louis to Texas and Louisiana cities only, with East Coast cars via the PRR and B&O.

The celebration which accompanied the inauguration of the new *Eagles* was an occasion of mixed emotions for the late Paul Neff, chief executive of the Missouri Pacific. For the first time in 20 years (since February 5, 1928) there was to be no luxury train from St. Louis to Mexico. Neff could not help but reflect on the great international service which he had worked so hard to create and which had earned him Mexico's

DINING CAR 10035 was a 36-seat vehicle built by Pullman in 1924. In 1934 Mopac shops rebuilt six such cars into diner-lounges 10230-10235 with interior décor of beamed ceiling with candelabra, white walls with pottery niches, red ceramic tile floors.

SUNBURST, a sunroom-lounge-buffet, 2-compartment, 1-drawing-room Pullman, was one of eight built in 1927 for Sunshine Special Service.

Shower | Heater locker | Shower | GENERAL LOUNGE | PANTRY | Desk | Ceiling fandoliers | Serving table
Radio locker | MEN'S TOILET | WOMEN'S TOILET | Pullman standard lower berth | OBSERVATION ROOM

LOUNGES Texas & Pacific 1401 and Missouri Pacific 10302 were part of an order of five such cars built in 1930. In 1933-1934 Mopac refurnished eight full-length lounges in Spanish decor with beamed ceiling, tapestry, grillwork, red ceramic-tile floor, and leather club chairs.

MEXICANO DE LUJO!

The SUNSHINE SPECIAL

SPECIAL entertainment-recreation cars Coliseum, Lyceum, and Trocadero of Land Cruise trains (see page 24) contained gym (left) with lockers and shower room; recreation hall (with Victrola or radio for dancing); barbershop; and library-lounge.

467

DIESEL power draws a postwar Sunshine Special from beneath the 600-foot-wide trainshed of St. Louis Union Station which spans 32 tracks.

DINING CAR 840 of Missouri Pacific was built by ACF in 1948 for St. Louis-Ft. Worth Eagle; seated 44 in a serpentine-style interior (below).

MEXICANO DE LUJO! / ROUTE OF THE *Eagles*

Order of the Aztec Eagle — the highest honor which that nation confers upon a citizen of another country — for his efforts "to promote friendly relations between the United States and Mexico."

With the advent of the *Texas Eagles*, Mexico-bound passengers were forced to transfer to heavyweight conventional Pullmans at San Antonio for the remainder of their journey. The connecting train bravely continued the *Sunshine* name until August 15, 1955, when it was discontinued.

EAGLE CANYON, a 5-double-bedroom-lounge, was delivered by Pullman-Standard to T&P in 1948; included a soda fountain in 26-seat lounge.

EAGLE FLIGHT, a 14-roomette, 2-double-bedroom, 1-drawing-room car built by Pullman-Standard for T&P in 1948, once ran from West Texas to Chicago via T&P-MP-GM&O. It had gray roof, skirting, and pier panels; blue letterboard and girder sheets; yellow striping.

Pullman-Standard.

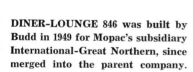

Budd.

EAGLE HAVEN (above) was one of six 10-roomette, 6-double-bedroom cars with six-wheel trucks (right) Budd delivered to Missouri Pacific in 1956. The only other non-articulated lightweight sleepers built with six-wheel trucks were Canadian National's 24-duplex-roomette cars. Eagle Haven had bedrooms in the center of the car, with 4 roomettes at one end and 6 at the other. Eagle Haven operated in St. Louis-Mexico City service; it was sold to NdeM in 1969 and renamed Panama.

Budd.

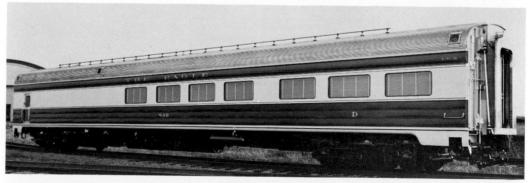

DINER-LOUNGE 846 was built by Budd in 1949 for Mopac's subsidiary International-Great Northern, since merged into the parent company.

Budd.

PLANETARIUM-DOME 893 was delivered by Pullman-Standard in 1952; operated in Texas Eagle, Colorado Eagle, Missouri River Eagle.

Pullman-Standard.

Mexican Government Tourism Department.

RAIL GATEWAY to the nation is modern (built in 1959) concrete-and-glass Buenavista Grand Central Station in Mexico City, head-quarters of National Railways of Mexico. Narrow-gauge 0-4-2T No. 601 stands outside on pedestal as a reminder of NdeM's past.

Streamliners south of the border

The new trains which the National Railways of Mexico have placed on the *Aguila Azteca* route represent an improvement which starts a new era in Mexican transportation: Perfect service, luxurious atmosphere, and unprecedented comfort. — *The New Aguila Azteca Trains*, brochure, 1953.

THE streamlined era in Mexico began with the new *Aguila Azteca* (*Aztec Eagle*) service on August 7, 1953.

BROCHURE announcing Aztec Eagle streamliner.

Three beautiful new red-and-cream trains were constructed by the firm of Schindler Waggon AG of Pratteln, Switzerland, as part of a Mexican-Swiss trade agreement. They had a distinctive European character — a reminder of Old World capitals, legendary vacation resorts, and the world-renowned Continental expresses of the Wagons-Lits Company. Each train consisted of a mail-baggage car, one standard coach, two first-class coaches with showers, two sleeping cars with sections and bedrooms, one sleeper containing bedrooms and drawing rooms (with private showers), 44-seat dining car, and bar-observatory car.

Architects and designers succeeded in blending authentic Aztec themes within the modern décor. Interior finishes included precious woods, silk and cotton fabrics and tapestries, and woolen carpets — all in contrasting colors. Expert chefs and personnel of the Pullman Company served delicious, select meals with specially designed crystal and china, napery and cutlery.

Although the cars were beautiful, their patented lightweight trucks — each equipped with eight oil-fed shock absorbers — proved unsatisfactory. These trucks, which were advertised as "conforming completely to the exacting standards of the American Association of Railroads [sic]," did not function properly in the rugged Mexican operation. Consequently, the new equipment spent much time in the repair shops, making operation of the *Aguila Azteca* difficult. One by one the new cars were re-equipped with *norteamericano*-type trucks, but not in time to save the new streamliner.

The Swiss cars were supplemented with modern lightweight rolling stock purchased secondhand from the U. S. Cars built for the streamlined *20th Century, Empire State,* and *Broadway* were sold to the NdeM in the postwar decades when the cars became surplus because of reductions in service. By 1965 nearly 200 lightweight Pullmans were operating in Mexico.

At midnight on November 12, 1970, Pullman service in Mexico was nationalized. The *Agencia Coches Dormitorio* (Sleeping Car Agency) assumed the operation of 426 cars — 254 lightweight and 172 conventional.

A typical 1972 evening at Buenavista Grand Central Station in Mexico City provided excitement for the train-watcher.

470

Schindler Waggon AG.

RED AND CREAM rolling stock for Aztec Eagle glides through mountains beneath Swiss Federal catenary shortly after completion in 1953 by Schindler works located in Pratteln, Switzerland.

Adolfo Gonzalez Arrellano.

CLUB AGUASCALIENTES, an ex-New York Central Budd-built (in 1948) lounge, carried illuminated tail sign of El Fronterizo. Stainless steel was painted green and white for the south-of-the-border run.

MEXICANO DE LUJO!

Long de luxe trains arrived and departed in rapid succession.

First in the parade was the *Aguila Azteca*, which arrived from Nuevo Laredo at 1721. (NdeM uses the 24-hour clock in its Spanish-language timetables.) No. 71, *El Regiomontano (The Mountain Region)*, with six sleeping cars, a diner, and an observation car, departed for Monterrey, the great industrial city of the North, at 1920. *El Regiomontano* was placed in service on December 1, 1962, between the capital and Monterrey. The de luxe consist and fast overnight schedule proved so popular that within 2 months of the train's inauguration, Mexicana Airlines discontinued two jet flights on the route.

No. 7, *El Fronterizo (The Frontiersman)*, left at 1950 for Ciudad Juárez with four sleeping cars (three to be set out at León, Aguascalientes, and Chihuahua), a diner, coaches, and an ex-New York Central Budd-built observation car.

At 2010 No. 49, *El Meridano*, pulled out on its two-night, 1029-mile run to Merida via Córdoba and Coatzacoalcos and the United South Eastern Railways line along the Yucatán Peninsula.

At 2030 First No. 5, *El Tapatio*, departed for Guadalajara, Mexico's beautiful second city, with club car, dining car, and sleepers. One sleeper was one of the Swiss-built 7-bedroom, 2-drawing-room cars; two other sleepers were destined for Nogales via the Pacific Railroad. Second No. 5 followed 20 minutes later with a similar consist that included one sleeper for Mexicali, handled north of Guadalajara by the Pacific Railroad and

the Sonora-Baja California Railway. *El Tapatio*, named for the natives of Guadalajara, required a pool of 50 sleeping, dining, and club cars.

Promptly at 2101 No. 53, *El Jarocho (The Native of Veracruz)*, departed with coaches and sleepers for Veracruz via the former Mexican Railway. This line, the first mainline railway in Mexico, was built by the British. It was completed in 1873 and offers some of the most spectacular scenery in the world.

Departing along with these name trains were locals carrying sleepers for Morelia, Uruapan, Tapachula, and Oaxaca.

In 1964 the National Railways of Mexico operated nearly 10,500 miles of track and carried 35 million mainline passengers. Despite the growing competition from bus and air transportation, the number of passengers increased steadily. Mexican rail officials attribute much of this growth to the establishment of luxury trains for overnight services.

Although rail operation in Mexico is expensive owing to the difficulties of terrain, the prices for passenger transportation are exceptionally low (about 1.4 cents per mile, plus space charge for sleeping-car travel). By this token, the government-owned railways perform a great social service in carrying an enormous passenger load, 90 per cent of which comprises people of the lowest economic level. In Mexico rail travel is the cheapest mode of transportation, and in some regions of the country it is the only one available.

ELECTRO-MOTIVE F2's prepare to depart from old Buenavista Station with heavyweight consist of El Tapatio for Guadalajara

Both photos, Everett L. DeGolyer Jr.

BALDWIN Centipede 6401 bulks big on head end of southbound pro-Swiss equipment Aztec Eagle during station stop in Saltillo.

471

OBSERVATORY cars Club Maya, Club Mexica, and Club Olmeca featured round bar (left) decorated with pre-Cortesian themes. Crystalware, fine woodwork finish, and tapestries produced unique effect.

DINING cars Tarasco, Tolteca, and Totonaca — also Swiss-built — combined serpentine seating (above) with specially designed carpet, crystal, china, cutlery, and napery.

MEXICANO DE LUJO!

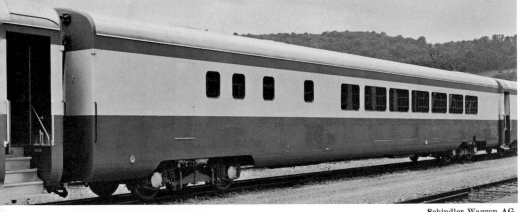

VILLA RICA — ex-New York Central Budd dining car John Jay built for 1941 Empire State Express — served a tequila cocktail for 36 U.S. cents, as well as a filet mignon dinner complete with wine for only $2.40.

ISLANDIA, a 10-roomette, 6-double-bedroom car, was one of 22 lightweight Pullmans built for New York Central in 1948 and sold to NdeM in 1964. All were rebuilt and named for countries or constellations. Islandia (Iceland) ran on the NYC with the name Beaver River.

MP.

CUYUTLAN, U.S.-imported diner (ex-C&O No. 961), was purchased in 1950 and painted red and cream for the Aztec Eagle streamliner.

Everett L. DeGolyer Jr.

GUASAVE, a traditional 12-section, 1-drawing-room heavyweight Pullman, was delivered in 1925 as Red River and operated on C&NW-UP-SP Overland Limited. Sleeper is shown in olive green, orange stripe.

Everett L. DeGolyer Jr.

NORTHBOUND Aztec Eagle at San Luis Potosi with ex-New York Central Budd lounge Club Coahuila.

Everett L. DeGolyer Jr.

Some

Exotic Trains

Trains of all shapes and sizes

1   AMERICAN passenger-train history after World War II was marked by the appearance of exotic trains — trains composed of strange and intriguing locomotives and cars. Most of them were the products of joint ventures of the railroads, consultants, and manufacturers working to produce experimental trains to test their ideas for improving railroad travel. The results of these collaborations were innovative trains of many styles and configurations: standard-size lightweight, low-profile, low center-of-gravity, high-level, and bi-level.

General Motors joined with Pullman-Standard to produce the *Train of Tomorrow*. The Chesapeake & Ohio Railway, Baldwin Locomotive Works, and the Budd Company developed the *Chessie*. American Car & Foundry experimented with *Talgo*. Several Eastern railroads, notably New Haven, Chesapeake & Ohio, New York Central, and Pennsylvania, concentrated on low center-of-gravity designs. Budd built its successful Rail Diesel Car (RDC) and the *Pioneer III* car. Unrestrained by the critical clearances of the East, the Santa Fe and the Chicago & North Western examined the possibilities of two-story trains and ultimately purchased new two-level consists over 15 feet tall, almost 2½ feet taller than conventional streamlined equipment.

Some of the exotic trains were utter failures, and some were outstanding successes. Their part in the history of American passenger railroading is significant and fascinating.

LOW-SLUNG lightweight trains like New York Central's Xplorer, built by Pullman-Standard, embodied the hopes of the railroads and the carbuilders for a renaissance of the passenger train.

TRAIN OF TOMORROW was blue-green with stainless-steel trim and a large red star on the side of the locomotive. Here it poses at Pullman on May 14, 1947. In 1950 Union Pacific purchased the train (right). The E7 entered UP's motive-power fleet, and the four cars ran for many years as UP's contribution to the Portland-Seattle pool trains.

Pullman-Standard.

The Train of Tomorrow

THE central idea for the *Train of Tomorrow* originated with General Motors in 1944. Subsequent suggestions from consultants and railroad executives were incorporated in a four-car Astra-Dome train which was completed in Chicago in 1947. The train consisted of a 2000-h.p. Electro-Motive E7 passenger diesel and four streamlined, domed passenger cars built by Pullman-Standard: coach *Star Dust*, dining car *Sky View*, sleeping car *Dream Cloud*, and observation-lounge *Moon Glow*.

Engineers of GM's Electro-Motive Division worked with

General Motors.

General Motors.

THE Astra-Dome was the chief design feature of the train. Dining car Sky View offered "roof garden" dining (above). Dream Cloud (below) had 8 duplex roomettes, 2 drawing rooms, and, under the dome, 3 compartments (left) with two lengthwise lower berths.

UP.

476

stylists from GM's Detroit plants and Pullman-Standard engineers and designers to produce the equipment. The spectacular train made its initial run from Chicago to French Lick, Ind., over the Monon in May 1947. On subsequent exhibition tours in the East and West it traveled 65,000 miles and attracted wide attention. Thousands of visitors were intrigued by its many design innovations.

In 1950 the *Train of Tomorrow* was purchased by the Union Pacific for service between Seattle and Portland. The train remained intact until 1958, when *Moon Glow* was reconstructed for midtrain operation. *Sky View* was scrapped in 1961, and the other cars were scrapped in 1964 and 1965.

THE California Zephyr was ordered while the Train of Tomorrow was still being planned, but in 1947 the Train of Tomorrow was able to give the Feather River Route an idea of things to come. Here the GM train crosses WP's Spanish Creek trestle at Keddie, Calif.

MOON GLOW, the observation-lounge car (below), offered conventional dome seating, a rear observation lounge, and cocktail lounges forward and below the dome (the Top O' the Rail). Rear view of the car (above) shows an unusual "bumper" concealing the coupler. UP later rebuilt Moon Glow for midtrain service.

IN 1946 C&O's Huntington, W. Va., shops completely rebuilt four 20-year-old Pacifics into streamlined Hudsons, like L-1 No. 490.

The locomotives, clad in stainless steel and orange paint, were intended for the Newport News-Charlottesville connection.

C&O.

C&O.

THIS 1947 advertising display, with its representation of the steam turbine-electric, gave the public a hint of the train that never ran.

THE steam turbine-electrics made up in size — 154 feet long with tender, almost 16 feet high — for what they lacked in performance.

The Chessies

CHESSIE'S domes, such as observation 1875, were to be the first domes in the East. The cars were stainless steel with an orange letterboard.

The stillborn Chessie

IN 1942 Robert R. Young, an imaginative financier, became board chairman of the Chesapeake & Ohio. Part of his plan for the modernization of the C&O after World War II was a luxury passenger train to be operated between Washington and Cincinnati on a daylight schedule, with a connecting link between Newport News, Richmond, and Charlottesville, Va.

In 1944 a C&O research group designed and contracted for three steam turbine-electric locomotives. These coal-burning monsters were termed "the world's largest passenger locomotives." During 1945 plans for the new streamlined train began to take shape. An order for 46 stainless-steel cars was placed with the Budd Company for three 14-car consists plus the Virginia connection (Budd, because Young was battling for control of the Pullman Company). C&O and Budd planners designed an extraordinary train filled with special features:

lounges in every car, a playroom for children, luggage lockers, movies, and domes, to list only a few. The train was to be named *The Chessie*, after the cat which was C&O's trademark.

Suddenly the entire picture changed. Robert Young and the C&O were beset with economic problems, and the *Chessie* project was quietly terminated. The stillborn streamliner was abandoned without ever turning a wheel in revenue service. The steam turbine-electrics were returned to Baldwin in 1950, having failed to meet expectations, and all but four of the Budd-built cars were sold. Only four rebuilt L-1 streamlined Hudsons, three diner-lounge-observations, and a combine remained on C&O rails.

Almost half of *Chessie*'s cars eventually were purchased by Amtrak, while Auto-Train Corporation bought the twin-unit diners for its Virginia-Florida automobile-on-train service.

COMBINATION baggage-coach seated 28 passengers and carried their luggage. Amtrak bought No. 1402; the other two were sold to Argentina.

C&O.

THE family coaches, 1700-1702, had a playroom for the youngsters. To assist was (or would have been) a stewardess-nurse (below).

FOCAL POINT of the tavern-lounge cars, 1900-1902, with their aquamarine, vermilion, and yellow decor, was the illuminated aquarium (above). A bad omen, though, was the death from train-sickness of the goldfish, less hardy than C&O's feline mascot.

DOUBLE-UNIT dining cars embraced a lunch counter-kitchen car (above) and a full dining car (below) that became a movie theater after meals. These cars have worn two different paint schemes involving purple — those of Atlantic Coast Line and Auto-Train.

Pullman Company.

THE 5-roomette, 3-drawing-room, 1-bedroom cabin dome cars were the operation center of the train and provided crew space. In 1948 they were rebuilt for sleeper service by Dwight Austin & Associates, and in 1950 they were sold to the Baltimore & Ohio.

The Chessies

AFTER a brief tour of duty on the Pere Marquette streamliners, the dome-observation-coaches went west to work on the Rio Grande.

IN 1949 American Car & Foundry completed three Talgo trains at Berwick, Pa., and Wilmington, Del. (above). One remained in the U. S. for experimental service, and the other two were delivered to the Spanish National Railways. The articulation of the cars is evident (below) in the view of the interior, which was spacious even with the low profile of the train. The view of the uncoupled car (bottom) shows details of the suspension and offers a height contrast with a conventional car.

Talgo

DURING the late 1930's, engineers in the U. S. and Spain developed new passenger-car suspension systems. In California C. T. Hill, grandson of "Empire Builder" James J. Hill, designed the Preco "pendulum car," of which three were built. The Spanish design was named *Talgo*, an acronym of Tren (train), Articulado (articulated), Ligero (light), Goicoecha (the inventor), and Oriol (the project's financial backer).

The pendulum car was not repeated after World War II, but development continued on *Talgo*. The train proved successful in Spain, but in the U. S. performance of *Talgo* was disappointing. The lightweight construction and exotic mechanisms fell prey to problems at high speeds, and passengers preferred the solid comfort of conventional equipment. The trains soon were scrapped, stored, or relegated to suburban service.

Train X shared *Talgo*'s low center-of-gravity, guided-axle principles, while General Motors' *Aerotrain* was based on GM's intercity bus body supported on two single-axle trucks. Both *Train X* and *Aerotrain* suffered the same fate as *Talgo*. Many of *Train X*'s design features were used later for *TurboTrain*.

ROCK ISLAND'S Jet Rocket, a silver-and-maroon Talgo train powered by an Electro-Motive LWT12, entered Chicago-Peoria service
on February 11, 1956, making two round trips a day. The consist included a diner (right) and a parlor car. Rock Island officials had high hopes for the train, and even considered overnight service to Colorado for which the Pullman Company planned
sleeping cars. The low-profile equipment proved unpopular, and
standard-size equipment returned to the run in less than 2 years.

IN 1938 a low-slung two-unit articulated car was built by Pacific Railway
Equipment Company in Los Angeles
to test the pendulum principle. In
1941 three full-size pendulum coaches followed for Burlington (left),
Great Northern, and Santa Fe. The
cars ran together during testing.

NEW HAVEN experimented extensively with lightweight trains during the presidency of
Patrick B. McGinnis. Purchased in 1957 was the John Quincy Adams, a Talgo powered by two
Fairbanks-Morse diesels (above). Uncomfortable and unreliable, it was soon withdrawn from
service. When McGinnis took control of Boston & Maine, he ordered a similar Talgo for Bos-
ton-Portland service (left). By 1958, when it was delivered, B&M's traffic had shrunk, and
the unnamed white, blue, and black train spent its life in Boston-Reading commuter service.

Author's collection.

FROM April to October 1956, Aerotrain No. 1000 operated as New York Central's Great Lakes Aerotrain, first between Chicago and Detroit and later between Chicago and Cleveland. The train offered coach seats and "Cruisin' Susan Seatside Hot Meals."

UNION PACIFIC'S
NEW STREAMLINER
"City of Las Vegas"
BETWEEN LOS ANGELES — LAS VEGAS

Aerotrain

GENERAL MOTORS entered the lightweight train market in 1956 with two 10-car *Aerotrains*. The locomotives, model LWT-12, were EMD's bid for the lightweight-train power market. The coaches were an adaptation of GM's intercity bus body, widened and lengthened and riding on two air-spring single-axle trucks. The two *Aerotrains* logged nearly 600,000 demonstration miles in the U. S., Canada, and Mexico, ran in revenue service on NYC, PRR, and UP, and were sold in 1957 to the Rock Island, where they operated in suburban service until 1965.

UP.

CHUCK WAGON buffet car (above) served complimentary meals on the City of Las Vegas. The interiors of the coaches (below) were wider and longer than the buses from which they were developed.

General Motors.

AEROTRAIN No. 1001 operated on Union Pacific as the City of Las Vegas between Los Angeles and Las Vegas from December 18, 1956, to September 14, 1957.

UP.

NEW YORK CENTRAL'S Xplorer entered Cleveland-Cincinnati service on June 3, 1956, and ran for more than a year on that route. The blue-and-yellow train was built by Pullman-Standard.

NYC.

The **X** *plorer*

Train X

ALONG with *Chessie*, Robert R. Young was interested in *Talgo* for possible use on C&O. He authorized studies for *Train X* in 1947. Ultimately C&O began working with Pullman-Standard on the project. When Young moved to the New York Central he continued his interest in *Train X*, and in 1955 NYC ordered *The Xplorer* from Pullman-Standard. The New Haven under Patrick B. McGinnis ordered a similar train, named the *Dan'l Webster*. Both trains were powered by Baldwin-Lima-Hamilton 1000-h.p. diesel-hydraulic locomotives, one on the NYC train and two, one at each end, on the NH train.

Pullman-Standard.

THE Train X test car, lettered "Railplane" to protect a Pullman-Standard copyright, pauses at La Crosse, Ind., on C&O in 1952.

Pullman-Standard.

NEW HAVEN's version of Train X, the Dan'l Webster, (above) differed from NYC's in its motive power. NH's train had a locomotive on each end to obviate the need for turning the train at Boston and New York. In addition, the diesel-hydraulic locomotives, otherwise the same as NYC's, carried traction motors and third-rail shoes for operation into Grand Central Terminal, New York. The train was gray and white with orange doors. Train X interiors (right) were bright.

Pullman-Standard.

Pullman-Standard.

PULLMAN posed a Train X car (using dolly wheels at one end) beside a contemporary Union Pacific sleeper to show the contrast in size.

Edward G. Budd, "Father of Streamliners"

THE Edward G. Budd Manufacturing Company of Philadelphia was founded in 1912 by Edward Gowan Budd to produce steel automobile bodies. Soon the company entered into a license agreement with the Michelin Company, a French tire manufacturer, to produce Michelin steel-disc automobile wheels. The association eventually led to Budd's production of railroad passenger cars.

In 1929 Michelin undertook the development of a light-rail-motor car mounted on pneumatic rubber tires for branchline service. Budd officials who observed the French experiment developed the Budd-Michelin rubber-tired rail car, the first of which was built in January 1932. Similar units for Reading, Pennsylvania, and Texas & Pacific followed. *Pioneer II,** the Burlington's *Pioneer Zephyr* of 1934, was Budd's first steel-

wheeled train. More *Zephyrs*, the first *Super Chief*, the *Crusader*, and a fleet of *Rockets* established Budd as a versatile and innovative railroad carbuilder.

In 1949 Budd introduced its Rail Diesel Car (RDC), a self-propelled car available in various combinations of coach, mail, and baggage space. A total of 342 were built for service in North America, and others operated in such faraway places as Australia and Saudi Arabia.

During 1956 Budd completed a number of exotic stainless-steel cars. The eight-car *Keystone*, Pennsylvania Railroad's "Tubular Train," was followed by the *Pioneer III*, an 85-foot lightweight economy passenger car adaptable for service as a coach, a high-capacity diner, a tavern-lounge, a sleeper, or a multiple-unit electric commuter coach, the only configuration in which it was actually built. Except for contemporary pessimism about the future of the American passenger train, *Pioneer III* might have been an overwhelming success. The same year saw *El Capitan*, Santa Fe's Chicago-Los Angeles extra-fare coach streamliner, completely re-equipped with Budd Hi-Level cars. In 1957 Budd produced the *Hot Rod*, a six-car train of modified RDC's for the New Haven. Budd's later production included Long Island's *Metropolitan* cars and the *Metroliner* multiple-unit electric trains.

*Pioneer I was a stainless-steel amphibian biplane built by Budd in 1931.

THIS Budd-Michelin rail car, the Green Goose, was Budd's first railroad car. The stainless-steel car was almost 41 feet long and powered by Chrysler and Junkers engines. The wheels had steel flanges and a steel inner wheel inside the tire.

Budd.

All photos, unless otherwise credited, Lawrence S. Williams, courtesy of Budd.

KEYSTONE power car 9600 (above) had a food-service galley and a generator providing electricity for lighting, heating, and cooling.

The PENNSY KEYSTONE

TUBULAR construction of the Keystone dispensed with the usual center sill and used heavy side sills instead, permitting a lowered floor in the car center and a lower center of gravity. Coach 9604 (below) was one of seven purchased by the Pennsylvania (and later by Amtrak). Exterior was stainless steel, with red letters and numbers. The car seated 68 in reclining seats (right), plus 14 more in a smoking lounge at one end of the car.

NEW HAVEN'S third experimental was the Roger Williams, a six-car train of modified RDC's (above). The biggest differences from standard RDC's, such as Pacific Great Eastern BC-12 (right), were single-vestibule cars, locomotive-style control cabs, third-rail shoes and traction motors for use in New York's tunnels, and more luxurious interior appointments.

PIONEER III (right) was adaptable to several configurations — coach (above), diner, lounge, or sleeper. It was the most successful lightweight design and was used for more than 60 multiple-unit commuter cars for the Pennsylvania and the Reading.

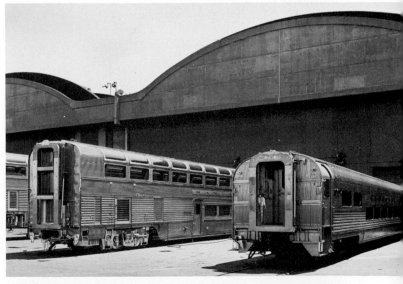

BUDD produced a wider variety of unconventional equipment than the other builders — witness the Hi-Level El Capitan lounge and the tubular Keystone photographed at Budd's Red Lion (Pa.) plant.

BOUND for New Mexico, Arizona, and California, El Capitan climbs the grade of Raton Pass, south of Trinidad, Colo., with Hi-Level coaches, diner, and lounge.

AT&SF.

Santa Fe Hi-Levels

IN the summer of 1954, the Santa Fe received a pair of experimental coaches from Budd. Termed "Hi-Levels," they were the very antithesis of *Talgo* and *Aerotrain*. They were long-distance coaches with two levels. The upper level contained **68** reclining leg-rest seats, half again as many as in Santa Fe's conventional coaches, and the lower level was devoted to entranceways, luggage racks, lavatories, and mechanical equipment. The cars were built with a second-level train door at one end and a conventional-level door and stairs at the other so they could be used with conventional equipment. The two cars were coupled together for the period of the test.

Polls conducted by the Santa Fe indicated that passengers enjoyed the ride, the view, the comfort, and the quietness. On the strength of the findings Santa Fe ordered 47 more Hi-Level cars in 1956 — coaches, diners, and lounges — to re-equip *El Capitan*. Drawings and specifications were prepared for spectacular Hi-Level sleeping cars for the *Super Chief*, but the project was abandoned. In 1963 and 1964 the purchase of 24 more Hi-Level coaches allowed the luxury cars to be added to the *San Francisco Chief*.

The Hi-Levels were considered a success by both the Santa Fe and the traveling public. The fleet of cars was eagerly purchased by Amtrak in 1971.

HI-LEVEL coaches 526 and 527 were the experimental cars that tested the idea of "see-level" seating for all.

Lawrence S. Williams, courtesy of Budd.

DINER 654 had an air-conditioned all-electric kitchen below and penthouse dining for 80 above. The car's weight, 97 tons, required six-wheel trucks.

Budd.

488

HI-LEVEL lounge car (above) had seats for 60 in the Top of the Cap lounge upstairs and room for 26 more in the Kachina Coffee Shop on the lower deck (right). Curved roof glass created an open feeling in the upper lounge (below).

HI-LEVEL *El* CAPITAN Santa Fe

BAGGAGE-DORMITORY 3481 (right) was rebuilt from baggage-dorm of El Capitan of 1938. The adapter-roof matched the profile of Hi-Levels.

Alternate end

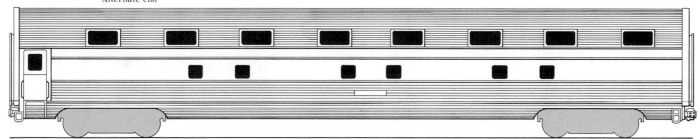

IN 1957 Budd proposed a Hi-Level sleeping car for the Super Chief. The car was to have 6 single bedrooms at normal floor level and 8 full-width "Vista Bedrooms" for two persons on the upper level. The rooms were arranged in duplex fashion, with crosswise beds in the upper rooms over those in the lower rooms, and lengthwise beds in the upper rooms over the passageway up another step. The upstairs bedrooms would have provided a superb view of the Southwest.

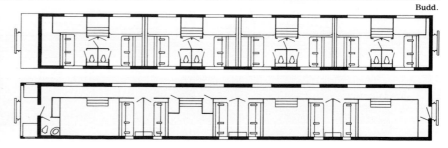

A report on Amtrak

The National Railroad Passenger Corporation

1 DURING each year from 1912 to 1923, about 1 billion revenue passengers were carried by Class 1 railroads in the United States. Intercity passenger trains enjoyed a transportation monopoly; rivalry from highway vehicles and commercial aircraft was negligible.

In the 1920's, competition from highways and airlines increased noticeably. Each year during that decade more than 2 million new automobiles were sold in the U. S. (compared with 4000 in 1900 and 181,000 in 1910). Motor coaches accounted for 15 per cent of intercity traffic, while fledgling commercial airlines were transporting increasing numbers of passengers: 13,000 in 1927 and 53,000 in 1928. During 1928 the railroads operated about 20,000 daily intercity passenger trains and carried 788 million revenue passengers — 77 per cent of public-carrier intercity traffic in the U. S.

By 1950 the railroads' share of public-carrier intercity traffic had dropped to 46 per cent (more than half of the 6000 post-World War II passenger trains had been discontinued). At the same time, motor-coach traffic had grown to 38 per cent, and airline traffic to 14 per cent.

By 1970 intercity railroad passenger traffic had dwindled to 7 per cent of the total for public carriers; only 450 daily intercity passenger trains remained in service. Commercial airlines dominated public-carrier traffic with 75 per cent of the total.

RED-NOSED Amtrak GG1 races newly refurbished Broadway Limited equipment to New York following exhibition at Amtrak's first anniversary party in Washington, D. C., on May 1, 1972.

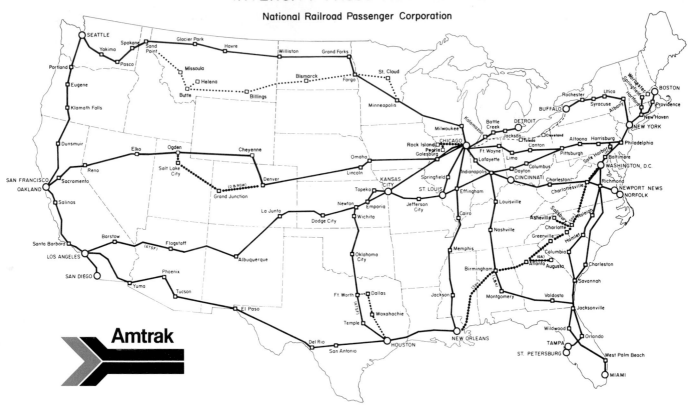

A new hope for rail travel

NOTWITHSTANDING a rapid growth in commercial aviation, the dominant mode of travel in the United States after World War I was the private automobile. Aided by a Federally subsidized national highway network, the automobile accounted for 87 per cent of all intercity transportation by 1970. The era of the intercity passenger train had all but ended.

Finally, the 91st Congress of the United States became concerned about the future of the passenger train. It voted to enact the Rail Passenger Service Act, which President Richard M. Nixon signed into law on October 30, 1970. This legislation specified that rail passenger routes and service standards be established, and that a corporation be organized to commence operation of intercity passenger trains no later than May 1, 1971. The National Railroad Passenger Corporation — first termed Railpax and later called Amtrak — was charged with the responsibility of managing the new service under contracts with the railroads.

To finance the new system, the corporation received a Federal grant of 40 million dollars in cash and 100 million dollars in Federal loan guarantees. In addition, 22 participating railroads paid approximately 197 million dollars in entry fees, a sum which represented 50 per cent of their combined passenger losses for the year 1969. (An additional appropriation for 179.1 million dollars of funding to cover the losses of international services and experimental routes until June 30, 1973, was approved by Congress in 1972.)

The "basic system" of routes was determined by the Department of Transportation (DOT) after careful consideration of comments and recommendations from many official agencies and groups including the Interstate Commerce Commission, railway labor, 43 states, and 15 railroads. In addition, views and opinions were received from many U. S. senators, House representatives, mayors, city councils, chambers of commerce, planning agencies, the National Association of Railroad Passengers (NARP), and nearly 3000 private citizens. The basic system was announced by Secretary of Transportation John A. Volpe on January 28, 1971. It contained 21 routes connecting pairs of cities designated as "end points" and included 29 U. S. cities with a population of more than 1 million.

Initially, the corporation signed contracts for service with 13 railroads: Atchison, Topeka & Santa Fe; Baltimore & Ohio/Chesapeake & Ohio; Burlington Northern; Chicago, Milwaukee, St. Paul & Pacific; Gulf, Mobile & Ohio; Illinois Central; Louisville & Nashville; Missouri Pacific; Penn Central; Richmond, Fredericksburg & Potomac; Seaboard Coast Line; Southern Pacific; and Union Pacific. Six railroads declined contracts and by law were obliged to continue their intercity services until January 1, 1975: Chicago, Rock Island & Pacific; Chicago South Shore & South Bend; Denver & Rio Grande Western; Georgia; Reading; and Southern.

In April 1971 the corporation adopted the short, energetic name Amtrak, formed from elements of the words *American*, *travel*, and *track*. (The previous informal name, Railpax, was rejected.) Also adopted was an arrowlike logo using the colors of red, white, and blue.

On the appointed date — May 1, 1971 — Amtrak commenced operation of more than 184 trains over 22,000 miles of track. Amtrak would serve more than 350 cities in the United States in an area inhabited by 87 per cent of the population. Immediately the corporation began to plan and implement a series of improvements in trains, scheduling, stations, and services for what was termed "America's Nationwide Rail Passenger System." From its Washington, D. C., headquarters, Amtrak President Roger Lewis directed the new operation.

Soon, a new simplified nationwide timetable was issued, headquarters organization and staffing were undertaken, and train performance standards were established. Special inspectors selected the best locomotives and passenger cars available from the nation's railroads. A fleet of 116 locomotives and 1295 cars was purchased in 1971 and expanded to 368 locomotives and 1571 cars — owned or leased — in 1972. Because of pre-Amtrak deferred maintenance, it was necessary to embark on a massive rehabilitation program for the equipment.

From the beginning, Amtrak concentrated on upgrading service, attracting passengers, and rebuilding the image of the American passenger train. During its first 18 months, Amtrak made steady progress: Simplified operational procedures were implemented; a nationwide advertising campaign was launched;

Amtrak.

Nelson Stickler, courtesy of Penn Central.

PRETTY Patty Saunders, an Amtrak passenger representative (formerly a Seaboard Coast Line hostess on the Florida Special — see page 226) greets passengers aboard a Metroliner Metroclub car.

(ABOVE RIGHT) Aboard the first run of the refurbished Amtrak Broadway Limited, NRPC President Roger Lewis (right) discusses Amtrak with (left to right) the author; Rogers E. M. Whitaker, New Yorker editor; and Albert R. Karr, Wall Street Journal reporter.

PRIDE of Amtrak: The New York-Washington Metroliners (right).

Amtrak.

fares were restructured; tour packages were developed jointly with airlines, bus companies, and steamship operators; and international train service to Canada and Mexico was reinstated.

There were successes and, indeed, disappointments on the part of both Amtrak and the railroads. Generally unsolved during Amtrak's first 18 months were the important problems of improving and replacing Amtrak's rolling stock, and maintaining the railroads' rights of way and terminal facilities. Yet, there was guarded optimism when Amtrak issued its reports for 1972. Monthly revenues were up significantly compared with 1971 indicating that the historical 25-year decline in railroad passenger ridership had been reversed. In addition, a survey conducted by the respected firm of Louis Harris & Associates in June 1972 established that "there [was] a clear and decisive public mandate for providing and continuing and improving intercity passenger train travel in the United States."

Auto-Liner Corporation, courtesy of Amtrak.

SILVER SALON, ex-CB&Q baggage-buffet-lounge No. 801, was refurbished for Amtrak in May 1972. It was built by Budd in 1947.

WAGONS-LITS AND GRAND EXPRESSES

Madame la Compagnie

THE Compagnie Internationale des Wagons-Lits et du Tourisme (International Sleeping Car and Tourism Company), recognized as one of the foremost institutions of travel and transport in the world, was founded by Georges Nagelmackers in Brussels on December 4, 1876. Affectionately termed "Madame la Compagnie," its stately *Wagons-Lits* (sleeping cars), elegant *Pullmans* (parlor cars), *Grands Express* (international express trains), *Grand Hotels*, and catering and tourism services established standards for transportation luxury and service on three continents — Europe, Asia, and Africa.

CIWL.

IN a minute and a half the Night Ferry will depart London's Victoria Station for Paris and Brussels via Dover, the cross-channel ferry, and Dunkirk. A British Rail police sergeant stands watch over the blue-and-gold Wagons-Lits sleeping cars that impart a continental flavor to an otherwise English scene. Georges Nagelmackers (above) founded a company that became an international institution. The company's blason avec guirlande (coat of arms with garland) was familiar to travelers almost everywhere between Lisbon and Vladivostok.

497

SLEEPING - CAR 3541   VOITURE - LITS   N°5   SCHLAFWAGEN 3517   CARROZZA CON LETTI

From varnished teak to dark blue enamel

BY 1870 most of Europe's railway arteries were in operation, but the multiplicity of railways, each with its own technical characteristics, made through travel difficult. In order to journey from one country to another it was necessary to change trains. Moreover, the crossing of the frontiers was made rather more difficult by customs examinations and police interrogations. Rolling-stock design was slow to improve; passenger comfort was minimal, and the facilities were primitive.

Georges Nagelmackers, a Belgian mining engineer born in Liege on June 24, 1845, was the man to improve matters. During a visit to the United States in 1868 he became acquainted with the design and construction of the Pullman sleeping car. Upon returning to Europe in 1869 he set about to establish a European sleeping-car company. On October 1, 1872, with the financial backing of a few friends, he established the Compagnie Internationale de Wagons-Lits. Soon he obtained a contract to operate sleeping cars on the Paris-Vienna route. Contracts for other important lines followed.

In January 1873 Nagelmackers entered into an alliance with Col. William D'Alton Mann, the American inventor of the Boudoir Car. This venture ended in 1875 and Mann returned to the United States. (See page 98 and page 342.)

On December 4, 1876, the Nagelmackers company was reorganized in Brussels as the Compagnie Internationale des Wagons-Lits. One of the major shareholders was King Leopold II of Belgium. Management and operation headquarters were established in Paris at 40, Rue de l'Arcade.

The Wagons-Lits company continued to grow in spite of civil strife and two great wars in Europe which brought about the loss of the operation of internal services in Germany (1916), operations in Russia (1917), and operations in the Communist satellite countries (after 1947).

In 1883 the company inaugurated the world-renowned *Orient Express* by rail and steamer between Paris and Constantinople (later Istanbul), the first of its many *Grands Express Europeens*. In 1895 the company through its subsidiary, the International Palace Hotel Company, constructed its first Grand Hotel at Nice. The first all-steel sleeping cars, painted blue and trimmed with gold, were built in 1922.* In 1925 came the first of the great daytime trains composed of Pullmans ("Pullman" means parlor car in Europe). An alliance in 1928 with Thos. Cook & Son, the British travel organization, extended Wagons-Lits/Cook agencies throughout the world. After World War II an extensive modernization program was undertaken.

On May 2, 1967, the company was reorganized as the Compagnie Internationale des Wagons-Lits et du Tourisme. The new diversified organization was created to operate railway sleeping and dining services, hotels and motels, catering services (the users of which included 75 airlines), and travel agencies.

During 1973 the Wagons-Lits company employed more than 20,000 persons. Its rolling stock included 1051 sleeping cars and 83 restaurant cars operating in 21 countries. Leased to nine European railway administrations were 258 sleeping cars for pool service in accordance with an agreement signed July 1, 1971. The company also operated 280 hotel and catering establishments with 2400 rooms in 14 countries. During 1973 this remarkable organization transported more than 2.6 million sleeping-car passengers and served 4.3 million meals, the latter largely in the dining cars of *Trans Europ Express (TEE)* trains. The hotel and catering division provided more than 700,000 traveler-nights and served 7 million meals. Gross income for the company in 1973 was more than 16 billion Belgian francs (over 360 million dollars).

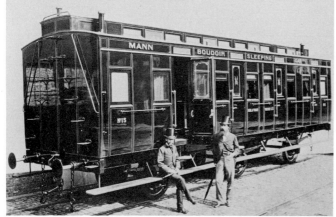

CIWL.

THE first Mann Boudoir Sleeping Car was built in 1873 by Simmering of Austria. The gentlemen are Nagelmackers (seated) and Mann.

*In September 1914 the Pullman Company (of Chicago) submitted complete plans and specifications to the Wagons-Lits company for a proposed 72-foot, all-steel sleeping car containing 8 compartments, each with two berths and private lavatory. The car was to be painted teak color with white roof and cast bronze letters and numerals.

THE Orient Express speeds along behind a Bavarian 4-6-2. In the consist are two fourgons (vans), a restaurant car, and four sleeping cars.

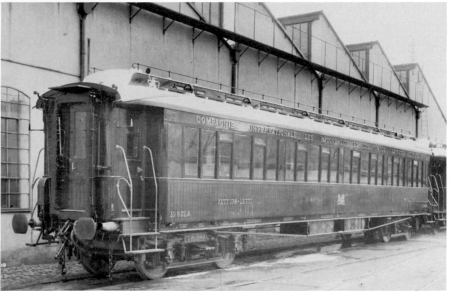

WAGONS-LITS cars are labeled "sleeping car" in various languages. Left to right: English, French, German, Italian, Swedish, and Greek. Plaque labeled "RIC" indicates the countries in which the car may operate and gives mechanical data.

Railphot: Maurice Mertens.

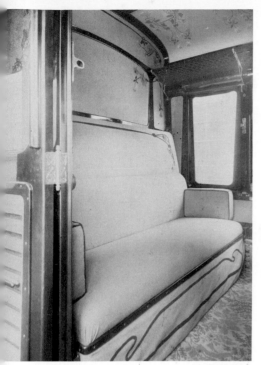

F. Ringhoffer.

F. Ringhoffer.

CAR 832, built in 1902 by Ringhoffer of Prague, exemplifies turn-of-the-century Wagons-Lits rolling stock. It had a varnished teak body, white roof, black running gear, and bronze letters and numbers. The painted and embroidered art-nouveau interior trim (left) was reminiscent of Maxim's restaurant in Paris during La Belle Époque.

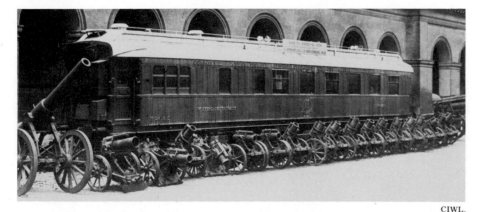

CIWL.

IN restaurant car 2419 Marshall Foch ended the fighting of World War I — November 11, 1918.

END VIEW of a 1927-built sleeping car shows the many connections for steam, air, electricity.

Enterprises Industrielles Charentais.

Archiv Bellingrodt.

THE Paris-Madrid Puerta del Sol changes bogies at the border between France (4 feet 8½ inches) and Spain (5 feet 6 inches).

WAGONS-LITS operated sleeping-car service in Egypt from 1898 to 1961. The Star of Egypt between Cairo and Luxor, 419 miles along the River Nile, made its first run in 1903. The sleepers were built in 1908 of teak and painted white to reflect the sun's heat.

DURING the summer of 1931 Wagons-Lits operated the Golden Mountain Pullman Express on the meter-gauge Montreux-Oberland-Bernois Railway in Switzerland. The cars of the electric railway were painted Wagons-Lits Pullman blue and cream for the service.

KING LEOPOLD II of Belgium (with beard) strolls on the platform alongside his special train at Beaulieu, near Nice on the Côte d'Azur in 1908 (above, far left). Kaiser Wilhelm II of Germany alights from his special train of Wagons-Lits cars at Bari, an Italian seaport on the Adriatic and burial place of St. Nicholas (above center). President Theodore Roosevelt, first American to be awarded the Nobel Prize for peace, greets well-wishers from a Wagons-Lits sleeping car.

THE Trans-Siberian Express traveled nearly 5300 miles between Moscow and the Sea of Japan. The luxurious broad-gauge salon car (above) built in 1900 had a piano and was decorated with pastoral scenes.

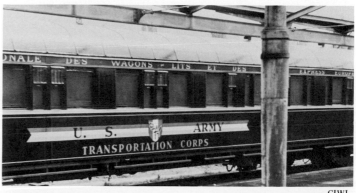

WARTIME complicated Wagons-Lits operation. Sleeping car 3310 (left) wore camouflage in 1945 when it served as an army headquarters car. The U. S. Army Transportation Corps operated the Mozart train (above) between Munich and Vienna. Its cars carried the insignia of the Corps.

501

The Rev. A. C. Cawston.

THE Night Ferry sleepers (left) from Paris and Brussels roll toward London behind a British Railways Merchant Navy-class 4-6-2. The Paris service began in 1936; steam was used in England until 1959.

(LEFT) The Night Ferry arrives at the Gare du Nord, Paris, on the advertised at 0840. (Below) Bilingual brochure includes schedules, notes about connections at Paris, information on restaurant cars, and a list of mineral waters available on board.

J. H. Price.

TRAIN DE WAGONS-LITS
PARIS · LONDRES
PAR FERRY-BOAT (Via Dunkerque-Douvres)
SLEEPING-CARS
LONDON · PARIS
BY FERRY-BOAT SERVICE (Via Dover-Dunkirk)

COMPAGNIE INTERNATIONALE DES WAGONS-LITS
ET DES GRANDS EXPRESS EUROPÉENS

Author's collection.

BR.

THE sleeping cars of the Night Ferry are shunted aboard the French National Railways ferry Saint-Germain at Dover. The ferry carries sleepers at night and freight cars during the day. The 20-mile English Channel crossing takes about 4 hours.

SIMPLON ORIENT EXPRESS

قطار اكسبريس سمبلون الشرق

Railphot: Maurice Mertens.

J. H. Price.

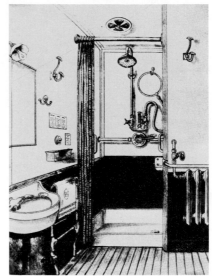

Author's collection.

Author's collection.

FIRST of the Wagons-Lits international expresses was the Orient Express, which made its maiden run from Paris to Constantinople (now Istanbul) on June 5, 1883. The Simplon-Orient Express, known familiarly as the SOE, once offered a fabulous luxury service linking London and Cairo: 7226 miles, 14 countries, 3 continents. An amenity of the SOE in the 1920's and 1930's was a shower (above) in a specially equipped fourgon (luggage, express, and mail van) built by Metro in 1929 (left). The Orient Express gained a reputation for the mysterious and the romantic and was the setting for many novels and films.

THE second Grand Express was the Calais-Méditerranée Express, which began service on December 8, 1883. The first blue-painted steel cars were assigned to this train, which was unofficially named the Train Bleu; later the name became official. The photographs show the Blue Train behind steam (left) and electric power (below).

Railphot: Maurice Mertens.

SNCF.

503

GRAND LUXE sleeping cars (above) with 10 single-berth compartments were built in England and France in 1929 for the Blue Train and other international expresses. The compartments (left) were furnished with oversize beds, special carpeting, and inlaid paneled walls. The lavatory facilities were concealed by curved double doors.

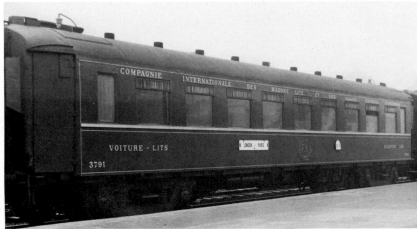

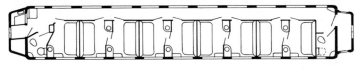

TYPE F sleeping cars for the London-Paris Night Ferry service were 62 feet 11 inches long and somewhat lower and narrower than standard Wagons-Lits cars (76 feet 11 inches over buffers) because of the tighter clearances in England. The compartments were for either single or double occupancy and included life jackets and luggage safety nets as protection against a rough channel crossing.

THREE Pullman (parlor) cars built in 1929 for the Côte d'Azure were rebuilt as salon-bar cars for the Blue Train (above). Half of the interior of the car was fitted with a bar and leather club chairs (right). The atmosphere of traditional elegance was enhanced by wall paneling inlaid with sculptured glass by famed artist René Lalique. The remainder of the car provided dining service in conjunction with an adjacent restaurant car.

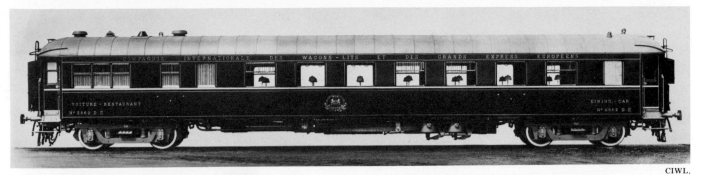

CIWL.

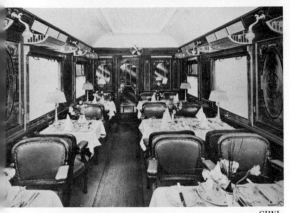

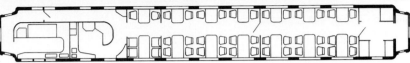

CIWL.

DINING CAR 2862 (above) was one of a group built in England during 1925 and 1926 for service on the Simplon-Orient Express. The car seated 42 persons for meals in a luxurious atmosphere of inlaid wood paneling and leather-upholstered chairs (left). The table lamps were a feature copied in the U.S. by the Pennsylvania Railroad.

CIWL.

IN 1925 Wagons-Lits launched the first of a fleet of Pullman trains which grew to include the Paris-Calais Flèche d'Or (part of a co-ordinated service that included a Calais-Dover channel crossing and the Dover-London Golden Arrow), the Paris-Brussels-Amsterdam Étoile du Nord (North Star), the Amsterdam-Zurich Edelweiss, the Paris-Brussels-Antwerp Oiseau Bleu (Blue Bird), and the Paris-Menton Côte d'Azur. No. 4005 (below) is a 7-mm-scale model of a Flèche d'Or Pullman made by Fulgurex of Lausanne. It carries the short-lived brown-and-cream livery that matched the English Pullmans. The artistic interiors of the 211-car Pullman fleet (above and right) were the ultimate in daytime travel luxury.

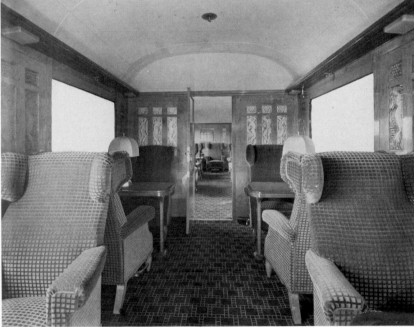

CIWL.

Hedrich-Blessing,

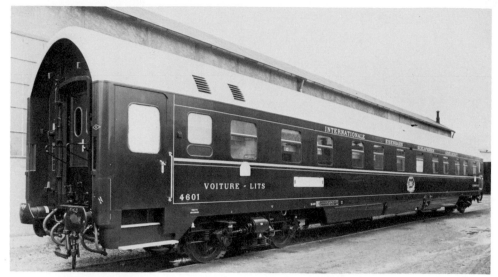

IN 1956 and 1957 the Hansa and Donauworth companies in Germany built 40 Class U (Universal) sleeping cars for Wagons-Lits as reparations for World War II damages. The blue-and-gold cars (right) were 81 feet 6 inches long and contained 11 convertible compartments for use in first-class service with one or two berths (below) or second class with three berths.

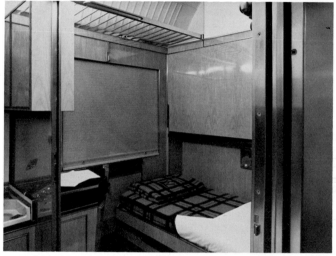

SIMILAR Class U car (below) was built by Orenstein-Koppel for the German Sleeping Car and Dining Car Company (DSG). Livery was red and gold. Compartment (right) is similar to U. S. bedroom.

TYPE P special sleeping car with 20 duplex single-berth compartments arranged in pairs (below) was designed by Albert Pillepich, technical and engineering chief of Wagons-Lits. The car (right) was built of stainless steel and utilized Budd Company patents. Eighty cars of this type were built in Belgium, France, and Italy.

SNCF.

CIWL.

CIWL.

TOURIST-CLASS car (right) contains 18 two-berth second-class compartments (above). Donauworth built 20 cars of this type in 1968 and 1969 for economy service in France and Italy.

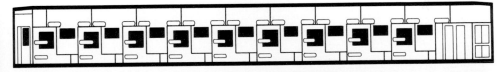

CIWL.

507

Index

RAILROADS AND OPERATING COMPANIES

1871

Acknowledgments

Without the generous help of the following person — railroad enthusiasts and professional railroaders alike — this book would not have been possible. For their considerable assistance the author acknowledges his gratitude:

Wallace W. Abbey; Donald E. Alexander, Canadian Government Travel Bureau; E. W. Anderson; F. F. Angus; Evalyn Antenucci, Altoona Public Library; Fred N. Arone; Laurence J. Barbeau, Chicago, Milwaukee, St. Paul & Pacific; John W. Barriger III, Federal Railroad Administration; John W. Barriger IV, Atchison, Topeka & Santa Fe; James Beck; Lucius Beebe; George Behrend; C. Bellingrodt, *Archiv* Bellingrodt; Henry Benz, Pullman Company; John Thomas Black; Sidney W. Bone, New York Central; Marie Thérèse Bonnet, Wagons-Lits; Lawrence E. Boone, ACF Industries; Peter A. Briggs, Burlington Northern; H. L. Broadbelt; James A. Bryant, Amtrak; William Bryce, Canadian National; Ralph Buckingham, Pullman Company; Charles Castner, Louisville & Nashville; the Rev. A. C. Cawston; Barry B. Combs, Union Pacific; Roger Chenault, Wagons-Lits; William H. Coo, Canadian National; John G. Coté, Canadian National; Jerry Curto, Atchison, Topeka & Santa Fe; Evelyn E. Danielson, Pullman-Standard; Dorothy B. Davis; Everett L. DeGolyer Jr.; Samuel Deloian, Pullman Company; C. C. Dilley, Chicago, Milwaukee, St. Paul & Pacific; Henry Dreyfuss; George Drury; Martin David Dubin; Brian Duff, Amtrak; W. H. G. Ebel; Edwin E. Edel, Amtrak; Harold A. Edmonson; W. E. Edson, Amtrak; Clarence C. Ehlert, Chicago & North Western; Donnette Englund; Rosemary Entringer; Peter A. Falles, Pullman Company; Charles E. Fisher; R. A. Fontaine, DDS; Leotis K. Frazier Jr.; Edward F. Gardner; Robert F. Gardner, Atchison, Topeka & Santa Fe; J. R. Getty, Seaboard Coast Line; Count Giansanti-Coluzzi; S. J. Gilfix; Jackson Gin; Gene V. Glendinning, Amtrak; George A. Gloff; Echo Goldman; Kenneth Gould, Edwin B. Luce Company; Marc Green, Chicago, Milwaukee, St. Paul & Pacific; Howard Greene; Octavio Gutierrez de Velasco, National Railways of Mexico; Barbara Hacker; Harry Hammer, Missouri Pacific; Zenon Hansen; Philip R. Hastings, MD; Edward Hedrich, Hedrich-Blessing Photography; Melvin Horn, Pullman-Standard; Freeman Hubbard; William C. Janssen; Phil Jefford, Wagons-Lits; Alfred W. Johnson; Richard D. Johnson, Pullman-Standard; Arnold J. Judge, Thomas J. Judge, Chicago & North Western; Stephen J. Kabala, Amtrak; Albert C. Kalmbach; Kendrick, British Railways Board; R. H. Kindig; James J. King; John Kniola, Pullman-Standard; James Konas, Chicago Great Western; Frank V. Koval, Chicago & North Western; Chester George Krambles, Chicago Transit Authority; William Kratville, Autoliner Corporation; Susan Kraus, Southern Pacific; Otto Kuhler; Ira Kulbersh, Chicago & North Western; Raymond Lott; Omer S. A. Lavallée, Canadian Pacific; Alan R. Lind, Illinois Central Gulf; Lawrence Luser; J. C. Lyon, The Budd Company; Marian Manasse; Richard P. Mann; Donald Wilson, Seaboard Coast Line; Andrew Merrilees; Maurice Mertens, *Railphot*; John J. Michiels; David P. Middleton; W. Llewellyn Millar, Penn Central; Arthur Million; Charles M. Mizell Jr.; John W. Moutoussamy; Margaret O'Dea, Amtrak; Thomas B. O'Rourke, Pullman-Standard; Lawrence A. Painter, Hawker Siddeley-Canadian Car & Foundry; Arthur Peterson; James Prokes; ACF Industries; H. W. Pontin; J. H. Price, Cooks Continental Timetable; The Catholic Church; Key Pugh; Roland de Quatrebarbes, Wagons-Lits; Thomas L. Quigley, The Louis Society; Charles Rank, Chicago, Milwaukee, St. Paul & Pacific; C. C. Roberts, St. Francisco; William E. Robertson; Albert M. Rung, Burlington Northern; Mike Schafer; Roy Pullman Company; Mark Sebby; B. M. Sheridan, Gulf, Mobile & Ohio; James Shields; Bill Shipler Photo; Paul O. Sichert Jr., The Budd Company; James Sloss; Nelson M. Stick, Ringham; Anne L. Sudeikis, Amtrak; Jackson C. Thode, Denver & Rio Grande Western; William Van Der Sluys, Pullman-Standard; V. Allan Vaughn, Chicago Great Western; Vaughn, Chicago Great Western; Nicholas B. Wainwright, the Historical Society of Pennsylvania; William G. Wait; David A. Watts Jr., Amtrak; Robert J. Wayner; Michael Weinman; Roger Whitaker; John H. White Jr., Smithsonian Institution; Lawrence S. Williams, Lawrence S. Williams Photography; Nora Wilson, Pullman-Standard; Edward J. Wojtas, Chicago, Rock Island; Douglas Wornom; S. S. Worthen; Richard K. Wright; D. W. Yungmeyer; Theodore Chicago, Rock Island & Pacific.

BACK ENDSHEET PAINTING
Grif Teller's "Serving the Nation" depicts No. 6100, Pennsylvania Railroad's experimental S-1 6-4-4-6 steam locomotive, sometimes referred to as the "Big Engine." Painting appeared on PRR's 1940 calendar.

512